First People, First Voices

Poundmaker

First People, First Voices

EDITED BY PENNY PETRONE

University of Toronto Press

Toronto Buffalo London

© University of Toronto Press 1983
Toronto Buffalo London
Printed in Canada

ISBN 0-8020-2515-3 (cloth)
Reprinted 1984

ISBN 0-8020-6562-7 (paper)
1985, reprinted 1987, 1989

Canadian Cataloguing in Publication Data

Main entry under title:
First people, first voices

Includes index.
ISBN 0-8020-2515-3 (bound)   ISBN 6562-7 (pbk.)

1. Indians of North America – Canada – History –
Sources. I. Petrone, Penny.

E78.C2F5   971'.00497   C83-098474-7

Some of the research costs of this book
were assisted by generous grants from
the Ontario Arts Council under its
writer's grant program.

Publication of this book was assisted by
a generous gift to the
University of Toronto Press from the
Herbert Laurence Rous Estate, and
further financial assistance was provided by
Multiculturalism Canada.

Contents

Illustrations

Preface

This book presents a selection of writing and speeches by Canadian Indians from the 1630s to the 1980s. Its principal aim is to show the beginnings and development in Canada of an Indian literary tradition in English; along the way, a good deal can be learned about the Indian view of Canadian history.

Indians in certain parts of Canada have been speaking in English for over three centuries. The words they spoke even earlier have been recorded and translated into English, often from the French and sometimes directly from one of the many native languages. From the early nineteenth century, Indians were increasingly educated in English and thus began to write in that language. Indians writing in Canada today draw on this long experience in English as well as on oral traditions in their own languages that stretch into the distant past.

The material gathered here is generally arranged in chronological order to give historical perspective and continuity. The first chapter includes Indian speeches recorded in eastern and central Canada in the seventeenth and eighteenth centuries. Chapter 2, stretching across the nineteenth century, deals for the most part with the often difficult struggle, at different times in different parts of the country, to come to terms with the arrival and settlement of Europeans. Chapter 3 presents the writings of a group of Indians who were active in various Christian missions in the middle and late nineteenth century, the first Indians to write extensively in the English language. Chapter 4 looks at the more secular side of things in the late nineteenth century and the first half of the twentieth, and it includes several of the ancient legends and myths that were being collected at the time; along with the songs and poems scattered throughout the book, these legends – only a few of the many available – are the real roots of Indian literature. Finally, Chapter 5 provides samples of contemporary Indian work, from essays and speeches to fiction and poetry and other genres of creative literature.

In this book the term 'literature' has been interpreted in the broadest sense, embracing not only imaginative prose and poetry but also letters, speeches, sermons, reports, petitions, diary entries, songs, essays, journals and travel writing, history, and autobiography. I have tried to give the collection as wide a scope as possible in form, content, regional coverage, and authorship. Although some items translated from French have been included, there is obviously room for a separate book of Indian writing in that language, as well as for work written in the various Indian languages. This book concentrates on the wealth of material in English. There is emphasis upon earlier works, as opposed to contemporary writing, because these items are less accessible and because the purpose is to show the depth of the tradition on which today's writers are building. Likewise, relatively few myths and legends are included because so many collections of these exist.

Apart from correcting a few obvious typographical errors and the standardizing of Indian names, the spelling, grammar, syntax, and punctuation of the original sources have been preserved, for these show development in the use of language. In order to give context and background, brief introductions have been provided to the items; it is my intention, however, as much as possible, that the various Indian spokesmen should speak for themselves with a minimum of interpretation.

This book resulted from a need that arose when I was asked to teach a course on Indian literature for the Native Teacher Education Program at Lakehead University. In preparing for the course I soon discovered that although many books had been written *about* Canadian Indians and much literature was being published by contemporary Indians, there was virtually nothing on Indian writing before this century. As time progressed I became more and more convinced of the necessity of locating works by early Indian writers if the course were to have historical base and meaning.

I am grateful for financial assistance provided by the Ontario Ministry of Education and the Ministry of Colleges and Universities for field research and by Lakehead University for the costs of typing the manuscript. During the eight years of research for materials I have been assisted by librarians and archivists across the country, at historical societies and university libraries, at the Public Archives of Canada in Ottawa; at the Ontario Archives, the United Church Archives, the Anglican Church of Canada Archives, the Metropolitan Toronto Library Board, the Royal Ontario Museum, all in Toronto; the Glenbow Museum in Calgary; the Provincial Museums of British Columbia, Nova Scotia, and New Brunswick; the Provincial Archives of Manitoba and New Brunswick; the Public Archives of Nova Scotia; the Saskatchewan Archives Board; the Detroit Public Library; the Lambton County Library in Wyoming, Ontario; the County of Grey Owen Sound Museum; and the Archives of the Grey Nuns in St-Boniface, Manitoba.

I am grateful to all the people at these institutions who helped me, especially Neil Semple at the United Church Archives, Kevin Neary at the British Columbia Provincial Museum, Robert Armstrong and Bill Russell at the Public Archives of Canada, Ruth Whitehead at the Nova Scotia Museum, Lillian Montour of the Woodland Indian Centre in Brantford, Ontario, Annette Saint-Pierre of the Centres d'études franco-canadiennes de l'ouest in St-Boniface, Manitoba, and to others too numerous to mention. Above all, I'm grateful to the Indian people who gave me their time and permission to use their work.

I am especially indebted to my editor, Gerry Hallowell, for his patience and valuable assistance in the evolution of the original manuscript to its present form.

PENNY PETRONE
Thunder Bay
April 1983

One of the Four Kings of Canada, 1710 – a European view of the 'noble savage'

1 'Bad meat upon our lands'

'You can have your way and we will have ours;
everyone values his own wares.'

Jesuit Relations, III (1611-16) 123

Address of a war-party to their women
on leaving the village,
Chippewa

Do not weep, do not weep for me,
Loved women, should I die;
For yourselves alone should you weep!
Poor are ye all, and to be pitied:
Ye women, ye are to be pitied!

I seek, I seek our fallen relations;
I go to revenge, revenge the slain,
Our relations fallen and slain,
And our foes, our foes shall lie
Like them, like them shall they lie;
I go to lay them low, to lay them low!

Anna Jameson, *Winter Studies and Summer Rambles in Canada*
(1838; Toronto: Coles Canadiana 1970) III, 223

From ancient times the Indians have lived in the lands now known as Canada.

Over the centuries they fed and clothed themselves off the usually bountiful land, lived in harmony with the Great Spirit, and made war upon their neighbours. They also sang songs, told stories, and passed traditions on by word of mouth through succeeding generations.

It was in the summer of 1534 that the Micmacs first discovered on their mainland shores strange white men with hairy faces, though many winters would pass before it became clear that the intruders had come to stay. Almost two and a half centuries later the Haidas and Nootkas on the west coast were similarly visited by newcomers from beyond the seas. In the meantime, the white man and his ways had spread, from the east coast and from Hudson Bay, across the continent.

In the early seventeenth century the French in the St Lawrence Valley – in pursuit of beavers and souls – began to learn the Algonkian and Iroquoian languages. The French missionaries, particularly in the *Jesuit Relations*, wrote of their experiences in the 'New World,' and in the process recorded in print for the first time the thoughts of the Indian people.

While the Algonkins and the Hurons became increasingly tied to the French, the nations of the Iroquois Confederacy, their traditional enemies to the south, were being pressed by the British in the Thirteen Colonies; thus the stage was set for a century and a half of conflict and turmoil. Pitted between two great rival European powers in their struggle to control a continent, the Indians held a balance of power. In this age of warfare, at least until the destruction of the Huron nation, the Indians in the east were equals and allies; they spoke as free men to free men. North and west of the Great Lakes, the Ojibwas, Crees, and others were similarly equal partners in the fur trade, exchanging goods with the British from Hudson Bay after 1670 and with the French traders and voyageurs on their long treks from Montreal.

The themes that emerge in this chapter have to do with war and trade, military and economic alliances, and the introduction of Christianity. It should be stressed that most of the Indian speeches presented here are English translations of French accounts of Indian words and ideas. It is not possible to know how accurately the words have been transposed or how well they represent the speakers' true form of expression. There were obvious difficulties in translating languages so foreign to French, and the interpreters' own tastes, abilities, purposes, and beliefs may be reflected in the passages.

None the less, the Indian voice comes through. A variety of opinions is expressed. If some Indians stood in awe of European technology, others frankly criticized notions of French superiority. If some abandoned their old religion with apparent ease and enthusiastically adopted Christianity, others had serious doubts about the new values being offered; still others saw their way of life being threatened and blamed the Europeans for bringing death and destruction.

The speeches illustrate above all the abilities of the Indian orator. The Europeans who first came into contact with the Indians marvelled that a people who had neither the wheel nor writing knew well the power of words: whether explorer or missionary, government official or trader, soldier or settler, French or English, all were amazed that the 'untrained savage mind' was capable of such eloquence. In the *New Relation of Gaspesia*, Chrestien Le Clercq, the Recollet priest, declared that the Indians 'are very eloquent and persuasive among those of their own nation, using metaphors and very pleasing circumlocutions in their speeches, which are very eloquent, especially when these are pronounced in the councils and the public and general assemblies' (pp 241-2). The Jesuit father, Paul Le Jeune, on listening to a speech by a Montagnais chief, remarked on the 'keenness and delicacy of rhetoric that might have come out of the schools of Aristotle or Cicero' (*Jesuit Relations*, v, 205).

When occasion warranted, the Indians made clear, straightforward statements, but they also delivered long, complicated discourses full of emotion, wit, irony, and sarcasm. Their orations were often graceful and poetic, drawing frequently on imagery from nature. Their predilection for figurative and symbolic language could contribute to the difficulties of exact translation, a problem recognized by a French missionary who warned: 'Metaphor is largely in use among these Peoples; unless you accustom yourself to it, you will understand nothing in their councils, where they speak almost entirely in metaphors' (*Jesuit Relations*, x, 219).

▶ If the Europeans sometimes regarded the Indians as barbarian children of the forest – 'les sauvages' – the Indians were equally not always impressed by the light-skinned strangers. Beards, in particular, they found odd, and some believed they 'weakened the intelligence.' A Huron, on seeing a bearded Frenchman for the first time, exclaimed 'in amazement':

O, what an ugly man! Is it possible that any woman would look favourably on such a man.

Gabriel Sagard, *The Long Journey to the Country of the Hurons* (1632) edited by G.M. Wrong, translated by H.H. Langton (Toronto: Champlain Society 25, 1939) 137

▶ The Europeans also had some peculiar habits and needs. A Montagnais man poked fun at the English because of their insatiable desire for beaver pelts.

The Beaver does everything perfectly well, it makes kettles, hatchets, swords, knives, bread; and, in short, it makes everything ... The English have no sense; they give us twenty knives like this for one Beaver skin.

The Jesuit Relations and Allied Documents: Travels and Explorations of the
Jesuit Missionaries in New France, 1610-1791, edited by Reuben Gold Thwaites
(Cleveland: The Burrows Brothers Company 1896-1901) VI (1633-4) 297-9

▶   Capitanal (fl. 1615-34) was a Montagnais chief and orator whose father had been killed at Samuel de Champlain's side in a raid against the Iroquois. In the spring of 1633 the French explorer complained because the Montagnais were trading with the British. Replying with 'grace' and apparent 'profound humility' in the following speech, Capitanal was in fact giving reasons for these contacts. The sending of skins was not for the purpose of economic exchange but rather to 'cut off the arms of our enemies,' that is, to make a political alliance with the British before the Iroquois did. The enemy controlled a large empire – they had 'long arms' – and the aim of the Montagnais was to preserve their own security.

I am only a poor little animal, crawling about on the ground; you Frenchmen are the great of the earth, who make all tremble. I do not know how I dare to talk before such great Captains. If I had some one behind me who would suggest what I ought to say, I would speak more boldly ... I am bewildered; I have never had any instruction; my father left me very young; if I say anything, I go seeking it here and there, at hazard, and it is that which makes me tremble.

Thou tellest us that the French have always loved us; we know it well, and we would lie if we said the contrary. Thou sayest that thou hast always been true, and we have always believed thee. Thou hast assisted us in our wars, we love thee all the more for it; what dost thou wish that we should answer? All that thou sayest is true.

Thou sayest that the French have come to live at Kebec to defend us, and that thou wilt come into our country to protect us. I remember well to have heard our fathers say that, when you were below at Tadoussac, the Montagnaits [sic] went to see you and invited you, unknown to us, to ascend [the river] above here, where our fathers, having seen you, loved you, and prayed you to make your home there ...

It was sieur de Caën, who believed that I had sent Beavers to the foreigners; I sent to those quarters a few Moose skins, not in trade, but to cut off the arms of our enemies. Thou knowest that the Hiroquois have long arms; if I had not cut them, we should have been taken by them long ago. I send presents to tribes who are their neighbors, to the end that they should not unite with them; it is not to offend the French, but to preserve ourselves.

Thou sayest that we wish to go to the English; I will tell my men that they should not go there. I promise thee that neither I myself, nor they who have any sense, will do that; but if there is some young man who jumps over there without being seen, I shall not know what to do; thou knowest well that youth cannot be restrained. I shall forbid every one from going there. Any one who does so has no sense. Thou canst do everything, place thy boats in the way and capture the Beavers of those who attempt to go ...

... Thou sayest that we must be careful what we do; grasp us by the arm, and we shudder; grasp us afterward by the heart, and the whole body trembles. We do not want to go to the English ...

Jesuit Relations, v (1632-3) 205-11

▶ Etienne Pigarouich (fl. 1639-43), a leading medicine man among the Algonkins of Trois-Rivières, was converted and baptized in 1639 by the Jesuit missionaries, who recognized his power as an able disputant. Here he explains, to a missionary he feels has slighted him, the difficulties of his conversion.

What dost thou think Pigarouich is? He is a great tree, strongly rooted in the ground; dost thou think to throw it down all at once? Strike, strike heavy blows of the axe, and continue a long time, and at last thou wilt overthrow it. It desires to fall, but it cannot, – its roots, that is, its bad habits hold it down, in spite of itself. Do not lose courage; thou wilt succeed.

Jesuit Relations, xvi (1639) 159

▶ Young converts were required to go through rigorous study before being accepted into the Roman Catholic faith – and they often asked provocative questions. In the late 1630s the Jesuit father Paul Le Jeune, in order to show 'the excellence of their minds,' recorded a few of the arguments presented to the French director 'by young Savage Seminarists between twelve and fifteen years old.'

You tell us that baptism is absolutely necessary to go to Heaven; if there were a man so good that he had never offended God, and if he died without Baptism, would he go to Hell, never having given any offense to God? If he goes to Hell God does not love all good people, since he throws that one into the fire.

You teach us that God existed before the creation of heaven and earth; if he did, where did he live, since there was neither heaven nor earth? You say also that the Angels were created in the beginning of the world, and that those who disobeyed were cast into Hell; elsewhere, you put Hell in the depths of the earth; these statements cannot agree very well, for, if the Angels sinned before the creation of the earth, they could not be thrown into Hell, or Hell is not where you place it.

Moreover, you declare that those who go to Hell do not come out of it, and yet you relate Stories of the damned who have appeared in the world; how is that to be understood? ...

Ah, how I would like to kill them [devils], since they do so much harm!

But if they are made like men and come among men, do they still feel the fire of Hell? Why is it that they do not repent of having offended God? If they did repent, would not God be merciful to them? If Our Lord has suffered for all sinners, why do not those receive pardon from him? ...

You say that the Virgin, Mother of JESUS CHRIST, is not God, and that she has never offended God, and that her Son has redeemed all men, and atoned for all; if she has done nothing wrong, her Son could not redeem her nor atone for her.

Jesuit Relations, XVI (1639) 183-5

▶ Joseph Chihwatenha (c. 1602-40), or Chihouatenhoua, was baptized in 1637, became a model Christian, and helped the Jesuits in their mission work throughout Huronia (in what is now southern Ontario); this was done at considerable personal risk, for the French priests were accused of being sorcerers and were held responsible for the epidemics that had killed more than half of the Huron population by the 1640s. Chihwatenha was one of the first Hurons to assimilate both the spiritual and material aspects of European culture. This 'pearl of our Christians,' as the missionaries referred to him, here chastises a group of his countrymen for their 'diabolical superstitions.'

I was called, in these past years, to all your councils ... I would be astonished not to have been invited to these, were it not that I well know that the Magician has not wished the believers to be present there. I would have gladly spoken there; and, although I honor you, and call you all my uncles, I would have told you publicly that in all these affairs you behave like children without intelligence. A sorcerer persuades you what he will;

he has promised to cure all your sick; you have believed him, and have made him great presents, according as he has desired them. The devil is a liar, and, for all that, you believe him; he is insolent in his demands, and yet, whatever it cost you, you obey him in every point. God is true in his promises; you refuse belief in him; his commandments are easy and reasonable; not one puts himself to the trouble of obeying him. The devil takes pleasure in receiving honors which are due only to God alone, and afterward he mocks you; the disease continues as strongly as ever; the mortality ravages your cabins, and those whom this false Magician has sprinkled most with his water, are the very ones who have died. You see that as well as I, and yet you persist in your blindness; open your eyes and you will acknowledge that the devil deceives you. Moreover, I hear that they speak of me as of a man who is in league with the black gowns. I wish them to know that I am allied with them, – not to ruin the country, as the slanderous tongues say, but to maintain the truths which they have come to announce to us. I shall be happy to die for this reason; I am quite ready to be burned for this cause. I aim at naught, in believing, save to honor the master of our lives, – not for the hope of any good that I expect from him in this world, but only in the hope of Paradise, whereof we had no knowledge before they came to teach us. That is why I do not fear to die; let them kill me for this cause, – I will not shun death. Tell that to every one; I tell it to all those who speak to me of my belief, to the end that they may plainly know the value which I attach to the Faith.

Jesuit Relations, xix (1640) 245-9

▶ During another altercation on the subject of religion, a missionary ridiculed the 'foolish notions' of a group of Algonkins; they, in turn, blamed him for their misfortunes.

Now, our dreams and our prophecies are no longer true, – prayer has spoiled everything for us ... you, you are the cause of it: for if you had lived in your own country without speaking to us of God, he would not say a word to us, since we would not know him or his will. You would then do much better to return to your country and live at rest; for it is you who kill us. Before you came here, the French did not say so many prayers; they only made the sign of the Cross, and even then, all did not know how to make it. They did not have all those prayers which you are introducing; it is you who have brought in all these novelties, and who teach them to the Savages, and overturn their brains and make them die.

Jesuit Relations, xxiv (1642-3) 211

►   Paul Tessouat (d. 1654), an Algonkin chief of the Allumette Island tribe (also called Le Borgne because he had only one eye), was one of the greatest orators of his time. His vanity and pride are revealed in this forceful speech delivered in the winter of 1640-1 during a quarrel between his people and a group of Christian Indians.

I had some intention of spending the winter here, but I am told that neither your Captain loves me nor do you. Perhaps you do not know that I have ruled from my youth, that I was born to rule. As soon as I open my mouth, every one listens to me; it is also true that I bear up and maintain the whole country during the life of my grandchildren and my nephews, it is thus he calls his people. Even the Hurons give ear to me, and I command among them; I rule them, as if I were Captain. I say not a word over there, – the rest speak; but there is nothing done except that which I have in my mind. I am like a tree, – men are the branches thereof, to which I give vigor.

> Quarrels were 'almost always on account of religion.' Tessouat once cleverly defended his actions before François de Champflour, the governor, explaining his reasons for throwing burning cinders in a Jesuit missionary's eyes and threatening to kill him with a rope.

... as for the rope which I took in my hand, it was never in my mind to bind the Father, much less to strangle him. But, when he reproached me with making the Savages die by my charms, and I, in my anger, reproached him with making them die by prayers, I took a noose, to show him that, if we both spoke truly, we both merited death; to have made an attempt upon his life, that is what never entered my head.

Jesuit Relations, xx (1640-1) 155-7, 265

►   Kiotseaeton (fl. 1645-6), a Mohawk chief and orator, was sent as the official ambassador of his nation to a great peace conference held at Trois-Rivières on 12 July 1645. The meeting was marked by ceremonial pomp and pageantry. Kiotseaeton presented seventeen wampum belts with their corresponding messages. When everyone was seated he 'rose and looked at the Sun, then cast his eyes over the whole Company and took the first of the seventeen collars of porcelain beads in his hand'; then he addressed the French governor, Huault de Montmagny.

Onontio, lend me ear. I am the mouth for the whole of my country; thou listenest to all the Iroquois, in hearing my words. There is no evil in my heart; I have only good songs in my mouth. We have a multitude of war songs in our country; we have cast them all to the ground; we have no longer anything but songs of rejoicing.

The tenth present was given to show a strong alliance. Kiotseaeton grasped a Frenchman, placed his arm within his, and with his other arm clasped that of an Algonkin.

Here is the knot that binds us inseparably; nothing can part us ... Even if the lightning were to fall upon us, it could not separate us; for, if it cuts off the arm that holds you to us, we will at once seize each other by the other arm.

He then turned around, caught the Frenchman and the Algonkin by their two other arms, and held them close. The eleventh collar was an invitation to feast.

Our country is well stocked with fish, with venison, and with game; it is everywhere full of deer, of Elk, of beaver. Give up those stinking hogs that run about among your houses, that eat nothing but filth; and come and eat good meat with us.

Jean-Baptiste Atironta (d. 1650), a Huron captain, also took part in the 1645 conference. At the close of the deliberations, he rejoiced at the results achieved.

It is done, we are brothers. The conclusion has been reached; now we are all relatives, – Hiroquois, Hurons, Algonquins, and French; we are now but one and the same people.

An unidentified Algonkin, following Atironta's example, also expressed happiness at the outcome.

I can no longer speak; my heart is too full of joy. I have large ears and so many good words crowd in there that they drown me in pleasure.

At a later, similar meeting, an Iroquois captain said:

Onontio, thou has dispersed the clouds; the air is serene; the Sky shows clearly; the Sun is bright. I see no more trouble; peace has made everything Calm; my heart is at rest; I go away very happy.

Jesuit Relations, XXVII (1642-5) 253-61, 289, 291, 303

▶   A seventy-year-old Huron was told that God had no pity on him because
    He had allowed a stroke to deprive him of the use of an arm. The old man
    replied wisely with a metaphor from nature.

What! Would you wish that there should be no dried trees in the woods
and no dead branches on a tree that is growing old?

Jesuit Relations, XXVIII (1645-6) 77

▶   At an assembly of Huron elders, a Christian was scolded and silenced for
    narrating the 'false' French story of the creation; he replied:

... I consented to listen to thee, and became silent without resistance, –
believing that thou wouldst teach us something better, and as true as
what I was saying. But seeing that thou tellest only fables, which have no
foundation but lies, I have more right to speak than thou. Where are the
writings which give us faith in what thou sayest? If each one is permitted
to invent what he will, is it strange that we know nothing true, since we
must acknowledge that the Hurons have been liars from all time? But the
French do not speak by heart; they preserve from all antiquity the Sacred
books, wherein the word of God himself is written, without permission to
any one to alter it the least in the world, – unless he would expose himself to the confusion of seeing himself belied by all the nations of the
earth, who cherish this truth more than they have love for life.

Jesuit Relations, XXX (1646-7) 63

▶   Louis Taondechoren (c. 1600-c. 1677), or Taiaeronk, was a Huron chief who
    fought alongside Dollard des Ormeaux at the siege of the Long Sault in
    1660. As spokesman for a group of Hurons who were fearful of losing
    Marie de l'Incarnation after a fire had destroyed the Ursuline chapel in
    1650, he comforted the sisters in their distress. By this time his own nation
    was in ruins.

Holy virgins, you see before you miserable carcasses, the remnant of a
country that once was flourishing and that is no more, the country of the
Hurons. We have been devoured and gnawed to the very bones, by war
and famine. These carcasses are able to stand only because you support
them ... Your hearts do not sorrow for the loss of earthly goods; we see
that they are raised too high in the desire of heavenly blessings; and
therefore we seek for no remedy in that respect. We fear but one thing
which would be a misfortune for us; we fear that, when the news of the

accident that has happened to you reaches France, it will affect your relatives more than it does yourselves; we fear that they will recall you and that you will be moved by their tears. How can a mother read, without weeping, letters telling her that her daughter is without clothes, without food, without a bed, and without the comforts of life in which you have been brought up from youth? The first thought that nature will inspire in those disconsolate mothers will be to recall you to them, and to procure for themselves the greatest consolation that they can have in the world, thereby procuring also your good. A brother would do the same for his sister; an uncle and an aunt for their niece; and afterward we would be in danger of losing you, and of losing in your persons the assistance for which we had hoped in the instruction of our daughters in the faith, the fruits whereof we have begun to taste with such enjoyment. Courage, holy virgins! do not allow yourselves to be persuaded by love of kindred; and show now that the charity that you have for us is stronger than the ties of nature ...

Jesuit Relations, xxxvi (1650-1) 215-19

▶ Noël Negabamat (c. 1600-66), or Tekouerimat, was one of the principal Montagnais chiefs of Sillery, a centre for Algonkin converts founded in 1637 by the Jesuit, Father Paul Le Jeune. A constant friend to the French cause, Negabamat worked indefatigably on behalf of his adopted God and country. He sent this letter in 1652.

Father le Jeune: I seem to see thee, when thy letter is read to me; and I seem to be with thee, when I speak to thee by the mouth, or the pen, of Father de Quen. I do not lie; it seems to me only yesterday that thou didst baptize me. I am growing old, but the faith is not growing old in me. I love prayer as much, at the end of fifteen years, as on the first day when thou didst instruct me. We are Changing in all things, we people of this country; but I assure thee that I never shall change in regard to what thou didst teach me, and what we are now taught by him who governs in thy place. Indeed, I make hardly any further change, even in my location; I shall pass the coming Winter at *Ka-Miskouaouangachit*, which you call St. Joseph, as I passed the last one. I am almost wholly French ...

Jesuit Relations, xxxviii (1652-3) 65

▶ The Flemish Bastard (fl. 1650-87), a Mohawk chief whose Indian name is unknown, delivered two French hostages at Quebec in July 1654 and complained that the Jesuit, Father Simon Le Moyne, had been sent on an embassy to the Onandagas instead of to the Mohawks, who were the closer neighbours of the French.

Ought not one to enter a house by the door, and not by the chimney or roof of the cabin, unless he be a thief, and wish to take the inmates by surprise? We, the five Iroquois Nations, compose but one cabin; we maintain but one fire; and we have, from time immemorial, dwelt under one and the same roof ... Well, then, will you not enter the cabin by the door, which is at the ground floor of the house? It is with us Anniehronnons [Mohawks], that you should begin; whereas you, by beginning with the Onnontaehronnons [Onandagas], try to enter by the roof and through the chimney. Have you no fear that the smoke may blind you, our fire not being extinguished, and that you may fall from the top to the bottom, having nothing solid on which to plant your feet?

Jesuit Relations, XLI (1654-6) 87-9

▶ Aaoueaté, a Huron captain, found himself a captive of the Iroquois; when they tried to reassure him that they were 'dropping the war-song' (that is, making peace), he replied:

You are faithless rogues, your hearts are full of venom, and your minds of knavishness; if you talk of peace, it is only to employ a treachery more baleful both for us and for the French. I know your wiles only too well. Content yourselves now with eating the head of the Hurons; but know that you do not yet hold the other members. My people still have feet and hands, legs and arms ... Burn me ... do not spare your tortures – all the more, as I am a dead man. My body has already become insensible; and neither your fires nor your cruelties will shock my courage. I would rather die to-day than be indebted to you for a life which you give me only with the intention of depriving me of it by some dire treachery ...

I know you well, your minds are furnished with seven linings, and when one of them is taken away, there are still six remaining. Tell me, I beg you, whether this treachery that you are devising with such skill is the last of your knavish tricks. You have forgotten the exchange of promises that took place between our Ancestors, – when they took up arms, the one side against the other, – to the effect that if a mere woman should undertake to uncover the Sweat-house and take away the stakes supporting it, the victors should lay down their arms and show mercy to the vanquished. You have violated this law; for not merely a woman, but the great Captain of the French has uncovered this ill-omened Sweat-house where decisions of war are adopted. By his presents he has taken away the stakes that support it, trying to win the Nations which you are upholding; and you, scorning his kindness, have trampled under foot the orders and the promise of your Ancestors. They blush with shame, in the land of souls, at seeing you violate, with an unbearable perfidy, the laws of nature, the law of Nations, and all human society.

Jesuit Relations, XL (1653) 179-81

▶ Prisoners taken in battle were often adopted by the tribe into whose hands they fell. If a woman wished to save a prisoner, she took him by the hand and led him into the hut, where she cut his bonds and gave him clothes, food, and tobacco.

I have given thee thy life, I have knock'd off thy chains, pluck up a good heart, serve me well, be not ill minded, and thou shalt have whereupon to comfort thee for the loss of thy Country and thy Relations.

New Voyages to North-America by the Baron de Lahontan (1703).
edited by Reuben Gold Thwaites (Chicago: A.C. McClurg & Co. 1905) II, 506

▶ As early travellers recorded, there were more gentle ways to find a partner.

A Lover's Proposal

Father, I love your daughter, will you give her to me,
that the small roots of her heart may entangle with mine,
so that the strongest wind that blows
shall never separate them.

A Bride's Love Song

It is true I love him only whose heart is like
the sweet sap that runs from the sugar-tree,
and is brother to the aspin leaf, that always
lives and shivers.

J. Long, *Voyages and Travels of an Indian Interpreter and Trader*
(London 1791; Toronto: Coles Canadiana 1971) 136, 113

▶ At a feast provided by the bishop, the Hurons, increasingly in good humour, began to make speeches interspersed with singing, as was their custom. The first to speak, 'with an eloquence as gracious as natural,' was one of the oldest Hurons present. His oration, according to the French interpreter, 'uttered with warmth, was all the more touching because it artlessly represented the last sighs of a dying nation,' but it also cleverly pointed out that the Hurons, although defeated in war by the Iroquois and ravaged by hitherto unknown infectious diseases, were still valuable to the French in their desire to expand westward and that they had a common interest in the destruction of the Iroquois.

We are now nothing, O Hariouaouagui [Monseigneur the Bishop – 'the man of the great work'] ... we are now nothing but the fragments of a once flourishing nation, which was formerly the terror of the Iroquois, and which possessed every kind of riches. What thou seest is only the skeleton of a great people, from which the Iroquois has gnawed off all the flesh, and which he is striving to suck out to the very marrow. What attractions canst thou find in our miseries? How canst thou be charmed by this remnant of living carrion, to come from so far and join us in the so pitiful condition in which thou seest us? It must needs be that the Faith, which works these marvels, is such as they have announced to us for more than thirty years. Thy presence alone, although thou shouldst say not a word to us, speaks to us quite audibly in its behalf, and confirms us in the opinion that we hold of it.

But, if thou wilt have a Christian people, the infidel must be destroyed; and know that, if thou canst obtain from France armed forces to humble the Iroquois, – who comes to us with yawning jaws to swallow up the remnant of thy people, as in a deep chasm, – know, I say, that by the destruction of two or three of these enemies' villages thou wilt make for thyself a great highway to vast lands and to many nations, who extend their arms to thee and yearn only for the light of the Faith. Courage, then, O Hariouaouagui; give life to thy poor children, who are at bay! On our life depends that of countless peoples; but our life depends on the death of the Iroquois.

Jesuit Relations, XLV (1659-60) 41-3

▶ The Jesuit priest, Father Claude Allouez, in 1670 penetrated into an Algonkin village never before visited by a white man. Startled by his pale complexion and long black robe, the Indians, who took him for some sort of a divinity, invited him to the council lodge. One of the elders approached him with a double handful of tobacco. The phrase 'take pity on us' was frequently used by Indians at the time and might now more accurately be translated as 'look kindly upon us' or 'be our friend and helper' rather than the literal 'pity us.'

This is well, black Gown, that thou comest to visit us. Take pity on us; thou art a Manitou; we give thee tobacco to smoke. The Nadouessious and the Iroquois are eating us; take pity on us. We are often ill, our children are dying, we are hungry. Hear me, O Manitou; I give thee tobacco to smoke. Let the earth give us corn, and the rivers yield us fish; let not disease kill us any more, or famine treat us any longer so harshly! ...

Jesuit Relations, LIV (1669-71) 229

▶   Otreouti (fl. 1659-88), called Garangula or La Grande Gueule (Big Mouth) by the French because of his abilities as an orator, was an Onondaga chief who often acted as ambassador to the French. When, in 1684, the crafty French governor, Joseph-Antoine Le Febvre de La Barre, attempted to intimidate him with threats he knew could not be executed, Otreouti rose, strode several times around the council fire, and delivered the following speech.

Yonondio! – You must have believed when you left Quebec, that the sun had burnt up all the forests, which render our country inaccessible to the French, or that the lakes had so far overflown the banks, that they had surrounded our castles, and that it was impossible for us to get out of them. Yes, surely you must have dreamed so, and the curiosity of seeing so great a wonder, has brought you so far. *Now* you are undeceived. I and the warriors here present, are come to assure you, that the Senecas, Cayugas, Onondagas, Oneidas and Mohawks [the Five Nations of the Iroquois Confederacy] are yet alive. I thank you in their name, for bringing back into their country the calumet, which your predecessor received from their hands. It was happy for you, that you left under ground that murdering hatchet, so often dyed in the blood of the French.

Hear, Yonondio! – I do not sleep. I have my eyes open. The sun, which enlightens me, discovers to me a great captain at the head of a company of soldiers, who speaks as if he were dreaming. He says, that he only came to the lake to smoke on the great calumet with the Onondagas. But *Garangula* says, that he sees the contrary; that it was to knock them on the head, if sickness had not weakened the arms of the French. I see Yonondio raving in a camp of sick men, whose lives the Great Spirit has saved by inflicting this sickness on them.

Hear, Yonondio! – Our women had taken their clubs, our children and old men had carried their bows and arrows into the heart of your camp, if our warriors had not disarmed them, and kept them back, when your messenger came to our castles. It is done and I have said it.

Hear, Yonondio! – We plundered none of the French, but those that carried guns, powder and balls to the Twightwies and Chictaghicks, because those arms might have cost us our lives. Herein we follow the example of the Jesuits, who break all the kegs of rum brought to our castles, lest the drunken Indians should knock them on the head. Our warriors have not beaver enough to pay for all the arms they have taken, and our old men are not afraid of the war. This belt preserves my words.

We carried the English into our lakes, to trade there with the Uta-wawas and Quatoghies, as the Adirondacks brought the French to our castles, to carry on a trade, which the English say is theirs. We are born free. We neither depend on Yonondio nor Corlear [the English governor of New York]. We may go where we please, and carry with us whom we please, and buy and sell what we please. If your allies be your slaves, use them as such, command them to receive no other but your people ...

We knock the Twightwies and Chictaghicks on the head, because they had cut down the trees of peace, which were the limits of our country. They have hunted beaver on our lands. They have acted contrary to the customs of all Indians, for they left none of the beavers alive, – they killed both male and female. They brought the Satanas into their country, to take part with them, after they had concerted ill designs against us. We have done less than either the English or French, that have usurped the lands of so many Indian nations, and chased them from their own country ...

Hear, Yonondio! – What I say is the voice of all the Five Nations. Hear what they answer. Open your ears to what they speak. The Senecas, Cay-ugas, Onondagas, Oneidas and Mohawks say, that when they buried the hatchet at Cadarackui, in the presence of your predecessor, in the middle of the fort, they planted the tree of peace in the same place, to be there carefully preserved: that in the place of a retreat for soldiers, that fort might be a rendezvous for merchants: that in place of arms and ammuni-tion of war, beavers and merchandize should only enter there.

Hear, Yonondio! – Take care for the future that so great a number of soldiers as appear there, do not choke the tree of peace planted in so small a fort. It will be a great loss, if, after it had so easily taken root, you should stop its growth, and prevent its covering your country and ours with its branches. I assure you, in the name of the Five Nations, that our warriors shall dance to the calumet of peace under its leaves. They shall remain quiet on their mats, and shall never dig up the hatchet, till their brother Yonondio, or Corlear, shall either jointly or separately endeavor to attack the country, which the Great Spirit has given to our ancestors ...

B.B. Thatcher, *Indian Biography* (New York: Harper and Brothers 1832) II, 42-4

▶ In 1676 the Recollet priest, Chrestien Le Clercq, tried to persuade a group of Gaspesians (Micmacs) that it would be more advantageous to build houses in the French manner. Their chief, whose name is not known, replied in a way that must have surprised his listeners.

... I am greatly astonished that the French have so little cleverness, as they seem to exhibit in the matter of which thou hast just told me on their behalf, in the effort to persuade us to convert our poles, our barks, and our wigwams into those houses of stone and of wood which are tall and lofty, according to their account, as these trees. Very well! But why now do men of five to six feet in height need houses which are sixty to eighty? For, in fact, as thou knowest very well thyself, Patriarch – do we not find in our own all the conveniences and the advantages that you have with yours, such as reposing, drinking, sleeping, eating, and amusing ourselves with our friends when we wish? This is not all (addressing himself to one of our captains), my brother, hast thou as much ingenuity and cleverness as the Indians, who carry their houses and their wigwams with them so that they may lodge wheresoever they please, independently of any seignior whatsoever? Thou are not as bold nor as stout as we, because when thou goest on a voyage thou canst not carry upon thy shoulders thy buildings and thy edifices. Therefore it is necessary that thou preparest as many lodgings as thou makest changes of residence, or else thou lodgest in a hired house which does not belong to thee. As for us, we find ourselves secure from all these inconveniences, and we can always say, more truly than thou, that we are at home everywhere, because we set up our wigwams with ease wheresoever we go, and without asking permission of anybody. Thou reproachest us, very inappropriately, that our country is a little hell in contrast with France, which thou comparest to a terrestrial paradise, inasmuch as it yields thee, so thou sayest, every kind of provision in abundance. Thou sayest of us also that we are the most miserable and most unhappy of all men, living without religion, without manners, without honour, without social order, and, in a word, without any rules, like the beasts in our woods and our forests, lacking bread, wine, and a thousand other comforts which thou hast in superfluity in Europe. Well, my brother, if thou dost not yet know the real feelings which our Indians have towards thy country and towards all thy nation, it is proper that I inform thee at once. I beg thee now to believe that, all miserable as we seem in thine eyes, we consider ourselves nevertheless much happier than thou in this, that we are very content with the little that we have; and believe also once for all, I pray, that thou deceivest thyself greatly if thou thinkest to persuade us that thy country is better than ours. For if France, as thou sayest, is a little terrestrial paradise, art thou sensible to leave it? And why abandon wives, children, relatives, and friends? Why risk thy life and thy property every year, and why venture thyself with such risk, in any season whatsoever, to the storms and tempests of the sea in order to come to a strange and barbarous country which thou considerest the poorest and least fortunate of the world? Besides, since we are wholly convinced of the contrary, we scarcely take the trouble to go to France, because we fear, with good reason, lest we find little satisfaction there, seeing, in our own experience, that those who are natives thereof leave it every year in order to enrich themselves on our shores. We believe, further, that you are also incomparably poorer than we, and that you are only simple journeymen, valets, servants, and slaves, all masters and grand captains though you may appear, seeing that you glory in our old rags and in our miserable suits of beaver which can no longer be of use to us, and that you find among us, in the fishery for cod which you make in these parts, the wherewithal to comfort your misery and the poverty which oppresses you. As to us, we find all our riches and all our conveniences among ourselves, without trouble and without exposing our lives to the dangers in which you find yourselves constantly through your long voyages. And, whilst feeling compassion for you in the sweetness of our repose, we wonder at the anxieties and cares which you give yourselves night and day in order to load your ship. We see also that all your people live, as a rule, only upon cod which you catch among us. It is everlastingly nothing but cod – cod in the morning, cod at midday, cod at evening, and always cod, until things come to such a pass that if you wish some good morsels, it is at our expense; and you are obliged to have recourse to the Indians, whom you despise so much, and to beg them to go a-hunting that you may be regaled. Now tell me this one little thing, if thou hast any sense: Which of these two is the wisest and happiest – he who labours without ceasing and only obtains, and that with great trouble, enough to live on, or he who rests in comfort and finds all that he needs in the pleasure of hunting and fishing? It is true that we have not always had the use of bread and of wine which your France produces; but, in fact, before the arrival of the French in these parts, did not the Gaspesians live much longer than now? And if we have not any longer among us any of those old men of a hundred and thirty to forty years, it is only because we are gradually adopting your manner of living, for experience is making it very plain that those of us live longest who, despising your bread, your wine, and your brandy, are content with their natural food of beaver, of moose, of waterfowl, and fish, in accord with the custom of our ancestors and of all the Gaspesian nation. Learn now, my brother, once for all, because I must open to thee my heart; there is no Indian who does not consider himself infinitely more happy and more powerful than the French.

> In contrast to the feelings of security and pride expressed above are the pathos and grief of separation evident in this oration, delivered in 1686 by an unidentified chief of the Gaspesians to Father Le Clercq, just before his return to France.

Well then, my son, the resolution has been taken; thou wishest to abandon us and return to France. For there lies the great wooden canoe ... which is going to steal thee from the Gaspesians in order to take thee to thine own land, to thy relatives and thy friends. Ah, my son, if thou couldst see my heart at present, thou wouldst see that it weeps tears of blood, at the very time that my eyes are weeping tears of water, so much is it affected by this cruel separation ... dost thou not know my son, that I am thy father, and the Chief of the Gaspesian nation? And as I am thy father, thou canst not be ignorant thus far of the sincerity of my friendship. I assure thee that I will even love thee always as tenderly as one of my own children ...

... thou hast said to our children that they were bound, under penalty of being burned in Hell, to honour their fathers and their mothers, and that it was a monstrous crime to abandon their parents, and to refuse them the aid which they had a right to expect from their children in their need. Thy instructions and the commandment of God which says, *Koutche, kitche chibar, chaktou, baguisto skiginouidex*, 'Honour and fear thy father and thy mother and thou shalt live long,' have kept my eldest son in my wigwam, who, nevertheless, wanted to abandon me in the middle of winter, in our greatest need. He has killed a great number of moose, he has made thee fare well and has given thee abundantly of the grease to eat, and of the oil of bear to drink in our feasts, as much of it as thou hast been able to desire. Frenchman! here is another argument; my eldest son has remained with his father and mother because of the respect which he had for the comandment of JESUS, and the friendship which he bore for the Patriarch. Do then now, after his example, for me, for my wife, and for him, that which he has done so generously for thee. Thou callest me thy father; my wife, saidst thou to all the Indians, was thy mother; ever since we both had given thee birth in our wigwams, my children were thy brothers and thy children. Well now! is it then a good deed for a child to leave his father, his mother, his brothers, and his sisters? Is it thus that thou despisest the commandment of God which says, *Koutche, kitche chibar, chaktou, baguisto skinouidex*? If it is true that the children who honour their parents live long, art thou not in fear of perishing in the great lake, and of suffering shipwreck in these salt waters after having abandoned us in the need that we have for thine aid? Alas, my son, ... if some one of us comes to die in the woods, who will take care to show us the road to Heaven, and to aid us to die aright? Was it then needful to take so much trouble to instruct us, as thou hast done up to the present, only to leave us in an evident peril of dying without the sacraments which thou hast administered to my brother, my uncle, and several of our dying old men? If thy heart remains still insensible to everything I have said, learn, my son, that mine sheds and weeps tears of blood in abundance so great that it chokes my utterance.

Chrestien Le Clercq, *New Relation of Gaspesia, with the Customs and Religion of the Gaspesian Indians* (1691) translated and edited by William F. Ganong (Toronto: Champlain Society 5, 1910) 103-6, 308-13

▶ Another Indian sympathetic to the French refused an English clergyman's proposal to administer to his needs.

Thy words astonish me, and I wonder at the proposition that thou makest me. When thou camest here thou sawest me a long time before the French Governors did; neither those who preceded thee, nor thy Ministers, ever spoke to me of prayer or of the Great Spirit. They saw my furs, my beaver- and elk-skins, and of those alone did they think; it was those that they sought with eagerness; I was not able to furnish them enough, and, when I brought many, then I was their great friend, and that was all. On the contrary, my canoe having one day been misguided, I lost my way and wandered at random for a long time, until at last I landed near Quebec, at a large village of the Algonkins, where the black Robes were teaching. I had hardly landed when a black Robe came to see me. I was loaded with furs, but the French black Robe did not deign even to look at them ...

Jesuit Relations, LXVII (1716-27) 211

► Theyanoguin (c. 1680-1755), better known as King Hendrick, Mohawk warrior, sachem, and orator, was taken to England in 1710 along with three lesser chiefs to appeal to Queen Anne for help against the French. They were escorted by Peter Schuyler and Colonel Francis Nicholson, who later became governor of Nova Scotia. While in London the Indians were lionized and fêted lavishly; the Queen presented them with a silver communion service and lent her patronage to missions in North America. An account of the visit to the court of Queen Anne was published in London in 1710 under the title *The Four Kings of Canada*; it contained a speech 'that even in the Translation carries along with it something of natural Eloquence and Simplicity, peculiar to that Sort of People, who, tho' unpolish'd by Art and Letters, have a large Share of good Sense and natural Reason.' The speech reveals some of the patterns of Indian-white diplomacy.

Great Queen,
We have undertaken a long and tedious Voyage, which none of our Predecessors could ever be prevail'd upon to undertake. The Motive that induc'd us, was that we might see our *Great Queen*, and relate to her those Things we thought absolutely necessary for the Good of her, and us her Allies, on the other side of the great Water.

We doubt not but our *Great Queen* has been acquainted with our long and tedious War, in Conjunction with her Children (meaning subjects) against her Enemies the *French*; and that we have been as a strong Wall for their Security, even to the Loss of our best Men. The Truth of which our Brother *Queder*, Colonel *Schuyler*, and *Anadagajaux*, Colonel *Nicholson*, can testify, they having all our Proposals in Writing.

We were mightily rejoyc'd, when we heard by *Anadagarjaux*, that our *Great Queen* had resolv'd to send an Army to reduce *Canada*; from whose Mouth we readily embrac'd our *Great Queen*'s Instructions: And in Token of our Friendship, we hung up the *Kettle,* and took up the *Hatchet*, and with one Consent join'd our Brother *Queder*, Colonel *Schuyler*, and *Anadagarjaux*, Colonel *Nicholson*, in making Preparations on this Side of the Lake, by building Forts, Store-houses, Canows, and Battows; whilst *Anadiasia*, Colonel *Vetch*, at the same Time, raised an Army at *Boston*, of which we were inform'd by our Embassadors, whom we sent thither for that Purpose. We waited long in Expectation of the Fleet from *England*, to join *Anadiasia*, Colonel *Vetch*, to go against *Quebeck* by Sea, whilst *Anadagarjaux*, *Queder*, and we went to *Mont-Royal* by Land; but at last we were told, that our *Great Queen*, by some important Affair, was prevented in her Design for that Season. This made us extremely sorrowful, lest the *French*, who hitherto had dreaded us, should now think us unable to make War against them. The Reduction of *Canada* is of such Weight, that after the effecting thereof, we should have *free Hunting*, and a great Trade with our *Great Queen*'s Children: And as a token of the Sincerity of the six Nations, we do here, in the names of all, present our Great *Queen* with these *Belts* of *Wampum*.

We need not urge to our *Great Queen* more than than the Necessity we really labour under obliges us, that in our Case our *Great Queen* should not be mindful of us, we must with our Families forsake our Country, and seek other Habitations, or stand neuter; either of which will be much against our Inclinations.

Since we have been in Alliance with our *Great Queen's* Children, we have had some Knowledge of the *Saviour* of the World, and have often been importun'd by the *French*, both by the Insinuations of their Priests, and by Presents, to come over to their Interest; but have always esteem'd them *Men of Falsehood*. But if our *Great Queen* will be pleas'd to send over some Persons to instruct us, they shall find a most hearty Welcome.

We now close all with Hopes of our *Great Queen's* Favour, and leave it to her most gracious Consideration.

The Four Kings of Canada, being a Succinct Account of the Four Indian Princes
lately arriv'd from North America (London: John Baker 1710)

▶ During Queen Anne's War (1702-13) the French fort at Port Royal in what is now Nova Scotia fell to Colonel Francis Nicholson in 1710; by the Treaty of Utrecht of 1713, France ceded Acadia to Great Britain. When a group of Indians was informed that peace had been declared, a spokesman expressed relief.

It is well that the Kings should be at peace; I am very glad, and I no longer have any difficulty in making peace with thee. It is not I who have been striking thee for twelve years; it is the Frenchman who has used my arm to strike thee. It is true, we were at peace, I had even hurled away my hatchet, whither I know not; and while I was in repose upon my mat, thinking of nothing, some young men brought me a message that the Governor of Canada sent me, and which said to me: 'My son, the Englishman has struck me, help me to avenge myself; take thy hatchet and strike the Englishman.' I who have always listened to the word of the French Governor – I sought my hatchet, but I found it all rusty; I put it in order, and hung it to my belt, that I might come to strike thee. Now, when the Frenchman tells me to lay it down, I throw it far away, that we may no longer see the blood with which it is reddened. Therefore, let us live in peace, I am agreed.

Jesuit Relations, LXVII (1716-27) 207-9

▶ By the early eighteenth century the Anglo-French rivalry was being felt west of the Great Lakes. The Hudson's Bay Company had been formed in 1670 to trade for furs in the west, and the first white men seen by many western Indians were British traders operating out of Hudson Bay. In the meantime, explorers from New France, most notably Pierre Gaultier de Varennes, Sieur de La Vérendrye, were beginning to set up trading posts in the area. In June 1736 La Vérendrye's eldest son, Jean-Baptiste, along with Father Jean-Pierre Aulneau and some twenty voyageurs, was killed by a party of Sioux. La Colle (fl. 1736-42), the principal chief of the Monsonis at Rainy Lake, wanted to avenge their deaths, but La Vérendrye objected. At a council on 15 October, La Colle, presenting La Vérendrye with a collar and suggesting an exchange of persons to cement the alliance, makes it plain that the main need of his people was for economic security; next year the alliance would be continued by planning for warfare against the common enemy, the Sioux.

... My Father, when you came into our land you brought us things that we needed, and promised to continue doing so. For two years we lacked nothing, now we lack everything through default on the part of the traders. You forbade us to go to the English and we obeyed you, and if now we are compelled to go there to get guns, powder, kettles, tobacco, etc., you must only blame your own people.

This collar is to tell you to go yourself to see our Father at Montreal and represent our needs to him so that he may have pity on us. You will assure him that we are his true children, having all a French heart ever since we have known him. We give you the brother of La Mikouenne to accompany you; he will speak to our Father in the name of the three tribes. While awaiting your return we shall remain here with your children to keep your forts, and next spring we shall all go on a campaign against the Sioux to avenge the shedding of French blood, which is our own, and to protect your children against aggression. It is no longer you who are taking part in it, it is I and the chiefs of the three tribes. We beg you to send us from Michilimackinac the word of our Father in order that we may obey and follow it.

Journals and Letters of Pierre Gaultier de Varennes de la Vérendrye, and His Sons, edited by Lawrence J. Burpee (Toronto: Champlain Society 16, 1927) 231-2

▶ The following speech, made by a Cree to a Hudson's Bay Company factor,
  was typical of Indian bargaining in the fur trade and provides evidence of
  fur trade diplomacy and economy involving the complicated system of *over-
  plus*. The factor 'cheated' the Indians by giving short measure, not because
  of a greed for profits but because he needed to generate a material surplus
  which could then be distributed free to the Indians in the diplomatic ceremonies of the trade. The surplus could only be generated in this way
  because the Indians, who determined most fur trade practices, would not
  accept fluctuating prices. The speech also shows that the Indians determined the quality and type of goods traded.

You told me Last year to bring many Indians, you See I have not Lyd.
here is a great many young men come with me, use them Kindly! use
them Kindly I say! give them good goods, give them good Goods I say! –
we Livd. hard Last winter and in want. the powder being short measure
and bad, I say! – tell your Servants to fill the measure and not to put their
finger's within the Brim, take pity of us, take pity of us, I say! – we come
a Long way to See you, the french sends for us but we will not here, we
Love the English, give us good (brazl. tobacco) black tobacco, moist &
hard twisted, Let us see itt before op'n'd', – take pity of us, take pity of us
I say! – the Guns are bad, Let us trade Light guns small in the hand, and
well shap'd, with Locks that will not freeze in the winter, and Red gun
casses, (for if a gun is bad, a fine case oft'n putts it of, being great admir-
ers of Differt. Colour's) – Let the young men have Roll tobacco cheap,
Ketles thick high for the shape, and size, strong Ears, and the Baile to Lap
Just upon the side, – Give us Good measure, in cloth, – Let us see the old
measures, Do you mind me!, the young men Loves you by comming to
see you, take pity, take pity I say! – and give them good, they Love to
Dress and be fine, do you understand me!

James Isham's Observations on Hudson's Bay (1743) edited by E.E. Rich
(Toronto: Champlain Society 1949) 85-7

▶ Minavavana (c. 1710-70), also known as Minweweh, 'The one with the
  silver tongue,' or Le Grand Sauteux because of his six-foot height, was a
  chief of the Ojibwas on Mackinac Island. During the Seven Years' War he
  was allied to the French, and after their defeat refused to accept English
  sovereignty. However, he did allow Alexander Henry, one of the first English traders to arrive at Fort Michilimackinac in 1761, to trade unmolested
  in the area.

Englishman, it is to you that I speak, and I demand your attention!

Englishman, you know that the French King is our father. He promised to be such; and we, in return, promised to be his children. – This promise we have kept.

Englishman, it is you that have made war with this our father. You are his enemy; and how, then, could you have the boldness to venture among us, his children? – You know that his enemies are ours.

Englishman, we are informed, that our father, the king of France, is old and infirm; and that being fatigued, with making war upon your nation, he is fallen asleep. During his sleep, you have taken advantage of him and possessed yourselves of Canada. But, his nap is almost at an end. I think I hear him already stirring, and enquiring for his children, the Indians: – and, when he does awake, what must become of you? He will destroy you utterly!

Englishman, although you have conquered the French, you have not yet conquered us! We are not your slaves. These lakes, these woods and mountains, were left to us by our ancestors. They are our inheritance; and we will part with them to none. Your nation supposes that we, like the white people, cannot live without bread – and pork – and beef! But, you ought to know, that He, the Great Spirit and Master of Life, has provided food for us, in these spacious lakes, and on these woody mountains.

Englishman, our father, the king of France, employed our young men to make war upon your nation. In this warfare, many of them have been killed; and it is our custom to retaliate, until such time as the spirits of the slain are satisfied. But, the spirits of the slain are to be satisfied in either of two ways; the first is by the spilling of the blood of the nation by which they fell; the other, by *covering the bodies of the dead*, and thus allaying the resentment of their relations. This is done by making presents.

Englishman, your king has never sent us any presents, nor entered into any treaty with us, wherefore he and we are still at war; and, until he does these things, we must consider that we have no other father, nor friend, among the white men, than the king of France; but, for you, we have taken into consideration, that you have ventured your life among us, in the expectation that we should not molest you. You do not come armed, with an intention to make war; you come in peace, to trade with us, and supply us with necessities, of which we are much in want. We shall regard you, therefore, as a brother; and you may sleep tranquilly, without fear of the Chipeways. – As a token of our friendship, we present you with this pipe, to smoke.

Alexander Henry, *Travels and Adventures in Canada and the Indian Territories between the years 1760 and 1776*, edited by James Bain (Edmonton: Hurtig Publishers 1969) 43-5

▶ The Indians lost patience when pestered; in response to Alexander Mackenzie's persistent questioning about 'what obstacles might interrupt' him in his
travels, one man replied sarcastically:

What ... can be the reason that you are so particular and anxious in your
inquiries of us respecting a knowledge of this country: do not you white
men know every thing in the world?

> *Alexander Mackenzie's Voyage to the Pacific Ocean in 1793*
> (1801; Chicago: Lakeside Press 1931) 190-1

▶ Waub-ojeeg (c. 1747-93), or White Fisher, was an Ojibwa chief in the Lake
Superior region. His strong feelings about white men were expressed on one
occasion when John Johnston, a young Irish fur trader, fell madly in love
with his beautiful eldest daughter, O-shaw-gus-co-day-way-qua (Daughter
of the Green Mountain) and immediately asked the chief to give her to him
in marriage. Waub-ojeeg refused.

White Man, I have noticed your behaviour; it has been correct; but,
White Man, *your colour is deceitful*. Of you, may I expect better things?
You say you are going to Montreal; go, and if you return I shall be satis-
fied of your sincerity and will give you my daughter.

> Edward S. Neill, *History of the Ojibways, and their Connection with Fur Traders,*
> *based upon official and other Records*, Collections of the Minnesota Historical Society 5
> (St Paul 1885) 447-8

Waub-ojeeg was known for his eloquence and poetry as well as his warlike
daring. Here is one of his war songs translated into English verse by John
Johnston, who did in the end win the hand of the chief's daughter (one of
their daughters became the mother of Jane Schoolcraft, whose poetry
appears later in this book).

Waub-ojeeg's Battle Song

On that day when our heroes lay low, lay low,
On that day when our heroes lay low
I fought by their side, and thought, ere I died,
Just vengeance to take on the foe,
Just vengeance to take on the foe.

On that day, when our chieftains lay dead, lay dead,
On that day, when our chieftains lay dead,
I fought hand to hand at the head of my band,
And here on my breast have I bled, have I bled,
And here on my breast have I bled.

Our chiefs shall return no more, no more,
Our chiefs shall return no more –
Nor their brethren of war, who can show scar for scar,
Like women their fates shall deplore, deplore,
Like women their fates shall deplore.

Five winters in hunting we'll spend, we'll spend,
Five winters in hunting we'll spend,
Till our youth, grown to men, we'll to the war lead again,
And our days like our fathers' will end, will end,
And our days like our fathers' will end.

James Cleland Hamilton, 'Famous Algonquins: Algic Legends,'
Transactions of the Canadian Institute, VI (1898-9) 306

▶ Pontiac, or 'He who unites or joins together' (c. 1720-69), a chief of the
Ottawas, was an unwavering ally of the French. He resented and feared
British expansion into the interior, and successfully united a large number
of tribes to drive them from his country. He tried to take Fort Detroit, but
when it became apparent he would receive no help from the French he was
forced to raise the siege (he reluctantly made peace with the British in
August 1765). In a formal council-of-war at Detroit on 23 May 1763, unin-
formed of the Peace of Paris by which Great Britain had acquired a vast
empire in North America from the French, Pontiac attacked his friends and
allies as traitors to his cause.

My Brothers! ... I have no doubt but this war is very troublesome to you,
and that my warriors, who are continually passing and re-passing through
your settlements, frequently kill your cattle, and injure your property. I
am sorry for it, and hope you do not think I am pleased with this conduct
of my young men. And as a proof of my friendship, recollect the war you
had seventeen years ago, [1746] and the part I took in it. The Northern
nations combined together, and came to destroy you. Who defended you?
Was it not myself and my young men? The great Chief, Mackinac, [the

Turtle] said in Council, that he would carry to his native village the head of your chief warrior, and that he would eat his heart and drink his blood. Did I not then join you, and go to his camp and say to him, if he wished to kill the French, he must pass over my body, and the bodies of my young men? Did I not take hold of the tomahawk with you, and aid you in fighting your battles with Mackinac, and driving him home to his country? Why do you think I would turn my arms against you? Am I not the same French Pontiac, who assisted you seventeen years ago? I am a Frenchman, and I wish to die a Frenchman ...

My Brothers! I begin to grow tired of this *bad meat* which is upon our lands. I begin to see that this is not your case, for instead of assisting us in our war with the English, you are actually assisting them. I have already told you, and I now tell you again, that when I undertook this war, it was only your interest I sought, and that I knew what I was about. I yet know what I am about. This year they must all perish. The Master of Life so orders it. His will is known to us, and we must do as he says. And you, my brothers, who know him better than we do, wish to oppose his will! Until now, I have avoided urging you upon this subject, in the hope, that if you could not aid, you would not injure us. I did not wish to ask you to fight with us against the English, and I did not believe you would take part with them. You will say you are not with them. I know it, but your conduct amounts to the same thing. You will tell them all we do and say. You carry our counsels and plans to them. Now take your choice. You must be entirely French, like ourselves, or entirely English. If you are French, take this belt for yourselves and your young men, and join us. If you are English, we declare war against you.

Thatcher, *Indian Biography*, II, 117-18

Maquinna's ancestor, 1788

Joseph Brant

Tecumseh

Big Bear

Crowfoot

Piapot

2 'Listen to our grievances, fulfil your promises'

'Truly the Aborigines of America are a doomed race!'

Peter Dooyentate Clarke, *Origin and Traditional History of the Wyandotts*
(Toronto 1870) 76

A Feasting Song

I approach the village,
Ya ha he ha, ya ha ha ha;
And hear the voices of many people;
Ya ha he ha, ya ha ha ha;
The barking of dogs,
Ya ha he ha, ya ha ha ha;
Salmon is plentiful,
Ya ha he ha, ya ha ha ha;
The berry season is good,
Ya ha he ha, ya ha ha ha.

John McLean's Notes of Twenty-Five Years' Service in the Hudson's Bay Territory,
ed. W. Stewart Wallace (1839; Toronto: Champlain Society 19, 1932) 157

Micmac Vengeance Song

Death I make, singing,
Heh-yeh!heh-yeh!heh-yeh!heh-yeh!
Bones I hack, singing,
Heh-yeh!heh-yeh!heh-yeh!heh-yeh!
Death I make, singing,
Heh-yeh!heh-yeh!heh-yeh!heh!

Translated by Dr Silas T. Rand

New France had fallen. The Indians from coast to coast would eventually find themselves under British rule.

The wars were not over, however. In the late eighteenth and early nineteenth centuries, Indian leaders in central and eastern Canada led their people into battle on one side or other of the civil war that became the American Revolution. Joseph Brant supported the British in the revolutionary war (1775-83), as did Tecumseh in the War of 1812. Since the Indians no longer held a balance of power, their role as allies was of less importance, and their sacrifices did not always bring the rewards they deserved.

With peace came more settlers. Throughout the nineteenth century white farmers took over the land in the east and Indians were pushed onto reserves; increasingly their lives became regulated at the same time as their lands shrunk and they had to contend with poverty and disease.

Later in the century the signing of treaties in the west led to the same miserable conditions on the prairies. The great chiefs of the plains, Crowfoot, Big Bear, Poundmaker, did the best they could for their people, but with the disappearance of the buffalo herds the old way of life was gone forever. The crushing of the rebellion on the Saskatchewan in 1885 signified the end of Indian dominance on the prairies.

The Indian writing of this period is dominated by what might be called 'official' literature – innumerable petitions, letters of protest, memorials, speeches in council and at treaty-signing sessions. The language used contains less rhetoric and conceit than in the earlier period. The statesmanship, courtesy, and respect that distinguished the orations of their forefathers are still present, but there is an underlying urgency in their appeals, an immediacy of need.

The over-riding theme is a sense of loss – loss of land, hunting and fishing rights, loss of self-sufficiency and dignity, loss of nationhood.

There is a sadness in the protests but also a will to survive, a determination to conserve what was possible, of land and customs, as accommodation to the white man, who was busy subduing a continent, became inevitable. At age eighty-five, in 1865, Peter Paul found himself none too impressed by modern Nova Scotia – 'steamboat make water dirty ... scare'em fish ... everything noise, bustle, all change'; and a chief in Fort Frances, in 1873, observed that food was less plentiful since the white man came, a fact that 'deranges a little my kettle.' As the nineteenth century drew to a close, the chief Maquinna, in British Columbia, protesting the outlawing of the potlatch, pointed out that this ancient Indian custom was hardly less respectable or less efficient than the white man's banks.

▶ During the American Revolution, the Malecites in the Saint John Valley (now New Brunswick) were caught between Nova Scotia, loyal to the British, and rebellious Massachusetts to the south. They were believed to hold the balance of power north of the Bay of Fundy, and both sides vied for their support. The Indians, as former allies of the French, had suffered attacks from the Americans, and they were in bad economic straits because of the decline of the fur trade; they were therefore reluctant to fight and tried to accommodate both sides, with some success. In the speech that follows, Pierre Tomah (fl. 1775-80), a Malecite chief and a staunch Roman Catholic, negotiates with the Americans in council at Machias (Maine) on 27 December 1779. Eventually the Indians themselves split, with Tomah's people settling on the British side.

Brother,

By the Grace of the Almighty, who Conducts all his People we are permitted to meets togeather at this place [Machias] where we formerly did our Undertakings, – The Old men, the Sachems, the Captains & the Young men Salute, all the Officers & Gentlemen here present as well as all the rest of the Americans –

Brother, You now see we have Complyed with the request you made when on St. Johns, & all those who are with me have come & are ready for any thing you may order us to do –

Brother, When you sent for me before I was ready to obey your Commands in behalf of America, I am now come, & left all I have, and depend on you for our Subsistance for something to Eat, & to keep our backs Warm, –

Brother, some Difficultys arose between you & me when I was on St. Johns, But I assure you any thing I did was through fear, as our Situation was such as the Enemy Cou'd Distroy us & our Familys – I am now Come to obey you in any thing for the Good of America & the Thing [King] of France you may order.

Brother you are Sencible I am not Acquainted with writing and Reading – I did Receive Letters from the Britains, I went & meet them, but never acted any thing against the Americans, – but any thing I did was thro fear, as I was old & infirm & for fear of their hurting me & family I was on the River & Loath to leave what I had, I only acted as I see many Americans, at this Day, that is to keep peace on both sides, but my heart was for America, –

Brother, When I was on the Road half way to Meete you, and Express over Took me, from some of our Colour who entreated us not to Come & Join you, but Continue on the River where we was, & remain friends to Britain & with our Brothers who were friends with them – & not to Come to you, & fight against Britain & them, – I in answer mentioned that I was attach'd to America & General Washington as well as our old Allie's the French, & was Determined to Come, for which reason you now see me here, ready with all here to do any thing for the Good of America, –

Brother, I forgot to Mention something more respecting this Express, they said it was a pity that as we were the same Colour & Religion, for us to Take up the Hatchet for America, as then we must fight against them – and shoud be Compelled to Kill one another, – that the Britains wou'd be friends to us & Give us whatever we stood in Need off, –

Brother, I now have repeated over what I have to say respecting News, – I now have to mention respecting our Situation, – We have Come here to Join you, all we Desire is to have some support, We have no body to look too but you, to Assist us in whatever we stand in need off –

Brother, You see our Situation, & you must Know it – we are now like Birds lett out off a Cage & Depend on people who are better Acquainted with the world then ourselves – You know the Nature of Indians, they often Ask for more then is promised them – their Demands likely will be Great, but we depend on you to Give what you think is absolutely Necessary –

Brother, I must repeat to you respecting our Situation, there is a number of Old people among us who must be supported – if there shoud not any thing Come Down this fall, if you Lett us Know it in time we will send the Young Men a hunting for Subsistence – But the Old ones must be Round you & supported at all events –

Brother, We have now Risen from our Beads & left our former Place of abode & come to Join you for the Reguard we had for America & the King of France, and hope by the blessing of God that we shall be preserved thro all our Difficultys & Distresses, which Doubt not we shall be able to go thro by the Assistance you will afford us –

Brother, I forgot further to mention, People may have an odd opinion of us, for our being of a Different Principle of Religion, but we Act from Principle, & must beg you will do your Endeavour to get a Priest from our old Father the King of France to settle among us, so that we may have every thing Done According to our own manner of Religion,

Brother this is all I have to say at this Time –
The foregoing was Literally Interpreted
Attest
Jas. Avery, Secy to Supr Intn
Easn Dept

W.D. Hamilton and W.A. Spray, eds., *Source Materials Relating to the New Brunswick Indian* (Fredericton: Hamray Books 1977) 53-4

▶ Joseph Brant (1742-1807), or Thayendanegea, 'He who sets or places together two bets,' was a Mohawk chief who fought with the British against the French and later against the Americans, eventually leading his Six Nations people to take refuge in Upper Canada where they were given a tract of land on the Grand River (the town of Brantford was named after him). In frank and forceful English, Brant delivered an address to Lord Sidney, His Majesty's secretary for colonial affairs, in London on 4 January 1786.

My Lord,
... We hope it is a truth well known in this country, what a faithful part we took in their behalf [the British] in the late dispute with the Americans: and though we have been told peace has long since been concluded between you and them, it is not finally settled with us, which causes great uneasiness through all the Indian nations ...
... we were struck with astonishment at hearing we were forgot in the treaty [1783]. Notwithstanding the manner we were told this, we could not believe it possible such firm friends and allies could be so neglected by a nation remarkable for its honor and glory, whom we had served with so much zeal and fidelity. For this reason we applied to the King's Commander-in-chief, in Canada in a friendly and private way, wishing not to let those people in rebellion know the concern and trouble we were under. From the time of delivering that speech, near three years, we have had no answer, and remain in a state of great suspense and uneasiness of mind ...
It is, my Lord, the earnest desire of the Five United Nations, and the whole Indian Confederacy, that I may have an answer to that speech ...

In this extract from a letter written about 1786, Joseph Brant answers Indian commissioner Thomas Eddy's question as to whether 'civilization is favourable to human happiness.' 'There are degrees of civilization,' he argues, 'from Cannibals to the most polite of European nations.'

... I was, Sir, born of Indian parents, and lived while a child among those whom you are pleased to call savages; I was afterward sent to live among the white people, and educated at one of your schools; since which period I have been honored much beyond my deserts, by an acquaintance with a number of principal characters both in Europe and America. After all this experience, and after every exertion to divest myself of prejudice, I am obliged to give my opinion in favor of my own people ... In the government you call civilized, the happiness of the people is constantly sacrificed to the splendor of empire. Hence your codes of criminal and civil laws have had their origin; hence your dungeons and prisons ... we have *no* prisons; we have no pompous parade of courts; we have no written laws; and yet judges are as highly revered amongst us as they are among you, and their decisions are as much regarded.

Property, to say the least, is well guarded, and crimes are as impartially punished. We have among us no splendid villains above the control of our laws. Daring wickedness is here never suffered to triumph over helpless innocence. The estates of widows and orphans are never devoured by enterprising sharpers. In a word, we have no robbery under the color of law. No person among us desires any other reward for performing a brave and worthy action, but the consciousness of having served his nation. Our wise men are called Fathers; they truly sustain that character. They are always accessible, I will not say to the meanest of our people, for we have none mean but such as render themselves so by their vices.

The palaces and prisons among you form a most dreadful contrast. Go to the former places, and you will see perhaps a *deformed piece of earth* assuming airs that become none but the Great Spirit above. Go to one of your prisons; here description utterly fails! Kill them, if you please; kill them, too, by tortures; but let the torture last no longer than a day. Those you call savages, relent; the most furious of our tormentors exhausts his rage in a few hours, and dispatches his unhappy victim with a sudden stroke. Perhaps it is eligible that incorrigible offenders should sometimes be cut off. Let it be done in a way that is not degrading to human nature. Let such unhappy men have an opportunity, by their fortitude, of making an atonement in some measure for the crimes they have committed during their lives.

But for what are many of your prisoners confined? – for debt! – astonishing! – and will you ever again call the Indian nations cruel? Liberty, to a rational creature, as much exceeds property as the light of the sun does that of the most twinkling star. But you put them on a level, to the everlasting disgrace of civilization ... Great Spirit of the Universe! – and do you call yourselves Christians? Does then the religion of Him whom you call your Saviour, inspire this spirit, and lead to these practices? Surely no. It is recorded of him, that a bruised reed he never broke. Cease, then, to call yourselves Christians, lest you publish to the world your hypocrisy. Cease, too, to call other nations savage, when you are tenfold more the children of cruelty than they.

William L. Stone, *Life of Joseph Brant-Thayendanegea, including the Border Wars of the American Revolution* (New York 1838) II, 253-4, 481-3

▶ John Deserontyon, 'Struck by Lightning' (c. 1742-1811), a cousin of Joseph Brant, was a Mohawk captain and chief who fought on the side of the British in the American revolutionary war. In 1784 he accepted General Frederick Haldimand's offer of a grant of land along the shores of the Bay of Quinte on Lake Ontario and led the first group of Mohawk United Empire Loyalists to settle there. The importance Deserontyon attached to education and religious instruction is witnessed in the following letter addressed to Colonel Daniel Claus, deputy superintendent of Indians in Montreal.

Bro^r Solsitsyowane [Claus]   La Chine, 10th April 1784

    Mr Vincent the Schoolmaster came here about what you was speaking to him the other day of instructing the Mohawks of this settlement for which we give you thanks. We have been long thinking about a Schoolmaster to go with us, having been used to such a person in the Mohawk Country thro' the Bounty of our most gracious King by whose order one Mr. Lealand was appointed but he being then six years of no Service to us having stayed behind. For which reason we wish that the General would consider our case, and appoint such a person, as we never had more occasion for one than at present for the teaching of our Children who have been much neglected in that respect since we left home. And likewise to be instructed in religious Matters, in which points we think Mr. Vincent very capable, we find he will likewise answer another good purpose which is to be Interpreter to our Minister as he speaks our Language as well as his own, & had an English Education in Dartmouth College, and shews a great Desire of living with us in our New Settlement. – We would not speak about these Matters before we knew how the War would end, and where we were to sit down with our families for good. We have been these two years in an unsettled state at La Chine with regard to our future abode, but knowing now where to go we would be glad to enjoy the priviledge of a School-Master, & Clerk as before; and by Sir Johns, and your assistance, & recommendation to General Haldimand how much we and our children stand in need of such a person, and would be glad to have the General's answer as soon as convenient upon that head as well as upon the Letter we wrote you the other day about our Settlement near Cataraghkon in regard to a Deed from the General for the Tract of Land we pointed out to His Excellency, as we would be glad to set out as soon as possible in order to get some Indian Corn in the Ground. We salute you, & Sir John wanonghsisohon [Johnson, superintendent-general of Indian affairs in British North America]
(signed) Jno Deserontyon

Public Archives of Canada, Haldimand Papers, MG21, vol. B114

The new settlement on the shores of the Bay of Quinte required Deseron-tyon's leadership in all types of councils. He recorded the following Mohawk form of ritual condolence, which was recited at the Mourning Council. Based on an ancient prescribed form of set speeches and formulaic expressions, the ritual is not only a public lamentation for the death of a chief but also an induction ceremony for the new chief. This ancient cultural pattern, which guarantees the continuity of Iroquois society and government, still survives.

Lachine, April 9th, 1782.

We of Caughnawaga, may we give utterance to our voice, we, the Tekari-hoken [the Mohawk], we, whose clans number three, we, whose settlements number 2, concerning what befell him in person, him, the Seven Nations (of Canada) in number, in that he now died, he who was a chief, he who was Asharekowa [= He, the Great Knife] (the chief who died 25 March 1782).

1. The first thing is 'The Forepart of the Ceremony.' The tears, we have borne them elsewhere. And also from his open throat we have dislodged the several lodgments. And also from his outspread mat [his abiding-place], we have wiped away the several blood spots. Thoroughly again have we readjusted the things (there).

Indeed, there a wampum string (is required).

The Gorah [i.e., the Superintendent (Colonel Daniel Claus)], Shot-sitsyowanen, he and I are unanimous (in this).

None the less, there are many matters.

2. The Second Matter. Go to, my brother, thou, the Seven Nations in number. Now, again, it is an awful thing that has befallen thy person. Now, thou has lost that upon which thy two eyes rested trustfully, he was a warrior, the establishment of welfare by law was his duty. Now our Master [our God] has withdrawn him again. That, then, do I remember, I, who am the Mohawk (I, the Tekarihoken), how that they, our grandsires who were, had made it an ordinance; did they not say (that) wherever it might be that one, whose mind is left fresh and untouched, shall at once readjust all the several things again. Now, therefore, my brother, may I say it, I have smoothed over the rough earth whereon, indeed, landed the flesh of him, who was our Business, the late Ashre-kowa [Great Knife], that is, we as one had him as the embodiment of our affairs, so then that we speak words over the corpse, that is it, he and I, the Gorah, *Shotsitsyowanen* [= He whose flower is great; i.e., the Super-intendent], are unanimous.

There (i.e., at this point), a wampum belt (is required).

Many, lo, are the matters in number.

The Third Matter (Rite) in Order.

3. Thou and I are brothers [= my brother]; thou, the Seven Nations (in number). Now, do thou continue listening along as I continue reciting the words (of the ceremony). Did I not intend that only once would I speak words on what has befallen thy person today. May I, therefore, say, my brother (*lit.*, thou and I are brothers) that I again draw together thy people at the place where thou art wont to environ the fire (i.e., around the hearth of the home, as well). And also I have again rekindled thy (Council) fire where all manner of things come to thee as duties. Go thou forward. Have courage, my brother. Thou hast the charge of public affairs, as many in number as still remain.

Do thou not suffer it, that thy mind should be borne hence (by grief). The only thing now to which thou must continue to give attention is our Law (and welfare). It is that over which thou, the Seven Nations, art administrator. And also, is it not true, that they, our late grandsires, said, perhaps, we should die were it to take along with it, one's mind, no matter where it may be, among those who have united their affairs, will (it) slay with a single blow, only thou [deprecatively] must continue thinking that He, the Master [i.e., God], foreordains what befalls our persons in the course of things.

There [at this point in the ceremony] a wampum belt (is required).

Many, lo, are the matters in number.

4. It is the Fourth Matter. My brother [i.e., thou and I are brothers], do thou keep listening along to my recital of the matter of the ritual. Now, am I not today saying, Go thou forward, do thou have courage. Thou hast charge of public affairs. So then let me say, my brother [thou and I are brothers], do you two, nephew and uncle, thy nephew who is heed to anything that is good to which he may give utterance.

And also thou too, thou, warrior, wait to hear anything thy uncle, the royaner [i.e., the nobleman] of many things, to which he may give utterance.

So then, just that will come to pass, that anything in relation to our Law that you two may ordain shall be firmly established.

There [i.e., here] at this place a string of wampum (is required).

Many, lo, are the things (of the ceremony) in number.

I have written it. John Deserontyon.

Canadasege (At Newtown).

John Deserontyon, *A Mohawk Form of Ritual of Condolence*, 9 April 1782, translated by J.N.B. Hewitt (New York: Museum of the American Indian Heye Foundation 1928)

► Tecumseh (1768-1813), 'He who crosses over,' was a Shawnee chief who supported the British in the War of 1812, in which he was given the regular commission of brigadier-general in command of more than two thousand Indian soliders (he was killed in action at the Battle of Moraviantown on 5 October 1813). Sir Isaac Brock said of him: 'A more sagacious or more gallant warrior does not exist.' When Colonel Henry Procter, the British commander, began to withdraw his forces from Fort Malden before the advancing American army, Tecumseh objected to the retreat, delivering this celebrated appeal at Amherstburg on 18 September 1813.

Father, listen to your children, You see them now all before you. The war before this, our British father, gave the hatchet to his red children when our old chiefs were alive. They are now all dead. In that war our father was thrown on his back by the Americans, and our father took them by the hand without our knowledge, and we are afraid our father will do so again at this time.

Summer before last, when I came forward with my red brethren, and was ready to take up the hatchet in favor of our British father, we were told not to be in a hurry – that he had not yet determined to fight the Americans.

Listen! When war was declared, our father stood up and gave us the tomahawk, and told us that he was now ready to strike the Americans – that he wanted our assistance; and he certainly would get us our lands back, which the Americans had taken from us.

Listen! You told us at the same time to bring forward our families to this place – we did so, and you promised to take care of them, and that they should want for nothing, while the men would go to fight the enemy – that we were not to trouble ourselves with the enemy's garrisons – that we knew nothing about them, and that our father would attend to that part of the business. You also told your red children that you would take care of your garrison here, which made our hearts glad.

Listen! When we last went to the Rapids, it is true we gave you little assistance. It is hard to fight people who live like ground-hogs.

Father – Listen! – Our fleet has gone out; we know they have fought; we have heard the great guns; but know nothing of what has happened to our father with one arm [Commodore Robert H. Barclay]. Our ships have gone one way and we are much astonished to see our father tying up every thing and preparing to run away the other, without letting his red children know what his intentions are. You always told us to remain here and take care of our lands; it made our hearts glad to hear that was your wish. Our great father, the King, is the head, and you represent him. You always told us you would never draw your foot off British ground; but now, father, we see you are drawing back, and we are sorry to see our father doing so without seeing the enemy. We must compare our father's conduct to a fat animal, that carries its tail upon its back, but when affrighted, it drops it between its legs and runs off.

Listen father! The Americans have not yet defeated us by land; neither are we sure that they have done so by water; we therefore wish to remain here, and fight our enemy, should they make their appearance. If they defeat us, we will then retreat with our father.

At the battle of the Rapids, last war, the Americans certainly defeated us; and when we retreated to our fathers fort, at that place, the gates were shut against us. We were afraid that it would now be the case; but instead of that we now see our British father preparing to march out of his garrison.

Father! You have got the arms and ammunition which our great father sent for his red children. If you have any idea of going away, give them to us, and you may go in welcome, for us. Our lives are in the hands of the Great Spirit. We are determined to defend our lands, and if it is his will, we wish to leave our bones upon them.

Major John Richardson, *War of 1812* (Brockville, Canada West 1842) 119-20

▶ Ocaita, an Ottawa chief and the official spokesman for the Ottawa, Chippewa, and Wenabago Indians, at a council held on Drummond Island, 7 July 1818, recalled the contribution his people had made to the British cause in the War of 1812 and charged the British with false promises. The sense of betrayal stems from the situation at the end of the revolutionary war, when the British retained control of their posts in the Ohio country west of the former Thirteen Colonies. Although most of the Indians were technically living on American land, they were tacitly allied to the British because of their connections to the fur trade and they received annual gifts from the Canadian government. Even before the War of 1812 the pressures of American settlement were forcing both Indians and the British north of the Great Lakes. Ocaita's people were caught amongst the uncertainties of a shifting international boundary.

Father
Your children now seated round you salute you sincerely they intend to talk to you a great deal and beg you will listen to them with patience for they intend to open their hearts to you [explain their sentiments].

Father

When the Great Master of Life made us he set us down on the Ottawa Island [Great Manitoulin, in Lake Huron] – we were all white [pure] – we were then unacquainted with the whites and did not value guns gunpowder or iron we wore skins, were independent and lived happy in our natural state: –

Father

Our ancestors one day on looking towards the rising sun, saw people of a different colour to themselves and not long after they [the French] stretched out their hands to us [supplied them with goods] we were delighted at the appearance of these strangers – They treated us well and appeared to become our relations [to live in the country], We consented and soon, after they kindled a fire at Old Mackinac [built a fort] and called us their children they told us we should never be in want or miserable with them but they would always give us good supplies and furnish us with Traders they did so my father they never told us a lie neither did they deceive us. –

Father

While we were living in this happy state, you was at play [at war] with our Father. He desired us to join and assist him in keeping you out of our Country – Our Ancestors cryed but notwithstanding our assistance you beat the french, drove them off our lands and took us under your arm [made peace with them]

Father

On making peace you promised to treat us with the same attention that the french had done, that we should receive a bounty annually of fine things, that would make us comfortable and happy – You also told us your breasts would never be dry, but that we should have plenty of milk [rum]

Father

Some time after you had got quietly seated on our lands a neighbouring Nation of ours, acted like fools [when the Chippawas cut off the garrison at Michilimackinac], they killed the greater part of your Soldiers then at Michilimackinac the surviving ones my father we collected together and took care of them – We went to the Green Bay brought away all your soldiers and delivered them safe in a Strong place [Montreal], our father at Montreal was delighted at our conduct returned us many thanks, and said he would again build a fire [a Fort] and plant a tree on our lands that would never die the bark would be taken off [a flag staff] and that round the tree you would raise a strong hill [a fortification]; all this my father has come to pass Your words have been true, your words were smooth and pleasant. (Holding the Belt of 1764 in his hand he said:)

Father

This my ancestors, received from our father [Sir William Johnson, super-intendent of Indian affairs] – You sent word to all your red children to assemble at the crooked place [Niagara]. They all heard your voice [obeyed the message] and the next summer met you at that place – You then laid this Belt on a Mat and said Children you must all touch this belt of Peace – I touch it myself that we may be all brethren [united] and hope our friendship will never cease. I will call you my children, will send warmth [presents] to your country, and your families shall never be in want. Look towards the rising sun. My Nation is brilliant as it is, and its word cannot be violated. –

Father

Your words were true – all you promised came to pass. On giving us the belt of peace you said if you should ever require my assistance shew this belt and my hand will be immediately stretched for to help you. (Here the speaker laid down the Belt, and took up eight strings of white Wampum.)

Father

Listen with attention to what I have to tell you – It is the voice of my Chiefs and the Ottawa Nation, not long ago you sent for us to St. Josephs, and spoke to us with a strong voice [entreated]. We never until that moment hesitated to obey your orders, but my Father something whispered in our ears that it would be good policy for us to sleep [remain neutral] during the war, and Cultivate our Lands for the support and comfort to our families, but my father when one of your warriors [Captain Roberts] as it was for our good and that you would never make peace with them until you would drive them over the Mississippi and that you would make a large road [boundary line] that would drive them from us that they should never be allowed to step over it, and that when you would make peace all your red Children that would join you should be consulted and included as your sincerest friends [allies] – at the same time that you implored our assistance you won the influence of our sensible chiefs, who talking to us incessantly, til with one voice we raised the hatchet and made the Americans run out of their Fort [Michilimackinac].

Father

We were not anxious to raise the hatchet, for fear the Americans should be too strong for you and in that case we should lose your support and be obliged to fight them ourselves in defence of our women and children, and to prevent them from taking from us our lands, that the Great Master of life planted us on but knowing your words to be the breath of truth we seized the Hatchet painted our faces and made the woods echo with the songs of war –

Father

Though many of our young men were mixed with the earth [killed] we were happy, and took to your chiefs the hair of a great many of the heads of your enemies; and tho' we were enjoying ourselves and every thing going on well, we were astonished one morning [spring] to hear by a little bird [messenger], that you had buried the Hatchet and taken our enemies by the hand. –

Father

We of course supposed the enemy had been crying over your head [imploring] to be charitable to them to make Peace, and to save their lives – We were glad to hear the news, not doubting that all you told us was now coming to pass. –

Father

My heart now fails me. I can hardly speak – We are now slaves and treated worse than dogs – Those bad spirits [the Americans] take possession of our Lands without consulting us they deprive us of our English traders They even tie us up and torture us almost to death [flog them].

Father

Our chiefs did not consent to have our lands given to the Americans – but you did it without consulting us. and in doing that you delivered us up to their mercy – They are enraged at us for having joined you in the play [in the war] and they treat us worse than dogs

Father

We implore you to open your ears to listen to our Grievances fulfill your promises that we may be released from Slavery, and enjoy the happiness we did previous to the War. –

Father

The Great Master of Life made the Water the Land, deer, Fish and Birds, for the good of mankind. You are our Great father placed by the Master of Life to watch over us, you can make us enjoy those things, We – therefore implore you to take Pity upon us, and allow us to enjoy what the Great Master of Life made for us all –

Father

When you abandoned Michilimackinac you promised we would at this fire place riceive every thing we could wish for to make us comfortable until this year your words have true. we have now come a great distance, and all return nearly empty handed.

Father

You Mackay it is to you our chiefs speak they request you to put our parole in a fair road to reach our new Father at Quebec and also request that an answer may be sent to them this Fall, they have already sent several Paroles, respecting their situation, but they have not been listened to – The Paroles have been asleep – If a deaf ear is turned to this, the chiefs and warriors say they will go to Quebec themselves next spring and talk loud [explain their sentiments themselves personally] and if they should not be listened to, or should the store door be shut against us we Indians, will find the means to open them, and be heard. –

Father

What we have said is not intended to offend you we have merely reminded you of your promises and told you of our grievances.

Father

Should some of our People be in the fall employed gathering their Corn and not able to come for their presents could you not have their clothing sent to them by some of their relations that come here.

Father

I return thanks to the Great Master of Life for having afforded us a fine day to speak to our Great father – I have been talking a long time and am quite thirsty. Cannot you give me a drop of milk ... I most sincerely shake you by the hands as the representative of our Great father – I have nothing more to say –

Public Archives of Canada, Lt.-Col. William McKay Papers, MG19, F29

▶ Although fur traders had been exploring the west and trading their wares with the Indians for well over a hundred years, the first real white settlers in Manitoba were planted by Lord Selkirk on the Red River in 1812 on a grant of land given by the Hudson's Bay Company. Grandes Oreilles, a chief of the Chippewas, mentions these 'Landworkers from below' (that is, from the north, Hudson Bay) in this speech addressed to several partners of the rival North West Company of Montreal in the Indian Hall at the Forks of Red River on 19 June 1814. His fears that farming and the intense rivalry between the companies would result in the removal of his traditional trading partners from the area were realized seven years later, in 1821, with the absorption of the Nor'Westers into the Hudson's Bay Company.

Traders, my Children, when I first heard of the troubles you were in at this place, my heart became sorry, and the tears ran down my cheeks. I found, however, there was no time to indulge in grief, no time to be lost.

Our Traders, our Friends, the Protectors of our Children, were surrounded with dangers; I gave the call of war, and you see before you proofs that my voice was not exerted in vain; my young men have listened to it.

I find that you as well as the Indians are surrounded with difficulties and dangers. We are placed as if all were encircled within the ring of beads which I hold in my hands. We have the Sioux to oppose from above, and now it appears that we have to contend with Landworkers from below.

What are these Landworkers? What brought them here? Who gave them our lands? and how do they dare to prevent our Traders from purchasing whatever we have to give them, upon our own lands? But it would appear that these Strangers, these makers of gardens, look upon themselves as the real possessors of these lands, and presuming on this extraordinary right, would wish to prevent you from returning here, by depriving you of your stock of provisions traded on this River, in hopes thereby to drive you from the country, and make slaves of the Indians when deprived of their Friends and Protectors. As for them, we can never look on them as such.

Last summer I was called upon by you to go with my young men to Fort William, in order to give assistance against the Americans [in the War of 1812]; I listened to the call, and proceeded towards your great Lodge; but when we reached it, I found that our assistance was not required. I however left my war club in the Hall, in case I might again be called upon. I then could not have thought that I should ever have occasion for my club to serve against the Whites on these lands; and white people too, coming from the same lands with yourselves! and all of you, as well as the Indians, obeying the same Great Father. But we see that the Landworkers are unreasonable; that they are determined to impose upon us and upon you. We are therefore equally determined to break down whatever barriers they may set up against us, or against you. My young men are equally determined with myself: it is our wish, it is our interest, to preserve you amongst us at the risk of our lives; for if you leave us, who will have pity on our women and children?

You say, however, that for the present, you have come to an understanding with these people, that you have carried your point with them. I am glad of it: I thank the Master of Life, that my string of beads will not be stained with the blood of Whites residing on these lands. I should always wish to see you at peace. I would love you all, was it possible, but my heart and my life is at the service of those who have charge of the bones of my Father [Netam, the Great Chief, his father] and my Brother;

and if you cannot live in peace, and that these Landworkers will not allow you to trade with us as usual, they shall be destroyed, or driven out of the Assiniboine River.

To conclude what I had to say; I already see a great change. When we were accustomed to encamp round the Forts of our Traders on this river, our Children used to be fed with pounded meat and with grease; but this spring, hunger and starvation forced us to leave the Fort much sooner than I intended; for my wish was to remain until the black clouds which appeared hanging over the Fort were dispelled.

Some of you, my Children, thought perhaps then, that I wished to get out of the way. But no; I had no such intentions: seeing that you had not a mouthful of provisions, even for your young men, I was forced to go and seek something for my Children. It was not the sound of bad birds that drove me away; my readiness in appearing here to support your cause, ought to be a proof of my attachment to my Traders and to my Children.

These are my words, and I have not two mouths.

A Narrative of Occurrences in the Indian Countries of North America,
since the Connexion of the Right Hon. the Earl of Selkirk with the Hudson's Bay Company,
and his attempt to establish a colony on the Red River (London: B. McMillan 1817)

▶ Jane Schoolcraft (1800-42) was part Chippewa, a granddaughter of Waubojeeg, the celebrated war sachem. Educated in Europe under the care of her Irish father's relatives, in 1823 she married Henry Rowe Schoolcraft, the American explorer and ethnologist who was at the time Indian agent for the tribes around Lake Superior. She was equally well versed in the English and Algonkian languages, and on 23 March 1827 wrote this poetic tribute to the memory of her first-born son.

To my ever beloved and lamented Son
  William Henry

Who was it, nestled on my breast,
'And on my cheeks sweet kisses prest'
And in whose smile I felt so blest?
                    Sweet Willy.

Who hail'd my form as home I stept,
And in my arms so eager leapt,
And to my bosom joyous crept?
                    My Willy.

Who was it, wiped my tearful eye,
And kiss'd away the coming sigh,
And smiling bid me say 'good boy'?
                    Sweet Willy.

Who was it, look'd divinely fair,
Whilst lisping sweet the evening pray'r
Guileless and free from earthly care?
                    My Willy.

Where is that voice attuned to love,
That bid me say 'my darling dove'
But oh! that soul has flown above,
                    Sweet Willy.

Whither has fled the rose's hue?
The lilly's whiteness blending grew,
Upon thy cheek – so fair to view,
                    My Willy.

Oft have I gaz'd with wrapt delight,
Upon those eyes that sparkled bright,
Emitting beams of joy and light!
                    Sweet Willy.

Oft have I kiss'd that forehead high,
Like polished marble to the eye,
And blessing, breathed an anxious sigh.
                    For Willy.

My Son! thy coral lips are pale,
Can I believe the heart-sick tale,
That I, thy loss must ever wail?
                    My Willy.

The clouds in darkness seemed to low'r,
The storm has past with awful pow'r,
And nipt my tender, beauteous flow'r!
                    Sweet Willy.

But soon my spirit will be free,
And I my lovely Son shall see,
For God, I know, did this decree!
　　　　　My Willy.

▶ Henry Schoolcraft, who did a great deal to popularize Indian oral literature, made both a literal and a literary translation of this Chippewa song.

Chant to the Fire-Fly

Wau wau tay see!
Wau wau tay see!
E mow e shin
Tahe bwau ne baun-e wee!
Be eghaun – be eghaun – ewee!
Wau wau tay see!
Wau wau tay see!
Was sa koon ain je gun.
Was sa koon ain je gun.

Flitting-white-fire-insect! waving-white-fire-bug! give me light before I go to bed! give me light before I go to sleep. Come, little dancing white-fire-bug! Come, little flitting white-fire-beast! Light me with your bright white-flame-instrument – your little candle.

Fire-fly, fire-fly! bright little thing,
Light me to bed, and my song I will sing.
Give me your light, as you fly o'er my head,
That I may merrily go to my bed.
Give me your light o'er the grass as you creep,
That I may joyfully go to my sleep.
Come, little fire-fly, come, little beast –
Come! and I'll make you tomorrow a feast.
Come, little candle that flies as I sing,
Bright little fairy-bug – night's little king;
Come, and I'll dance as you guide me along,
Come, and I'll pay you, my bug, with a song.

A. Grove Day, *The Sky Clears: Poetry of the American Indians*
(1951; Lincoln: University of Nebraska Press 1964) 28

▶ Anna Jameson recorded this Chippewa love song.

'Tis now two days, two long days,
Since last I tasted food;
'Tis for you, for you, my love,
That I grieve, that I grieve,
'Tis for you, for you that I grieve!

The waters flow deep and wide,
On which, love, you have sail'd;
Dividing you far from me.
'Tis for you, for you, my love,
'Tis for you, for you that I grieve!

Anna Jameson, *Winter Studies and Summer Rambles in Canada*
(1838; Toronto: Coles Canadiana 1970) III, 223-4

▶ In central Canada the Indians were being settled on reserves. This petition
from the Ojibwas, dated River Credit, 24 January 1840, to Colonel Samuel
Peters Jarvis, chief superintendent of Indian affairs, is a straightforward
statement of Indian wants.

Father
We would again humbly solicit our Great Father, to secure to us and our
descendants for ever, the lands on which we reside.
Father,
It is our wish to be informed with regard to the relation your red children
stand to the British Government. Whether as subjects or Allies!
Father,
Having considered the future welfare of our children, and anticipating the
time when your Red children will be so crowded by your white children
as to compel them to leave their present settlements and seek a home
elsewhere – We therefore humbly pray that our beloved Great Mother the
Queen may be graciously pleased to Reserve a sufficient Tract of land in
the vicinity of the Saugeeng River, as the future home of all your Red
children.
Father,
We wish to be informed, whether the white people have power to prevent
the Indians from hunting on their wild lands. We ask this question on
account of our people having been repeatedly ordered off from the woods

where they had gone to hunt, and in some instances have had their venison taken away from them by white men ...

Father,

Last winter an Act was passed by the Parliament of this country, for the preservation of Game, and for the better observance of the Sabbath day, imposing fines and penalties against any [Indian] person or persons shooting game on the Sabbath. It is our desire that our Great Father may be pleased to recommend that the said Act may be so amended as to impose the same fines and penalities against any person or persons *fishing* on the Lord's day.

Public Archives of Canada, RG10, vol. 1011, pp 100-3

▶ Sir George Arthur, lieutenant-governor of Upper Canada, received this testimony when the monument to Sir Isaac Brock at Queenston Heights was dynamited, supposedly by Americans.

Amherstburgh, 22nd February 1841

Father

In our hearts we shake you by the hand and we thank the Great Spirit that he has preserved you to see the end of another year and that he has permitted us to assemble once more around the Council fire of Our forefathers.

Father

Our object in meeting together this day is to communicate to you the feelings and wishes of your red children.

Open your ears and listen.

Father

Twenty seven winters have past with the swiftness of the deer when startled by the tread of the young hunter, since you said 'The game is at an end, the Big Knife who dared to measure strength with me already pants for breath and has grown weak. He asks for rest and I have opened my ears to him. Therefore my red children let the war cry cease to be heard – let the Tomahawk be burried and let us once more smoke the pipe of peace with him.'

Father

When these words were spoken by you the war whoop was suppressed – the firm grasp of the Tomahawk was released – the pipe of peace was taken up because it was the command of our father beyond the great lake.

52

Father

But while the head of the red men is still bowed down with grief and while the eyes of his women and children are yet dim with tears for those who are not. He bears with abhorrence and indignation that the serpent with the double tongue has polluted the resting places of the illustrious dead. Yes father the bones of the venerated Chiefs, Brock and T'cumthey who were struck low while foremost in the fight, are sought after by him who works as a mole in the dark and are even now denied the repose of the grave.

Father

The heart of the Big Knife is hid in his breast – warm him in your bosom and he will requite you with death. Such father, is the nature of the reptile you pitied and placed under your wing.

Father

The bad feeling which prompted him to attempt the destruction of the last resting place of the gallant Brock we cannot sufficiently condemn, and to shew our veneration and respect for the memory of that great Chief we now offer our mite in aid of the building of a new monument to him, and may it ever stand firm as a rock in the midst of the great waters, defying the dashing of the angry waves.

Father

Our men women and children salute you. May the strong chain which has so long united us in friendship ever remain bright and may the Great Spirit give you a long life and a clear sky.

Ontario Archives, Brock Monument Papers, VI, Indian Papers 1840-57

▶   The Indians on the east coast also had their grievances, for their old way of life was rapidly disappearing in the face of expanding white civilization. This plaintive petition, received at the Colonial Office in London on 25 January 1841, was written by a Micmac chief, Paussamigh Pemmeen-auweet, to Queen Victoria a few years after she ascended the throne. It is typical of countless appeals that were written by Indians across the country.

To the Queen

Madam,

I am Paussamigh Pemmeenauweet, and am called by the White Man Louis Benjamin Porninout.

I am the Chief of my People the Micmac Tribe of Indians in your Province of Nova Scotia and I was recognized and declared to be the

Chief by our good Friend Sir John Cope Sherbrooke in the White Man's
fashion Twenty Five Years ago; I have yet the Paper which he gave me.

Sorry to hear that the King is dead. Am glad to hear that we have a
good Queen whose Father I saw in this Country. He loved the Indians.

I cannot cross the great Lake to talk to you for my Canoe is too small,
and I am old and weak. I cannot look upon you for my eyes not see so
far. You cannot hear my voice across the Great Waters. I therefore send
this Wampum and Paper talk to tell the Queen I am in trouble. My
people are in trouble. I have seen upwards of a Thousand Moons. When I
was young I had plenty: now I am old, poor and sickly too. My people
are poor. No Hunting Grounds – No Beaver – no Otter – no nothing. Indians poor – poor for ever. No Store – no Chest – no Clothes. All these
Woods once ours. Our Fathers possessed them all. Now we cannot cut a
Tree to warm our Wigwam in Winter unless the White Man please. The
Micmacs now receive no presents, but one small Blanket for a whole
family. The Governor is a good man but he cannot help us now. We look
to you the Queen. The White Wampum tell that we hope in you. Pity
your poor Indians in Nova Scotia.

White Man has taken all that was ours. He has plenty of everything
here. But we are told that the White Man has sent to you for more. No
wonder that I should speak for myself and my people.

The man that takes this talk over the great Water will tell you what
we want to be done for us. Let us not perish. Your Indian Children love
you, and will fight for you against all your enemies.
My Head and my Heart shall go to One above for you.
Pausauhmigh Pemmeenauweet, Chief of the Micmac Tribe of Indians in
Nova Scotia.
His mark +

L.F.S. Upton, *Micmacs and Colonists: Indian-White Relations in the Maritimes, 1713-1867*
(Vancouver: University of British Columbia Press 1979) 188-92

▶   The following item appeared in a Nova Scotia newspaper in 1865 under the
      heading: 'BIOGRAPHY of Peter Paul – Written February 16th, 1865, From
      His own Statement – By an Amanuensis.' In a chatty tone, Paul reflects on
      the changes, mostly not for the better, that have come to the Micmac coun-
      try since the arrival of the white man.

My name, Peter Paul; eighty-five years old last Christmas. People say,
that was 1779, the year of American Independence, and now, I just so old
as the American Constitution. Me little shakey, some say that government shakey too. My Father's name Joseph Paul, he die when ninety-nine

years and six months old; he die thirty years ago. My mother's name Madeline Paul; die when seventy-four years old; twenty-seven years ago. I had five brother and four sister; three brother and two sister die; two brother and two sister living. I just twenty two years when married; my wife's name Jennie Paul, she die three years ago, seventy years old. I had nine children, four living, five dead. I believe me oldest Micmac man. I was born at West River, (some greatest people born there.) When little boy, live Antigonish and Little Harbor ... Pictou small town; New Glasgow two or three houses. That time Mortimer dig coal at Mines, haul coal in carts, put'em in scow, take'em to Loading Ground and put'em in vessel.

That time every thing plenty; salmon, trout, eels, good many kinds fish. Plenty Moose, Carriboo, Bear, Beaver, Otter, Martin, Foxes, Wildcat and good many more. My father have'em coat – inside beaver, outside otter. That time plenty fresh fish in summer and dry'em for winter ... white men that time ... cut down woods, ... Spear'em salmon ... all gone now. Everything eat'em up make country cold – make rivers small; build saw mills, sawdust and milldam send all fish away. That time plenty codfish, white man set line scare'em all. White man burn up all wood for staves, baskets, everything scarce now. That time, great many Micmac's; white people learn'em to drink ... many bad things ... and great many die; not many Micmacs now. One time this Micmac country, our country; now white people say this their country, take'em from Indian and never pay'em. Indian speak'em 'bout that good many times.

Some white men very good; Edward Mortimer very kind to Indian – give'em flour, pork, and good many things to poor people. Squire Pagan very good man – Squire Pagan and Edward Mortimer married to two sisters. One Minister very good man, call'em Doctor McGregor; old Lulan and Mr McGregor almost same two brothers. John McKay at Narrows, Robert's father, good man, he almost same one brother to old Lulan; John McKay and old Lulan make first road to St. Mary's; me very small boy that time. Mr Carmichael call'em one vessel Lulan for my father-in-law. Squire Matheson, too, very good man; very well acquainted with my father – give my father plenty work; very good man to me too, always when meet'em, put hand in pocket and give me something.

One old man live at Middle River, call'em Deacan Marshall, and my father live at West River, all same two brother. All old men gone now; my friends most all gone too. If old man come back, would'nt know this country; nothing same now; vessels sail about, steamboat make water dirty, and scare'em fish; Railroad and steam engine make noise; everything noise, bustle, all change – this not Micmac country – Micmac country very quiet, no bustle; their Rivers make gentle murmur; trees sigh like young woman; everything beautiful. My father and mother Roman Catholic, me Roman Catholic, too, most all Micmac Roman Catholic. Believe not much difference if believe in Jesus Christ and do good; all same in heaven.

Now, me old man, can't work – soon die, then white people miss old Peter – good many people very kind, now I thank them all – white man you got my country; keep'em good, be kind to poor Indian – he have no country now – call'em stranger here.

Me very well pleased if white man make this country large – take'em Miramichi, St. Johns, Ressigouche, Prince Edward Island, and Nova Scotia, and put'em all together. Me not want Canada; too far away – I don't know'em very well, though I stay there four years. Some people not very good there, and Mohawk stay there – leave'em out.

Me think something wrong with white man's Council. When Micmac used to have Council, *old* men speak and tell'em young men what to do – and young men listen and do what old men tell'em; white man change that too: now *young* men speak'em, and old men listen; that's reason so many different kinds speak'em. Believe more.better, Micmac Council.

Me not like all trees cut down – better have some woods. White man should plant trees now, because take'em away old trees. White man should keep some woods for Indian, some place ...

I want all Micmac to be good people, (me never did take anything from white people,) now never steal – tell truth – don't get drunk – mind where bad people go, and where good people go, too.

This the first time ever I trouble Printer, I believe last time. Soon say Peter Paul dead. Good bye.

his
PETER   X   PAUL
mark

Public Archives of Nova Scotia, Press clipping scrapbook (no 5) of Dr George Patterson

▶ The Indians in northern Ontario were also feeling the effects of the white man's activities. Geologists had been searching for the mineral wealth that was believed to lie under the soil, and mining claims were being granted around Lake Superior. The Bruce Mine on the north shore of Lake Huron was discovered in 1846 and copper was produced there. A council was held by T.G. Anderson, vice-superintendent of Indian affairs, at Sault Ste Marie on 18 August 1848, to prepare for the signing of an Indian treaty (1850).

Peau de Chat (fl. 1840-50), chief of the Fort William Indians, here attempts to answer Anderson's query as to the authority by which the Indians claimed their lands.

Father
You ask how we possess this land. Now it is well known that 4000 Years ago when we first were created all spoke one language. Since that a change has taken place, and we speak different languages. You white people well know, and we Red Skins know how we came in possession of this land – it was the Great Spirit who gave it to us – from the time my ancestors came upon this earth it has been considered ours – after a time the Whites living on the other side of the Great Salt Lake, found this part of the world inhabited by the Red Skins – the Whites asked us Indians, when there were many animals here – would you not sell the Skins of these various animals for the goods I bring – our old ancestors said Yes. I will bring your goods, they the whites did not say any thing more, nor did the Indian say any thing. I did not know that he said come I will buy your land, every thing that is on it under it &c &c he the White said nothing about that to me – and this is the reason why I believe that we possess this land up to this day. When at last the Whites came to this Country where now they are numerous – He the English did not say I will after a time get your land, or give me your land, he said indeed to our forefathers, when he fought with the French and conquered them come on our Side and fight them, and be our children, they did so, and every time you wanted to fight the Big knives you said to the Indians wont you assist me, Yes! we will help you this Man (pointing to Shingua-conse) was there and he was in much misery – the English were very strong when we gave our assistance. When the war was over the English did not say I will have Your land, nor did we say you may have it – and this father You know, this is how we are in possession of this Land – It will be known every where if the Whites get it from us.
Father
You ask in what instances the Whites prevent our Farming, there are bad people among us who are continually saying to us dont Farm, live as Indians always did, You will be unhappy if you cultivate the Land, take your Gun go and hunt, bring the Skins to me, and leave off tilling the Soil – and the Queen says to me become Christian my children. Yes I say we will become Christians but when this bad man (the Trader) sees me he says leave it alone do as you formerly did, and this is the way he destroys my religion and farming this is the way I explain the question you have now asked me.

Father

The miners burn the land and drive away the animals destroying the land
Game &c much timber is destroyed – and I am very sorry for it – When
they find mineral they cover it once with Clay so that the Indians may
not see it and I now begin to think that the White man wishes to take
away and to steal my land, I will let it go, and perhaps I will accomplish
it. I wish to let the Governor have both land and Mineral, I expect him
to ask me for it, and this is what would be for our good. I do not wish to
pass any reflections on the conduct of the whites – ask me then, send
some one to ask for my land my Mineral &c. I wont be unwilling to let
it go to the Government shall have it if they give us good pay. I do not
regret a word I have said – You Father You are a White Man make Yourself an Indian, take an Indians heart come assist me to root out the evil
that has been among us and I will be glad answer me is there any thing
that requires explanation.

Father

The Indians are uneasy seeing their lands occupied by the Whites, taking
away the mineral and they wish that our Great Father would at once
settle the matter. Come and ask me for my land and mineral that there
be no bad feelings left, I am Sorry, my heart is troubled. I dont know
what would be good for us, it will not do for me an Indian to say to the
Governor come buy my land, yet this is what I think would be very good,
Yes very good for my people, then the White man the miner and trader
could do what he liked with the land and so could the Indian on that part
which we would like to reserve, when we give our land up we will
reserve a piece for ourselves and we, with our families will live happily on
it we will do as we please with it. There (pointing to Fort William) I will
find out a place for my self. perhaps you will come and arrange Matters it
would be well if you could, and if an officer cannot come this autumn to
settle our affairs I will look out for one in the Spring to do it for me and
this is nearly all I have to say, tell the Governor at Montreal to send a
letter and let us know what he will do and what our land is worth in the
mean time I will converse with my tribe on the subject. When I am
going to sell my land I will speak again and Settle Matters.

A great deal of our Mineral has been taken away I must have something for it. I reflect upon it, as well as upon that which still remains.
Certified

T.G. Anderson, V.S.I.A.

Public Archives of Canada, RG1, E5, vol. 8, ECO file 1157 of 1848

► Shinguaconse (c. 1773-1854), or 'Little Pine,' of Garden River near Sault Ste
Marie, fought with Brock in the War of 1812. So concerned was he for the
welfare of his people that he once walked all the way to York (Toronto) to
ask the governor for teachers.

My father ... you have made promises to me and to my children. You
promised me houses, but as yet nothing has been performed, although five
years are past. I am now growing very old, and, to judge by the way you
have used me, I am afraid I shall be laid in my grave before I see any of
your promises fulfilled. Many of your children address you, and tell you
they are poor, and they are much better off than I am in everything. I
can say, in sincerity, that I am poor. I am like the beast of the forest that
has no shelter. I lie down on the snow, and cover myself with the boughs
of the trees. If the promises had been made by a person of no standing, I
should not be astonished to see his promises fail. But *you*, who are so
great in riches and in power, I am astonished that I do not see your
promises fulfilled! I would have been better pleased if you had never
made such promises to me, than that you should have made them and
not performed them ... But, my father, perhaps I do not see clearly; I am
old, and perhaps I have lost my eye-sight; and if you should come to visit
us, you might discover these promises already performed! I have heard
that you have visited all parts of the country around. This is the only
place you have not yet seen; if you will promise to come, I will have my
little fish ... ready drawn from the water, that you may taste of the food
which sustains me.

Anna Jameson, *Winter Studies and Summer Rambles in Canada*
(1838; Toronto: Coles Canadiana 1970) III, 237-8

Shinguaconse expressed the sentiments of many Indians when he sent this
letter in 1849 to the governor at Montreal.

When your white children first came into this country, they did not come
shouting the war cry and seeking to wrest this land from us. They told us
they came as friends to smoke the pipe of peace; they sought our friendship, we became brothers. Their enemies were ours, at the time we were
strong and powerful, while they were few and weak. But did we oppress
them or wrong them? No! And they did not attempt to do what is now
done, nor did they tell us that at some future day you would.

Father,
Time wore on and you have become a great people, whilst we have
melted away like snow beneath an April sun; our strength is wasted, our
countless warriors dead, our forests laid low, you have hunted us from
every place as with a wand, you have swept away all our pleasant land,
and like some giant foe you tell us 'willing or unwilling, you must now go
from amid these rocks and wastes, I want them now! I want them to
make rich my white children, whilst you may shrink away to holes and
caves like starving dogs to die.' Yes, Father, your white children have
opened our very graves to tell the dead even they shall have no resting
place.
Father,
Was it for this we first received you with the hand of friendship, and gave
you the room whereon to spread your blanket? Was it for this that we
voluntarily became the children of our Great Mother the Queen? Was it
for this we served England's sovereign so well and truly, that the blood of
the red skin has moistened the dust of his own hunting grounds, to serve
those sovereigns in their quarrels, and not in quarrels of his own?
Father,
We begin to fear that those sweet words had not their birth in the heart,
but that they lived only upon the tongue; they are like those beautiful
trees under whose shadow it is pleasant for a time to repose and hope, but
we cannot forever indulge in their graceful shade – they produce no fruit.
Father,
We are men like you, we have the limbs of men, we have the hearts of
men, and we feel and know that all this country is ours; even the weak-
est and most cowardly animals of the forest when hunted to extremity,
though they feel destruction sure, will turn upon the hunter.
Father,
Drive us not to the madness of despair. We are told that you have laws
which guard and protect the property of your white children, but you
have made none to protect the rights of your red children. Perhaps you
expected that the red skin could protect himself from the rapacity of his
pale faced bad brother.

Ontario Indian, III, 12 (December 1980) 25

▶ By the mid-1850s pressure was growing in central Canada to expand into
the vast North-West. In the summer of 1857 an expedition under Henry
Youle Hind was sent by the Canadian government to explore the route
westward from Lake Superior as well as the resources and climate of the

lands by the Red and Assiniboine rivers. An Indian chief between the Lake of the Woods and Red River, made suspicious by reports of white settlement elsewhere, refused the expedition permission to cross his territory; his objections were 'couched in very poetical language, with a few satirical touches.'

The reason why we stop you is because we think you do not tell us why you want to go that way, and what you want to do with those paths. You say that all the white men we have seen belong to one party, and yet they go by three different roads, why is that? Do they want to see the Indian's land? Remember, if the white man comes to the Indian's house, he must walk through the door, and not steal in by the window. That way, the old road, is the door, and by that way you must go. You gathered corn in our gardens and put it away; did you never see corn before? Why did you not note it down in your book? Did your people want to see our corn? Would they not be satisfied with your noting it down? You cannot pass through those paths ...

It is hard to deny your request; but we see how the Indians are treated far away. The white man comes, looks at their flowers, their trees, and their rivers; others soon follow; the lands of the Indians pass from their hands, and they have nowhere a home. You must go by the way the white man has hitherto gone. I have told you all.

... Let not these men think bad of us for taking away their guides. Let them send us no presents; we do not want them. They have no right to pass that way. We have hearts, and love our lives and our country. If twenty men came we would not let them pass to-day. We do not want the white man; when the white man comes, he brings disease and sickness, and our people perish; we do not wish to die. Many white men would bring death to us, and our people would pass away; we wish to love and to hold the land our fathers won, and the Great Spirit has given to us.

Henry Youle Hind, *Narrative of the Canadian Red River Exploring Expedition of 1857 and of the Assiniboine and Saskatchewan Exploring Expedition of 1858* (London 1860; Edmonton: Hurtig Publishers 1971) I, 99-100

▶ The Indians in the west protested against white encroachments on their lands in the late nineteenth century with the same eloquence and dignity their eastern counterparts had used earlier. A portion of the dialogue in the proceedings of the North-West Angle Treaty, or Treaty no 3, signed with the Saulteaux on 3 October 1873 and covering lands in southwest Ontario and southeast Manitoba, reveals the uneasiness the Indians felt as well as their negotiating abilities: their demands for freedom of movement, recompense for loss of renewable resources, independence of military action, and removal of the Hudson's Bay Company.

GOVERNOR – I am sent here to treat with the Indians. In Red River, where I came from, and where there is a great body of Half-breeds, they must be either white or Indian. If Indians, they get treaty money; if the Half-breeds call themselves white, they get land. All I can do is to refer the matter to the Government at Ottawa, and to recommend what you wish to be granted.

CHIEF – I hope you will not drop the question; we have understood you to say that you came here as a friend, and represented your charitableness, and we depend upon your kindness. You must remember that our hearts and our brains are like paper; we never forget. There is one thing that we want to know. If you should get into trouble with the nations, I do not wish to walk out and expose my young men to aid you in any of your wars.

GOVERNOR – The English never call the Indians out of their country to fight their battles. You are living here and the Queen expects you to live at peace with the white men and your red brothers, and with other nations.

ANOTHER CHIEF – I ask you a question – I see your roads here passing through the country, and some of your boats – useful articles that you use for yourself. Bye and bye we shall see things that run swiftly, that go by fire – carriages – and we ask you that us Indians may not have to pay their passage on these things, but can go free ...

GOVERNOR – When the reserves are given you, you will have your rights. The Hudson's Bay Company have their rights, and the Queen will do justice between you.

CHIEF OF FORT FRANCES – Why I say this is, where I have chosen for my reserve I see signs that the H.B. Co. has surveyed. I do not hate them. I only wish they should take their reserves on one side. Where their shop stands now is my property; I think it is three years now since they have had it on it.

GOVERNOR – I do not know about that matter; it will be enquired into. I am taking notes of all these things and am putting them on paper.

CHIEF – I will tell you one thing. You understand me now, that I have taken your hand firmly and in friendship. I repeat twice that you have done so, that these promises that you have made, and the treaty to be concluded, let it be as you promise, as long as the sun rises over our head and as long as the water runs. One thing I find, that deranges a little my kettle. In this river, where food used to be plentiful for our subsistence, I perceive it is getting scarce. We wish that the river should be left as it was formed from the beginning – that nothing be broken.

Alexander Morris, *The Treaties of Canada with the Indians of Manitoba and the North-West Territories* (1880; Toronto: Coles Canadiana 1971) 69-74

▶ After Confederation in 1867 and the acquisition of the North-West Territories by Canada from the Hudson's Bay Company in 1870, but before Alberta and Saskatchewan were made provinces in 1905, treaties were signed with the Indians on the prairies (some were signed later with northern Indians). Crowfoot, or Isapo-muxika (1830-90), a Blood Indian, was the most influential chief in the Blackfoot Confederacy during the difficult period of transition: he led his people without bloodshed from a nomadic existence to a life on reserves, dominated by white Indian agents, because he realized resistance to change was futile. The Blackfeet were the last Indians on the open plains to sign a treaty with the government, no 7, on 22 September 1877, and they did not do so until Crowfoot had made up his mind.

While I speak, be kind and patient. I have to speak for my people, who are numerous, and who rely upon me to follow that course which in the future will tend to their good. The plains are large and wide. We are the children of the plains, it is our home, and the buffalo has been our food always. I hope you look upon the Blackfeet, Bloods and Sarcees as your children now, and that you will be indulgent and charitable to them. They all expect me to speak now for them, and I trust the Great Spirit will put into their breasts to be a good people – into the minds of the men, women and children, and their future generations. The advice given me and my people has proved to be very good. If the Police had not come to the country, where would we be all now? Bad men and whiskey were killing us so fast that very few, indeed, of us would have been left today. The Police have protected us as the feathers of the bird protect it from the frosts of winter. I wish them all good, and trust that all our hearts will increase in goodness from this time forward. I am satisfied. I will sign the treaty.

Morris, *The Treaties of Canada with the Indians* (1880) 272

Because of his loyalty during the 1885 North-West Rebellion, the Canadian Pacific Railway authorities presented Crowfoot with a framed railway ticket to be worn on his chest. He sent a telegram of thanks for the free life-time pass to the manager of the railway.

Blackfoot Crossing, 29th Feb., '86

Great Chief of the Railway, W.C. Van Horne: –

I salute you, O chief, O great; I am pleased with railway key, opening railway free to me. The chains, and rich covering of your name, writing its wonderful power to open the road, show the greatness of your chiefness. I have done.

his

Crow X Foot

mark

Public Archives of Canada, RG10, vol. 1137, p 1 (translated from the Blackfoot language)

Crowfoot died at Blackfoot Crossing on 25 April 1890. As he lay dying in his tipi – dressed in full regalia and surrounded by relatives and friends – he delivered a message to his people.

A little while and I will be gone from among you. Whither, I cannot tell. From nowhere we came; into nowhere we go. What is life? It is the flash of a firefly in the night. It is the breath of a buffalo in the winter time. It is as the little shadow that runs across the grass and loses itself in the sunset.

J.W. Grant MacEwan, *Portraits from the Plains* (Toronto: McGraw-Hill Ryerson 1971) 90

► The signing of the treaties on the prairies coincided with an influx of settlers and the decline of the traditional Indian way of life. The end of the great buffalo herds, on which the Métis but particularly the Indians relied for food, clothing, and shelter, was catastrophic, and life on the reserves, with hand-outs from the government and attempts at farming, seemed both confining and degrading. In the autumn of 1875 the Rev. George McDougall, a missionary familiar to the Indians, was sent by Alexander Morris, lieutenant-governor of Manitoba and the North-West Territories, to see if the Crees along the North Saskatchewan River would accept a treaty. Treaty no 6 was concluded a year later, but Big Bear, or Mistahimaskwa (c. 1825-88), a prominent chief, refused to sign for many years. His attitude was expressed in this speech to McDougall in 1875.

We want none of the Queen's presents; when we set a fox-trap we scatter pieces of meat all round, but when the fox gets into the trap we knock him on the head; we want no bait, let your Chiefs come like men and talk to us.

Morris, *The Treaties of Canada with the Indians* (1880) 174

The discontent along the Saskatchewan erupted into open rebellion in March 1885, under the Métis leader Louis Riel, who had led an uprising in Manitoba sixteen years earlier. Big Bear surrendered at Fort Carlton in July, was charged with treason, and confined in the Stony Mountain Penitentiary. At his trial he pleaded not for himself but for his people.

I have ruled my country for long. Now I am in chains and will be sent to prison ... Now I am as dead to my people. Many of them are hiding in the woods, paralyzed with fear. Can this court not send them a pardon? My own children may be starving and afraid to come out of hiding. I plead to you Chiefs of the white man's laws for pity and help for the people of my band.

I have only a little more to say. The country belonged to me. I may not live to see it again ... I am old and ugly but I have tried to do good. Have pity for the children of my tribe. Because Big Bear has always been a friend of the white man, you should now send a pardon to my people and give them help.

MacEwan, *Portraits from the Plains* (1971) 111-12

▶ Poundmaker, or Pitikwahanapiwtyin (c. 1842-86), another prominent Cree chief, the adopted son of Crowfoot, also took part in the rebellion and was sentenced to three years' imprisonment in the penitentiary; released in 1886, he died four months later. At his trial he made this appeal to the jury.

I am not guilty. A lot has been said against me that is untrue. I am glad of what I have done in the Queen's country. What I did was for the Great Mother. When my people and the whites met in battle, I saved the Queen's men. I took the firearms from my following and gave them up at Battleford. Everything I could do was to prevent bloodshed. Had I wanted war, I would not be here but on the prairie. You did not catch me. I gave myself up. You have me because I wanted peace. I cannot help myself, but I am still a man. You may do as you like with me. I am done.

John Peter Turner, *The North-West Mounted Police, 1873-1893*, (Ottawa: King's Printer 1950) II, 244

▶ Piapot (1828-1908), a Cree chief who had refused to take part in the rebellion, was noted for his whimsical sense of humour. When the superior-general of the Oblate Order visited Lebret in 1895, Piapot was sardonic.

In order to become sole masters of our land they relegated us to small reservations as big as my hand and make us long promises, as long as my arm; but the next year the promises were shorter and got shorter every year until now they are the length of my finger, and they keep only half of that.

Saskatchewan Archives Board, Regina, Clippings file Indians of North America – Biography of Chiefs, from *Indians of the West*, by Father Hugonard, p 3

When Lord Stanley of Preston, the governor-general, met an Indian gathering at Fort Qu'Appelle, Piapot criticized the Indian Department for its miserliness.

Why! ... our Agent is so mean he carries a linen rag in his pocket into which to blow his nose for fear he might blow away something of value.

Shortly after the appointment of W.M. Graham as Indian agent, Piapot said:

Now I know the Government is going to break the Treaty because when it was signed it was understood that it would last as long as the grass grew, the winds blew, the rivers ran, and men walked on two legs, and now they have sent us an Agent who has only one leg.

The Hon. A.E. Forget, Indian commissioner, asked Piapot why he had allowed a Sun Dance on his reserve when he knew it was against departmental policy. Piapot stood up, dropped the blanket from his shoulders, stretched out his arms in the approved gesture of the Indian orator, and began to speak.

Getchie Ogimow (the commissioner) arises in the morning. He has various dishes placed before him. He takes an iron implement and conveys something from a dish to his mouth, and if he doesn't like it, he takes the contents of another dish. He does not know what it means to be hungry. The poor Indians often know what it is to have an empty belly, and they just tighten their belts and pray to Getchie Manitou (the Good Spirit) to give them food. Their way of praying is to make a Sun Dance. That is all I have to say.

When Piapot (or 'Flash in the Sky') was quite elderly, he informed Father Hugonard that he thought there might be something in Christianity and asked to be instructed. Delighted, the priest suggested baptism.

Oh! No ... I am only going to accept half of your religion. I will belong half to the Christian Religion and half to the Indian, because you may turn out to be wrong after all, and the Indian Religion might happen to be right and then I would have nothing to fall back upon.

Saskatchewan Archives Board, Regina, 'Story of Piapot,' by Z.M. Hamilton, 1945, SHS file no 49, pp 14, 15, 13

▶ West of the Rocky Mountains the ancient Indian societies on the Pacific coast and in the interior of what is now British Columbia remained undisturbed by the Europeans until the late eighteenth century; Russian, Spanish, and British explorers arrived by sea, and fur traders came overland from the east to set up posts in the early nineteenth century. For many years the Indians continued to outnumber the newcomers, but they suffered terribly from the white man's diseases and their position was weakened. The following exchange between Gilbert Malcolm Sproat, an Englishman sent to establish a sawmill on Vancouver Island (and later a reserve allotment commissioner), and an unidentified Seshahts Indian, at Port Alberni in August 1860, portrays the Indians' fear and reluctance to end up on reserves.

'Chiefs of the Seshahts,' said I on entering, 'are you well; are your women in health; are your children hearty; do your people get plenty of fish and fruits?'

'Yes,' answered an old man, 'our families are well, our people have plenty of food; but how long this will last we know not. We see your ships, and hear things that make our hearts grow faint. They say that more King-George-men will soon be here, and will take our land, our firewood, our fishing grounds; that we shall be placed on a little spot, and shall have to do everything according to the fancies of the King-George-men.'

'Do you believe all this?' I asked.

'We want your information,' said the speaker.

'Then,' answered I, 'it is true that more King-George-men (as they call the English) are coming: they will soon be here; but your land will be bought at a fair price.'

'We do not wish to sell our land nor our water; let your friends stay in their own country.'

To which I rejoined: 'My great chief, the high chief of the King-George-men, seeing that you do not work your land, orders that you shall sell it. It is of no use to you. The trees you do not need; you will fish and hunt as you do now, and collect firewood, planks for your houses, and cedar for your canoes. The white man will give you work, and buy your fish and oil.'

'Ah, but we don't care to do as the white men wish.'

'Whether or not,' said I, 'the white man will come. All your people know that they are your superiors; they make the things which you value. You cannot make muskets, blankets, or bread. The white man will teach your children to read printing, and to be like themselves.'

'We do not want the white man. He steals what we have. We wish to live as we are.'

Gilbert Malcolm Sproat, *Scenes and Studies of Savage Life*
(London: Smith, Elder and Co. 1868) 3-4

▶ The government of British Columbia set aside reserves for the Indians and considered the matter settled, but the question of title to land would remain an issue for a long time to come. The rough handling of Indian claims led to much bitterness, as expressed in this letter to the editor in the *Victoria Daily Colonist* in 1880.

I am an Indian chief and a Christian. 'Do unto others as you wish others should do unto you' is Christian doctrine. Is the white man a Christian? This is a part of his creed – 'take all you want if it belongs to an Indian.' He has taken all our land and all the salmon and we have – nothing. He believes an Indian has a right to live if he can on nothing at all ...

The Indians are now reduced to this condition – THEY MUST ROB OR STARVE. Which will they do? I need not answer. An Indian is a man; and he has eyes. If you stab him he will bleed; if you poison him he will die. If you wrong him shall he not seek revenge? If an Indian wrongs a white man what is his humility? Revenge. If want compels us to execute the villainy they teach they may discover when it is TOO LATE that an Indian can imitate the lightning and strike in a thousand places at the same time. We are not beggars. In the middle of the magnificent country that was once our own we only ask for land enough to enable us to live like white men by working in the fields. If the Indians get no land this spring you MAY BE SURE the white man will have a very bad harvest this year, and the Indians will eat beef next winter. Fine talk won't feed an Indian. 'Her Majesty's Indian subjects,' whose rights are limited to living on noth-ing at all if they can, are prepared to face the worst – anything but death by starvation. In a court of justice we could prove that we are the only persons who have any right or title to this land. If the Queen has no

a consequence must have given 'potlatches' and now I am astonished that Christians persecute us and put us in jail for doing just as the first Christians.

Maquinna, ✗ (his mark)
Chief of Nootka

Victoria Daily Colonist, 1 April 1896, p 6

▶ The Nootka Indians' war preparations involved purification rituals, prayer, intense exercises, and abstinence from food, merriment, and sex. John R. Jewitt, when a prisoner of Maquinna early in the nineteenth century, recorded this war prayer.

Wocash Quahootze,
Teechamme ah welth,
Wik-etish tau-ilth-
Kar-sab-matemas-
Wik-sish to hauk matemas-
I ya-ish kah-shittle-
As-smootish warich matemas

Good, or great God, let me live –
Not be sick –
Find the enemy –
Not fear him –
Find him asleep,
And kill a great many of him.

Narrative of the Adventures and Sufferings of John R. Jewitt (The Jewitt Narrative), (Fairfield, Washington: Ye Galleon Press 1967) 121

▶ Other traditional west coast songs had to do with growing up and with hunting.

Kwakiutl Cradle Song

When I am a man, then I shall be a hunter, O father!
    Ya ha ha ha.
When I am a man, then I shall be a harpooner, O father!
    Ya ha ha ha.
When I am a man, then I shall be a canoe builder, O father!
    Ya ha ha ha.

When I am a man, then I shall be a carpenter, O father!
   Ya ha ha ha.
When I am a man, then I shall be an artisan, O father!
   Ya ha ha ha.
That we may not be in want, O father!
   Ya ha ha ha.

Franz Boas, 'Stylistic Aspects of Primitive Literature,' *Journal of American Folklore*, XXXVIII, no 149 (July-September 1925) 331

West Coast Mourning Song, for a lost child

CHIEF: Don't mourn any more, don't mourn.
CHORUS: We do not mourn any more.
CHIEF: He went up to play with his brethren the stars.
           Don't mourn any more.
CHORUS: We do not mourn any more.
CHIEF: There he is hunting with the hunters the nimble deer.
           Don't mourn any more.
CHORUS: We do not mourn any more.
CHIEF: We will see his beloved face in the new moon.
           Don't mourn any more.
CHORUS: We do not mourn any more.

Franz Boas, 'Poetry and Music of Some North American Tribes,' *Science*, IX (1887) 385

▶   The Nootkas were known as great hunters of whales. This 'Whaling Song'
     was sung to the giant mammals during whaling voyages.

Whaling Song

Whale, I have given you what you are wishing to get – my good harpoon.
And now you have it. Please hold it with your strong hands and do not
let go. Whale, turn toward the beach of Yahksis, and you will be proud to
see the young men come down on the fine sandy beach of my village at
Yahksis to see you; and the young men will say to one another: 'What a
great whale he is! What a fat whale he is! What a strong whale he is!'
And you, whale, will be proud of all that you will hear them say of your
greatness. Whale, do not turn outward, but hug the shore, and tow me to
the beach of my village at Yahksis, for when you come ashore there,

young men will cover your great body with bluebill duck feathers and with the down of the great eagle, the chief of all birds; for this is what you are wishing, and this is what you are trying to find from one end of the world to the other, every day you are travelling and spouting.

Edward S. Curtis, *The North American Indian* (1916; New York: Johnson Reprint Corporation 1970) XI, 23

▶ In 1912 a royal commission was set up under Dr J.A.J. McKenna, representing the federal government, and Sir Richard McBride, premier of British Columbia, to look into the whole complicated matter of Indian land claims in the province. Tsudaike, a chief of the Nackwacto tribe from Blunden Harbour, expressed his dissatisfaction with reserves at Fort Rupert, Vancouver Island, 8 June 1914.

I ask for the return of my country to me, and that the reserves be no more. It is not only just now that I came into possession of the country. It has always been mine from the beginning of time. There was a time when there was no whiteman in the country, and in those times I had full possession of all the country. What has been done to me with my country would be the other way – I would have measured pieces off for the whiteman, instead of the whiteman measuring off pieces for me. The one that has been selling my country has never been here – they have never seen it, and they have no right to sell it to the whitemen.

British Columbia Provincial Museum, McKenna-McBride Reserve Commission Report, Hearing of 1913-16

John Sunday

Henry Bird Steinhauer

Peter Jacobs

Allan Salt

Catherine Sutton

James Settee

Peter Jones

3 'We are yet babes in Christ'

'O wind be good to us, O sun shine on us brightly,
O Kitche Manitou we offer our thanks for the goodness of
our Mother Earth. Keep it ever so.'

Cree prayer, in William I.C. Wuttunee, 'Thirst Dance of the Crees,'
Beaver, 293 (Winter 1962) 23

'My father, you have spoken well, you have told me Heaven is very beautiful; tell me one thing more. Is it more beautiful than the country of the musk-ox in summer when sometimes the mist blows over the lakes and sometimes the water is blue, and the loons cry very often? That is beautiful; and if Heaven is still more beautiful, my heart will be glad and I shall be content to rest there till I am very old.'

Saltatha, in G.C. Monture, 'The Indians of the North,'
Queen's Quarterly, LXVI, no 4 (Winter 1959-60) 563

The nineteenth century was not only a time of loss and protest. Many Indians were being educated in the white man's ways, a task carried out mainly through the missions of the various Christian churches.

As the Roman Catholics had two centuries earlier, the Methodists and Anglicans in the early nineteenth century launched concerted campaigns to convert the Indians to their respective faiths. The activities of the Wesleyan Methodist Missionary Society in southern Ontario beginning in the 1820s resulted in a number of young Ojibwa Indians being trained as missionaries, teachers, and translators: a group including Peter Jones, George Copway, George Henry, Peter Jacobs, John Sunday, Henry Steinhauer, and Allan Salt. These remarkable men worked hard for the church and for their people, preaching and lecturing at home and abroad to win souls and help raise money for their growing missions. They generated enthusiasm within their own group, and became the first literary coterie of Indians in Canada, and the first to write extensively in English.

These men were of course acculturated to the increasingly dominant white society, and their writing reflects their Christian training; the Bible was the chief literary influence in their lives, and their work is pervaded by deep Christian piety and biblical cadences. Although they generally encouraged the adoption of white civilization and the blessings of progress, they could still appreciate the problems inherent in the difficult process of change. In his *History of the Ojebway Indians* (1861), Peter Jones went so far as to state: 'Oh, what an awful account at the day of judgment must the unprincipled white man give, who has been an agent of Satan in the extermination of the original proprietors of the American soil!' (p 29). The same Peter Jones affixed his signature to numerous protests the Mississauga Ojibwas of the River Credit sent to government authorities.

While this pioneer group was flourishing in Ontario, other promising native youths were being educated by the Church Missionary Society of the Church of England at the Red River; among them were Henry Budd, Charles Pratt, John Hope, Luke Caldwell, and James Settee. Missionary work in the North-West at this time was difficult and frustrating, a fact that likely accounts for the slight literary output of these men compared to their eastern counterparts. None the less, their journals and diaries are rich sources of social and historical information.

Education, among other things, allowed the Indians to speak for themselves, in English. They could express pride in their Indian past and explain their culture to the white man. George Copway's most famous work, *The Traditional History and Characteristic Sketches of the Ojibway Nation*, published in London in 1850, was prefaced by him as 'the first volume of Indian history written by an Indian'; he wrote it, he said, to 'awaken in the American heart a deeper feeling for the race of red men, and induce the pale-face to use greater effort to effect an improvement in their social and political relations.'

▶ At a council held in Orillia, Ontario, 30 July 1846, a number of Indian chiefs subscribed to the prevailing British attitude that civilizing the Indian was possible only through Christianity and education.

Brothers –
We have too long been children; the time has come for us to stand up and be men. We must all join hands like one family, and help one another in the great cause of Indian improvement: this is our only hope to prevent our race from perishing, and to enable us to stand on the same ground as the white man.

Let us then sound the shell, and summon every red man from the woods; let us give up the chase of the deer and the beaver; it is unprofitable: the white man's labour is fast eating away the forest, whilst the sound of his axe and his bells is driving the game far away from their old haunts; it will soon be all gone. Let us then leave the bush to the wolves and the bears, and come forth and build our wigwams in the open fields: let us exchange the gun and the spear for the axe and the plow, and learn to get our living out of the ground, like our white brethren.

Brothers –
Many summers have passed away since our forefathers forsook a wandering life, and built settled homes in cleared places; we may therefore, as elder brothers, testify to you how great are the advantages of changing your mode of life. We confess, with sorrow, that we have not improved, as we ought, the advantages we have enjoyed; we are desirous, therefore, that you should profit by our faults and not neglect your opportunities.

Brothers –
There is no reason why we should not become an intelligent, industrious, and religious people. Experience has proved that the Great Spirit has given us powers of mind and body, not inferior to those of our white neighbours; then, why should we be inferior to them? Besides, Government has given us sufficient land to cultivate which is carefully protected from encroachment; we are supplied with clothing as presents from our Good Mother the Queen, whilst our other wants are relieved by the sale of such of our lands as we do not want to use. Good and careful Fathers are appointed to watch over our interests and attend to all our wants; they

are anxious to do everything in their power to improve our people, and it is for this purpose they have called this Council.

Brothers –

Let us listen to all they have to say, with attention, and thankfulness. In all their dealings with us, though they are strong and we are weak, they never command us, they always use us like equals and brethren. In all they propose they have our good at heart; let us then meet their suggestions with generous confidence.

Brothers –

We understand one of the chief objects they have in view at present, is to improve our young people by means of Boarding Schools, at which they will not only be taught book and head knowledge, but also learn to work with their hands; in fact, to make our boys useful and industrious farmers and mechanics, and our girls good housekeepers. This seems to us very necessary, for most of our young people are both ignorant and indolent, and they must be taught and accustomed to work when young, or they will never learn it, nor like it, after they have been taught.

Feeling the great importance of this, we have authorized our Delegates to concur in any good plan for the purpose that may be settled in the Council.

Brothers –

In conclusion, we congratulate you all (we hope all) that you, like ourselves, have been led by the good Spirit of God, out of the darkness of heathenism into the light and knowledge of the true religion, and that, in addition to the ties of blood and colour, we are still more closely bound together by one Faith and one Hope, as believers in our Lord, Jesus Christ. We must not forget that we are yet babes in Christ, and have tasted but slightly of the benefits of Christianity; greater blessings are in store for our race, if we only diligently seek them.

Religion and civilization must go hand in hand, and then they will greatly assist each other in raising our respective Tribes to a safe and honourable position in the scale of society. If we are only faithful to our responsibilities and to ourselves, our Tribes will soon be raised from their present degraded and helpless condition, and be alike useful and respected, both as Members of society and as Christians.

Brothers –

We offer you the right hand of fellowship, and bid you farewell.

Minutes of the General Council of Indian Chiefs and Principal Men held at Orillia.
Lake Simcoe Narrows (Montreal: Canada Gazette Office 1846) 11-13

► John Sunday (1796-1875), Shawundais, 'Little South Man,' was a converted Ojibwa who took an active part in the Methodist missionary work among his people. With George Copway and other preachers he went on several missionary tours to the Ojibwas around Lake Superior. In 1837 he travelled extensively in England, pleading the cause of Canadian missions, and was presented to the Queen. Wherever he went, at home or abroad, as preacher or as public speaker, he attracted large crowds that delighted in his droll wit, irresistible humour, and gift for apt illustration. Themes of conversion and religious experience were popular with the early missionaries, and Sunday's account of his conversion is told in his own inimitable style.

Brother Scott want me that I shall write my conviction about nine years ago. First is, we had camped at Mr. James Howard's place one morning. I go to Mr. Howard to get some whisky; so I did get it some. After I took it, that fire-water, I feel very happy. By-and-bye, James Farmer he says to me, 'Do you want go see them Indians at Belleville? They want see all Indians.' I say to him, 'Why they want see Indians for?' He says to me, 'Them are preachers talk about God.' So I went home to my wigwam to tell others: and we took some our blankets. We hire with them, Mr. Howard with his team, to take us at Belleville. We got there about nine o'clock. We have no chance to go in the meeting-house: so we went to the wood pile; so we sit there all day in the wood pile, until about five o'clock in the evening. By-and-bye them came out from meeting-house; so we went to them, and shake hands with them. About seven o'clock in the evening went to meeting; I want to hear them very much, what they will say to us. By-and-bye one of them rose up talk to us; he begin talk about God, and soul, and body; he says this: 'All mankind is only two ways we have got to go when we come to die; one is broad way, and other is narrow way. All the wicked white men, and wicked Indians, and drunkards go there; but the good white people shall go in the narrow way; but if the Indians also become good, and serve the Lord, they can go in that narrow way.' Then now I begin think myself; I begin feel bad in my heart. This is, I think, I am one to go in that broad way, because I had hard drink last night. My father and my mother had taught me this ever since when I was little boy, 'All the Indians shall go where sun set, but the white people go in the Ish-peming.' That I had trouble in my heart. Next morning again they had talk to us; so they went off from us. As soon as they went off, some them Indian says, 'Let us get some more whisky to drink it. What them men say unto us, we shall not do so; we must do our own way.' So they went to get more whisky. So I take it

80

little with them; and immediately after I had drunk it, I went home, me and Moses. Is about seven miles to our house. All way along the road I thinking about these two ways. Four nights I do not sleep much. On Saturday we all went to Belleville again. There I saw Brother Case. He says to me, 'How you like Peter Jones' talk?' I say unto him, 'Four nights I do not sleep much.' And he began to talk about religion of Jesus Christ. O, I feel very bad again; I thought this, 'I am one of devil his men, because I so wicked.'

On next Monday we all went home again. That night I thought I would try pray: this is first I ever did intend to pray. I do not know how to pray – my heart is too hard – I cannot say but few words; I say this: 'O Lord, I am wicked, I am wicked man, take me out from that everlasting fire and dark place.' Next morning I went in the woods to pray; no peace in my heart yet. By-and-bye I went to other Indians to tell them about what them men had said unto us at Belleville; so I went home again. By-and-bye we went to cross the Bay on Sahgegwin Island. So Indians come there on Island. By-and-bye we begin have prayer-meeting in the evening, and in the morning. I talk with them all time. I had boy about six years old; by-and-bye he got sick, and died. I felt very bad. I thought this, 'I better not stop to pray to God'; I went to Belleville to all them Methodist men to come on Sahgegwin Island to pray for us. I asked one of them Methodist men for glass of beer to comfort in my heart. That man say to me, 'Beer is not good for you; better for you to have Good Spirit in your heart.' None them they do not want to come on our wigewaum. So I went home without glass of beer. So we have prayer-meeting. None of us had religion yet. By-and-bye I went to quarterly meeting at Mr. Ketche-son. I saw one man and one woman shouting; I thought they were drunk. I thought this, 'They cannot be drunk, because is them Christian: must be something in them' Brother Belton he preached that day: he says this, 'If any man be great sinner, Lord will forgive him, if only believe in Him.' I thought this, 'If I do well, maybe God will forgive me.' About one week after this, another quarterly meeting at Seventown, Mr. Dinge's barn. In the morning they had lovefeast; they give each other little bread and water; they give us some too, that piece and bread and water. I do not know what they do it for. When I took it, the bread had stop in my throat, and choke me. O how I feel in my heart! I feel very sick in my heart. I think this, 'Surely I belong to devil, because the Lord bread choke me: I know how that Great Spirit is angry with me.' I think this again, 'I do not know what must I do to be save my soul from that everlasting fire.' I thought, 'I will try again.' Take another piece and bread not that the Lord bread, but some I got at a house. I did swallow it down. I feel worse again, because I swallowed down that bread. O how I feel in my heart! I feel like this – if I in under the water.

In afternoon we went to prayer-meeting in the Old House, about five o'clock, and Peter Jones says to us, 'Let us lift up our hearts to God.' I look at him; I do not understand him. I think this, 'If I do this – take my heart out of my body, I shall be died.' However, I kneel down to pray to God. I do not know what to say to ask for religion; I only say this: 'O, Keshamunedo, shahnanemeshim!' 'O Lord, have mercy on me, poor sinner!' By-and-bye, the good Lord He pour His Spirit upon my poor wretched heart; then I shout and happy in my heart. I feel very light, and after prayer-meeting I went to tell Peter Jones how I feel in my heart. I say to him this, 'I feel something in my heart.' Peter says to me, 'Lord bless you now.' O how glad in my heart! I look around, and look over other side a Bay, and look up, and look in the woods; the same is everything NEW to me. I hope I got religion that day. I thank the Great Spirit what He done for me. I want to be like the man which built his house upon a rock. Amen.

Rev. Egerton Ryerson Young, *By Canoe and Dog-Train among the Cree and Saulteaux Indians* (Toronto: William Briggs 1890) 17-21

John Sunday wrote a letter in 1833 to Henry Rowe Schoolcraft, the American ethnologist, who found it of interest philologically, 'as its variations from the rules of English syntax and orthography, denote some of the leading principles of aboriginal construction.'

I received your kind letter. I understand you – you want here the Indians from this place. I will tell you what to the Indians doing. They worshiped Idol God. They make God their own. I understand Mr. D., he told all Indians not going to hear the word of God. So the Indians he believed him. He tell the Indians do worship your own way. Your will get heaven quick is us. So the Indians they do not care to hear the word of God.

But some willing to hear preaching. One family they love to come the meeting. That Indian, by and by, he got ligion. He is happy now in his heart. After he got ligion that Indian say, Indian ligion not good. I have been worship Idol god many years. He never make happy. Now I know Jesus. His ligion is good, because I feel it in my heart. I say white people ligion very good. That Indian he can say all in Lord's prayer and ten commandments, and apostle creed by heart. Perhaps you know him. His name is Shah-wau-ne-noo-tin.

I never forget your kindness to me. I thing I shall stay here till the May. I want it to do what the Lord say.

Henry R. Schoolcraft, *Personal Memoirs of a Residence of Thirty Years with the Indian Tribes on the American Frontiers* (Philadelphia: Lippincott, Grambo and Co. 1851) 434-5

▶ Peter Jones (1802-56), whose Ojibwa name was Kahkewaquonaby, 'Sacred Waving Feathers,' was the first Indian Methodist minister in Canada; he was also an interpreter, a translator, a supporter of the rights of his people, and a remarkable author. Scores of his letters, sermons, lectures, and speeches written in English attest to the vigorous part he played in the religious and secular life of his time. In this extract from a letter to his brother, John, written during his first visit to England to raise funds for his people, he gives his first-hand observations on the customs and manners of the English.

London, December 30th, 1831

The English, in general, are a noble, generous-minded people – free to act and free to think; they very much pride themselves on their civil and religious privileges; in their learning, generosity, manufactures, and commerce; and they think that no other nation is equal to them.

I have found them very open and friendly, always ready to relieve the wants of the poor and needy when properly brought before them. No nation, I think, can be more fond of novelties than the English; they will gaze upon a foreigner as if he had just dropped down from the moon; and I have often been amused in seeing what a large number of people a *monkey riding* upon a *dog* will collect, where such things may be seen almost every day. When my Indian name, *Kahkewaquonaby*, is announced to attend any public meeting, so great is the curiosity, the place is sure to be filled. They are truly industrious, and in general very honest and upright. Their close attention to business produces, I think, too much worldly-mindedness, and hence they forget to think enough about their souls and their God; their motto seems to be 'Money, money; get money, get rich, and be a gentleman.' With this sentiment they fly about in every direction, like a swarm of bees, in search of the treasure which lies so near their hearts. These remarks refer to the men of the world, and of such there are not a few.

The English are very fond of good living, and many who live on roast beef, plum pudding, and turtle soup, get very fat, and round as a toad. They eat four times in a day. Breakfast at eight or nine, which consists of coffee or tea, bread and butter, and sometimes a little fried bacon, fish, or

83

eggs. Dinner at about two, P.M., when everything that is good is spread before the eater; which winds up with fruit, nuts, and a few glasses of wine. Tea at six, with bread and butter, toast, and sometimes sweet cake. Supper about nine or ten, when the leavings of the dinner again make their appearance, upon which John Bull makes a hearty meal to go to bed upon at midnight.

The fashion in dress varies so much, I am unable to describe it. I will only say, that the ladies of fashion wear very curious bonnets, which look something like a farmer's scoop-shovel; and when they walk in the tiptoe style they put me in mind of the little snipes that run along the shores of the lakes in Canada. They also wear sleeves as big as bushel bags, which make them appear as if they had three bodies with one head. Yet, with all their big bonnets and sleeves, the English ladies, I think, are the best of women ...

> Peter Jones' essay on cannibalism reveals the Christian bias of an accul-
> turated Indian as well as a highly personal and literate anecdotal style.

It has been ignorantly stated by some persons, that cannibalism prevails among the North American Indians. In confirmation of this report, they adduce the fabulous sayings of Indians about *weendegoos*, or *giant men-eaters*, and also the sad fact that some northern Indians have been known through famine to eat one another. My firm conviction is, that North American Indians are not cannibals; and Mr. J. Carver, who travelled extensively through the interior parts of North America, among the Ojeb-ways, Sioux, Sanks, &c., makes no mention of cannibalism.

Having heard such assertions some years since, I took particular pains to ascertain whether or no this was a fact, and the result of my enquiries amounted to this: – First, that cannibalism does not exist among them as it does among the New Zealanders. Second, that such is their abhorrence of cannibalism, that they have a common law among them that when an Indian is known to have eaten human flesh through starvation, it is right to put such an one to death as soon as possible. A few years ago I met with a wretched Indian woman at the narrows of Lake Simcoe, who had fled for her life from the north-west country, in consequence of having eaten her husband through extreme hunger. She was a most pitiable object, and appeared as though an evil spirit haunted her, as she wandered about in the woods, hiding herself behind the trees and logs. She was the terror of all the people, as they supposed that Indians who have once tasted human flesh became deranged, possessing the nature of a racoon,

84

porcupine, or some other animal. They fall on such a person, and beat out his brains with a club. No doubt, if the Lake Simcoe Indians had not been Christians, this poor woman would have been put to death. Christianity saves in all ways.

That the poor Indians in the barren regions of the North should occasionally, through starvation, be driven to eat one another, is nothing more than might be expected. Has not the same thing often occurred among the white people when shipwrecked or cast upon some desolate island? Thirdly, the whole amount of cannibalism, if such it may be called, of some of the western war tribes, is this, – that they have been known to take the heart of their enemy, cut it into small pieces, and boil it in a large kettle of corn soup for a heathen feast or offering. Each warrior then takes a ladleful, as a bravado or triumph over his enemy. This, in Indian mode of speech, is called 'drinking the heart's blood of the enemy.'

In Alexander Henry's travels among the Indians in Canada, between the years 1760 and 1776, he mentions an Indian family who had been so reduced by famine as to be compelled to eat each other. One young man arrived at the author's wintering place. The Indian was suspected of what he had done, and search being made, it was found he had lately eaten his surviving companion. He confessed the crime, and was forthwith put to death by tomahawk. He also mentions that some French Canadians, in a time of extreme hunger, proposed to kill and eat an Indian woman who was in their company.

In no book of travels among North American Indians have I seen cannibalism mentioned as prevalent amongst them. Goldsmith, in his geography, says – 'Murder is seldom heard of among them. A murderer is detested by all the tribe, and obliged, like another Cain, to wander up and down forlorn and forsaken even by his own relations and former friends.'

Rev. Peter Jones, *History of the Ojebway Indians; with especial reference to their Conversion to Christianity* (London: A.W. Bennett 1861) 221-2, 69-70

▶ William Wilson was educated at Upper Canada Academy in Cobourg where he excelled at classics and enjoyed writing poetry. This excerpt from his poem 'England and British America,' a patriotic tribute to Canada and the British connection written in heroic couplets, was recited at a public examination on 19 April 1838 and published in the *Christian Guardian* on 23 May. It was commonplace for Canadians at the time to rejoice in the progress and triumph of their civilization, and their young queen, Victoria, had just ascended the throne. Peter Jones, who saw the poem as an example of 'Indian improvement,' declared: 'we hazard nothing in saying that it

exhibits an incipient genius which deserves cultivation.' The young man
died of smallpox in New York shortly after leaving the college.

The clime of Canada in fondness gleams,
And western wilds awake more pleasing themes:
From where the eagle gluts his hungry beak
On Labrador's far coast of barren peak,
To where the Rocky Mountains sternly rise,
O'erlook the land, and half invade the skies,
Its fair and undulating soil extends,
And to the eye its bright enchantment lends.
Here Nature's God in matchless splendour rears
His living fane, and in wild pomp appears.
Here placid lakes like molten silver beam,
The full-orb'd sun reflects the glassy stream, –
Alluvial mountains lift their verdant heads,
And on the prairies prone their influence spreads.
Here fertile vales their rich luxuriance show,
Where nature's works in loveliest beauty glow;
From whose retreats, or sounds the woodman's hymn,
Far from the bustling throng of madd'ning din,
Or 'mid their haunts aërial spirits stray,
While to the breeze they chaunt their roundelay.
Here cataracts vast the echoing forests wake,
And all the ground with quick vibrations shake;
Where dread Niagara in thunder roars,
As o'er the rocky steep his deluge pours, –
Along whose banks the lonely Indian wound,
And in the scene his kindred spirit found.
Here boundless plains in fragrant verdure stretch,
Bright landscapes there invite the artist's sketch;
Here forests dark their stately branches wave,
And rivers there in solemn silence lave.
But though this land with ev'ry good is crown'd,
And choicest gifts on ev'ry hand surround, –
Though Nature here has wrought her grandest plan,
Yet does the mind deplore the fate of man.
Those lordly tribes that lin'd these mighty lakes
Have fled, and disappear'd like wintry flakes.
Lo! on the mountain-tops their fires are out,

In blithesome vales all silent is their shout;
A solemn voice is heard from ev'ry shore,
That now the Indian nations are no more, –
A remnant scarce remain to tell their wrongs,
But soon will fade to live in poets' songs.

Hail to thee, Canada! the brightest gem
That decks Victoria's brilliant diadem;
Thine is the happy seat, the blissful clime
Where art and nature form one vast sublime;
Where temp'rate skies effuse their golden rays,
The fertile land the labourer's toil repays;
Plenty and peace at ev'ry footstep smile,
And sunny scenes to gentler thoughts beguile.
A voice is heard upon thy mighty floods,
A voice resounds throughout thy trackless woods, –
Heard in the plaintive rill and cataract's roar,
Heard in the whisp'ring breeze on ev'ry shore:
Tis Freedom's voice; 'tis on thy rivers roll'd,
That in their course the sacred theme have told,
And bid the dwellers on the mountains swell
The choral strain, and wake the joyful knell, –
Till all mankind shall hear the gladd'ning sound,
Rouse from the trammel yoke of sleep profound,
And o'er the earth Britannia's banner wave,
Each foeman crush'd – unshackled ev'ry slave.

Rev. Peter Jones, *History of the Ojebway Indians* (1861) 195-7

▶ George Henry, or Maungwudaus, 'Big Legging,' born about 1810, was an
Ojibwa Methodist preacher, interpreter, and translator who, according to the
American artist, George Catlin, 'spoke and wrote the English language very
correctly.' As leader and chief of an Ojibwa dance troupe, he toured the
United States and Europe in 1844 and was entertained and honoured as a
celebrity by royalty and high society alike. His reminiscences and impressions of this overseas tour appeared in a pamphlet he published in 1848.

While on the sea our middle mast got blown away. The waves were like
mountains; we did not get sea-sick, only got little hurt sometimes when
thrown out of our berths. Sometime got a good ducking with salt water

by the waves, pouring into our cabin. The flour and corn barrels got loose and knocked against one another and spilt all that was inside of them. The rats had great feasting. Every night after they had their bellies full they were very mischievous; they helped the waves in tormenting us, by biting us on our toes and noses. The sea in the night was like the blaze of fire.

We landed at Portsmouth on the 26th of the same month. Portsmouth is a great place for ships. We went to see Lord Nelson's war-ship and saw the place where he fell when he was killed. The officers living in this sea-house were very kind to us. The great sea-war chief took us into the navy yard where they are making many war ships. Another war chief invited us and showed us all his warriors under him in the barracks.

From Portsmouth we went to London, and we remained a long time in this wonderful city; performed every day in the Egyptian Hall, in Piccadilly. This city is about ten miles broad, but some parts of it is about twenty miles long. Like musketoes in America in the summer season, so are the people in this city, in their numbers, and biting one another to get a living. Many very rich, and many very poor; about 900 births and about 1100 deaths every week in this city alone. There are many stone and iron bridges over the river Thames. The steamboats in this river are not so handsome as those in America. The St. Paul's church and the Council House are very large buildings indeed. Most of the houses rather dark in color on account of too much smoke.

Many ladies and gentlemen ride about in carriages. The carriages, servants and horses are covered with gold and silver. Hundreds of them walk about in the parks, the servants leading little dogs behind them to air them. The English women cannot walk alone; they must always be assisted by the men. They make their husbands carry their babies for them when walking.

Mr. Harris took us into the Queen's house. She is a small woman but handsome. There are many handsomer women than she is. Prince Albert is a handsome and well built man. Her house is large, quiet country inside of it. We got tired before we went through all the rooms in it. Great many warriors with their swords and guns stands outside watching for the enemy. We have been told that she has three or four other houses in other places as large. The one we saw they say is too small for her, and they are building a much larger one on one side of it.

When she goes out she has a great many warriors before and behind, guarding her; most of them seven feet tall. Their coats and caps are of steel; long white horse-hair waves on their heads. They wear long boots, long gloves, and white buckskin breeches. Their swords, guns, and every-thing about them are kept very clean and bright. Their horses are all black, and much silver and gold about them. They do not shave the upper part of their mouths, but let the beards grow long, and this makes them look fierce and savage like our American dogs when carrying black squirrels in their mouths.

The nobility and ministers and the Society of Friends invited us most every day to take tea with them. Sometimes we were about two hours in eating; the plates, knives, forks, spoons and everything we used in eating were of gold and silver. The servants' heads were white powdered; they gave us many handsome presents, and caused us to see many things that others have never seen. We went to hear Lord John Russell and Sir R. Peel talk in the council; went also in the lower house and saw and heard the speakers in it. We were kindly invited to dine with Daniel O'Connell. He was very kind to us. We went through the tunnel under the bed of the river Thames. The ships were sailing over us while walking below.

Our war-chief shot a buck in the Park, through the heart, and fell down dead three hundred yards, before four thousand ladies and gentle-men. This was done to amuse them. Travelling on the Great Western Railway, the Engine knocked down several rooks or crows while flying over the railway. We saw three men out of the Zoological Gardens going up to the country of stars. They had something very large in the shape of a bladder over their heads; they called it a balloon. One man said to us, 'You see now that we Englishmen can go and see the upper world with our bodies.' Lord Bloomfield invited us to see the big guns at Woolwich; three of us got inside of one of them.

They say that there are eighty thousand common wives in the City of London. They say that they are allowed to walk in the streets every night for the safety of the married women. The English officers invited us to eat with them in the barracks in our native costume. When the tea got ready, the ladies were brought to the table like sick women; it took us about two hours in eating. The ladies were very talkative while eating; like ravens when feasting on venison. Indeed, they have a proverb which says, 'Thieves and robbers eat and drink a little, and make no noise when they eat.' They are very handsome; their waists, hands and feet are very small; their necks are rather longer than those of our women. They carry their heads on one side of the shoulder; they hold the knife and fork with the two forefingers and the thumb of each hand; the two last ones are of no use to them, only sticking out like our fish-spears, while eating.

The English officers are fine, noble, and dignified looking fellows. The voice of them when coming out of the mouth, sounds like the voice of a bull-frog. The only fault we saw of them, are their too many unneccessary ceremonies while eating, such as allow me Sir, or Mrs. to put this into your plate. If you please Sir, thank you, you are very kind Sir, or Mrs. can I have the pleasure of helping you?

Many of the Englishmen have very big stomachs, caused by drinking too much ale and porter. Those who drink wine and brandy, their noses look like ripe strawberries.

When we got ready to leave, one of the officers said to us, our ladies would be glad to shake hands with you, and we shook hands with them. Then they were talking amongst themselves; then another officer said to us, 'Friends, our ladies think that you do not pay enough respects to them, they desire you to kiss them'; then we kissed them according to our custom on both cheeks. 'Why! they have kissed us on our cheeks; what a curious way of kissing this is.' Then another officer said to us, 'Gentlemen, our pretty squaws are not yet satisfied; they want to be kissed on their mouths.' Then we kissed them on their mouths; then there was a great shout amongst the English war-chiefs. Say-say-gon, our war-chief, then said in our language to the ladies: 'That is all you are good for; as for wives, you are good for nothing.' The ladies wanted me to tell them what the war-chief said to them. I then told them that he said he was wishing the officers would invite him very often, that he might again kiss the handsome ladies. Then they said, 'Did he? then we will tell our men to invite you again, for we like to be kissed very often; tell him so.' They put gold rings on our fingers and gold pins on our breasts, and when we had thanked them for their kindness, we got in our carriage and went to our apartments.

The great war-chief with the big nose, Duke of Wellington, invited us, and he was very kind to us in his house. He and his son gave us handsome presents.

Sir Augustus d'Este, cousin to the Queen, son of the Duke of Sussex, invited us very often to take tea with him. He is a great friend to the Indians; he introduced us to many of his friends. This great man is an invalid, and not able to walk alone.

The Archbishop of Canterbury Cathedral was very kind of us; he showed us everything in the Cathedral, curious and wonderful works of the ancient Britons. He said that this building is thirteen hundred years old. This is the most curious, the largest, and beautiful one we have seen. The top of its steeple our arrows could not reach.

We went to see Dover; we went through the subterraneous roads in the Rocks ...

We crossed to Scotland and landed at the place called Adrosson; we went to see R. Burns's cottage, small, with straw-roof. We went to see Wallace's Oak Tree near Paisley; went to Glasgow and Edinburgh. Edinburgh is large of the Scotch people; the new town is very handsome, but the old town is rather filthy. All the dirt is thrown in the streets before people get up, and carts take it away, but still the smell of it is most offensive all day. One of the chiefs told us that a Scotchman some years ago, who was born in the city, was away from it for some years, and returning to it he said, 'There is nothing like home'; and when he began to smell the streets, he said, 'Ah! sweet auld Edinburgh, I smell thee now.' The Scotch chiefs showed us the Crown of Scotland in the Castle, also the Palace. We went to see about seventy young men, who are to be medicine men. They had thirty dead bodies, and they were skinning and cutting them same as we do with venison.

The Scotch people are very religious and industrious, very kind-hearted to strangers. They keep Sunday very strictly. A great many are teetotalers; their country is mountainous. The old men and women are very fond of snuff; they carry it in rams horns; they put one spoonful of it in each nostril at a time; this causes their words to sound nasal, something like pig grunting.

At Glasgow, two of my children died, another in Edinburgh; buried them in the burying ground of our friends the Quakers; and after we visited other towns at the North and South, we went to England again; my wife died at Newark. The vicar of that church was very kind to us, in allowing us to bury her remains near the church.

Riding through a town in our native costume, we saw a monkey performing in the street upon a music box, about fifty young men looking at him. He was dressed like a man. When the young men saw us, they began to make fun of us, and made use of very insulting language, making a very great noise; – at the same time when the monkey saw us he forgot his performances, and while we were looking at him, he took off his red cap and made a bow to us. A gentleman standing by, said to the audience, 'Look at the monkey take off his cap and make a bow in saluting those strangers; which of the two strangers will think are most civilized, you or the monkey? You ought to be ashamed of yourselves. You may consider yourselves better and wiser than those strangers, but you are very much mistaken. Your treatment to them tells them that you are not, and you are so foolish and ignorant, you know nothing about it. I have been travelling five years amongst these people in their own country, and I never, not once, was insulted, but I was always kindly treated and respected by every one of them. Their little children have far better manners than you. Young men, the monkey pays you well for all the pennies you have given him; he is worthy to become your teacher.' We then threw some money to the monkey, and he jumped down from his platform and picked up the money and jumped up again, and put the money into his master's mouth, and he made another bow to us as we were going away; at the same time heard one of the young men saying to his friends, 'See the teacher making another bow to the Indians.' 'Yes,' said another, 'this is to teach you, for you are the very one that was making fun and blackguarding the Indians.'

We visited New Castle upon Tyne, Hull, Leeds, York, Birmingham, and many other Towns; visited Shakspeare's house and his grave at Stratford on Avon. We visited Lord Byron's house. Col. Wildman was very kind to us; went to Nottingham and to London again.

We left London the 23d of April, 1848, with the ship called Yorktown, of New York. Capt. Seba was very kind to us all the way. Sixteen children of the Germans died on the way; also an English lady. Ourselves did not get sea sick. The waves were like mountains; saw seven whales and many porpoises; landed in New York city on the 4th of June, and we were very thankful to the Great Spirit for bringing us back again to America.

On the voyage Capt. Seba was very careful that there was no smoking with pipes and cigars inside the ship, drinking fire-water; quarrelling and fighting he prohibited, but when the sea had been very rough for two or three days, the English and Germans had little fighting, because there was no room for all their teapots in the cooking place; but no one got much hurt, only a few faces got little cut and scratched, and afterwards received four or five blows of rope by the powerful chief mate on their backs.

He allowed the religious minister to preach in the cabin every Sunday Every few days we had the inside of the ship cleaned; outside every day, that there might be no sickness among us. He was like a father to us; all the sailors loved him and were very obedient to him.

When the sun could be seen he would look at it with a little glass, curiously constructed with brass; and by this he could tell us where and how far we were from England and America. Sometimes he would get one of his men to sink a piece of lead with a long cord, some tallow on the bottom of it, and when it was hoisted up, there was sand on the tallow, and he, by looking at it and seeing its color, he knew exactly where we were, he received much wisdom by looking at the sun and sand.

He also had something in a glass tube look like melted lead, by which, in looking at it, he could always tell when the storm was coming, and had the ship ready for it. He is very good as well as a great man.

In Ipswich we dined with our friends the Quakers, about sixty in number; their names are Alexanders and Ransoms. After we had eaten many good things and all the plates taken away, a small round but high cheese was put on the table, and one of the oldest Friends said to us, 'Now, friends, this is our English cheese; the poor of our people cannot afford to eat this. We never think that our dinner is finished until we have ate some of it; will thou have litte of it.' I said yes. Will thou have little of it, &c., until every one of us had it before us, and we ate much of it, because it was from our friends. When our eating was over, a doctor, whose name is F.W. Johnson, placed on the table, what he calls microscope; it had three brass legs and a small glass to it, and when he had put a very small bit of the cheese we had to eat on a clean plate, he made us look at it through the little glass that was on the three legged brass, and we saw hundreds of worms moving in it. This made all our friends laugh, and we tried to laugh too, but we were very much frightened at the same time knowing that we must have swallowed thousands of them. When our friends saw that we were frightened, the medicine man dropped one drop of rain water in a clear glass, and he made us look at it again through the little glass, and we saw hundreds of living creatures swimming in it; some like beasts, some like snakes, some like fish, some had horns and some had no horns, some with legs and some had no legs; some had wheels on each side of their bodies, and with these they were moving about like steamboats, hooking, chasing, fighting, killing and eating one another. Then one of our oldest friends said to us, 'Now, friends, you must not think that this is the first time you have been eating worms. We swallow thousands of them every day either with food or water. They are floating in the air, and we inhale them, when we draw breath; thousands of them are also floating in our veins. The Great Spirit, who made us and all other beings is wonderful in power and wisdom. We sincerely hope that you will at all times love him, and obey what he tells you in your hearts.' We waited two or three days for the worms to bite. Sometimes we would be looking for them, thinking that they might have grown larger while they were in our bodies, but we did not feel their bites nor saw any of them. We have oftentimes been thinking since, that our friends must be something like bears, who love to eat living worms or maggots ...

... The Americans have been very kind to us in all places; they are not so fleshy as the English, but very persevering in all their ways. They pay more respect to their females than the English, and they like to see things belong to others without leave. The working classes of the English call their rich men 'Big Bugs,' but the Yankee call them, 'Top Notches.' They put their feet upon tables, chairs and chimney pieces when smoking their cigars or reading newspapers. They are not so much slaves to their civilization as the English; they like to be comfortable, something like ourselves, placing one leg upon the other knee, while basking ourselves in the sun. A real comfort is better than an artificial one to the human nature.

George Henry (Maungwudaus), *An Account of the Chippewa Indians,*
who have been travelling among the whites, in the United States, England,
Ireland, Scotland, France and Belgium (Boston: Published by the author 1848) 3-11

George Henry's impressions of France, which he visited during the same tour, are included in a letter he wrote to his cousin, Peter Jones.

Paris, *Oct. 19th*, 1854 [*sic*]

MY DEAR BROTHER,

... Last Saturday we saw the great chief of France, and his great chief woman; the great chief of Belgium, and his great chief woman; and some hundreds of their people ... These things we did for them: – We played the Indian ball-play, shot at marks with our own bows and arrows, false scalping, war dance, paddled one of our birch-bark canoes in a beautifully made river, among swans, wild geese, and ducks. After the two great chiefs and their great chief women had much talk with us, they thanked us, got into their carriages covered with gold, drawn by six beautiful horses, and drove to the wigwam of the great chief of France. We followed them, and the great chief's servant, who wears a red coat, and much gold and silver, and a hat in the shape of half-night-sun, took us into one of the great rooms to dine. Everything on the table was gold and silver; we had twelve clean plates. Many came in while we were eating, and it was great amusement to them all ...

Paris is much handsomer than the city of London; very clean.

The French people wear much hair about the mouth, which makes them look bold and noble; but our friend Sasagon, who has no taste for beauty, says that it would puzzle any one of our people to find where the French-man's mouth is; and that a person having much hair round his mouth makes him look like one of our Indian dogs in North America when running away with a black squirrel in his mouth.

The French women carry big and heavy loads on their backs, on what we call tetoomaugun, same as our women do; they do it because they are industrious. Here, again, Sasagon says, 'that the French women would make good wives for the Ojebway hunters.'

The French people are very gay in their dress, and yet I think they are not so selfish and proud as most of the English.

There are no ragged people or beggars in Paris. We have not seen a single person intoxicated since we have been here.

KEEKAUNIS,

MAUNGWADAUS

To KAHKEWAQUONABY,
or REV. PETER JONES.   or GEORGE HENRY.

Rev. Peter Jones, *History of the Ojebway Indians* (1861) 219-20

▶   Henry Bird Steinhauer (1820-84) was an Ojibwa born in Rama, Upper Canada. He studied at Upper Canada Academy in Cobourg and knew Greek and Hebrew. He devoted his life to missionary work among the Cree and Stoney Indians in the North-West and was the first Indian teacher in Alberta. This letter, addressed to the editor of the *Christian Guardian*, George R. Sanderson, on 15 August 1849, was sent from Rossville, a remote Wesleyan Methodist mission post three miles north of Norway House in the Hudson's Bay territory.

REV. AND DEAR SIR, – Though many a year has passed away since he who now addresses these few lines to you from this distant part of North America, had the pleasure of seeing you, since you and he sat under the instructions of the same masters, in the same recitation rooms, within the walls of the then U.C. Academy. By reverting to the period when you were there, you will perhaps recollect him who presumes to trouble you with a letter from the Hudson's Bay Territories. Since then many are the changes that have taken place. Our companions in the acquisitions of knowledge are now scattered into the different parts of the country; into various callings; some perhaps are now no more.

Though the living be scattered into different parts, yet blessed be God they are all under the care of the same God who careth for all. Although buried as it were, in this waste howling wilderness, I bless God, that thus he has been, my helper, that he can even here manifest himself to all that love and call upon him. I am truly happy to learn, by means of some few odd numbers of the *Guardian*, which by some means or other found their way into this country, that our beloved Wesleyan-Methodism is progressing, and that its members are prospering in godliness. I am happy to be able to say (though I can say but little) that it is also prospering at this mission station. The members of the society are endeavouring to walk worthy of their profession, holding fast that whereunto they have attained. That they are advancing in grace is evident from their love to the house of God and to the means of grace. We have a very nice chapel built by the Hon., the Hudson's Bay Company. Our Mission school is also in a state of prosperity, there are upwards of 73 attendants on the Day, but more than that number attend the Sabbath School. In this mission we have a printing establishment, and all our printing is in Indian, in the Syllabic characters, founded by the late superintendent of this mission [Rev. James Evans], which is very simple and easily learned. We know that the few little works that have been issued from the press tend greatly to increase the interest of the mission. It must be remembered that the field of labour is great; the labourers are few, and in this our day of small things, by means of the books that have been printed is knowledge spreading. These little books are finding their way even unto those parts where the missionary has not been. Pray for us. – There is only one solitary missionary in this part of the country, namely, the Rev. Wm. Mason. I am sorry I cannot write any more respecting the mission at this place. The Rev. Wm. Mason will in due time make known to the christian public the present state and future prospects of this mission; but before I close, I have one request to make of you, as I have learned that you are the Editor of the *Christian Guardian*, perhaps some christian friend will have pity on us and send it to us. I should have written more than I have done had I known sooner that there was an opportunity of sending letters to Canada. Hoping I may have another opportunity, till then adieu!

I am, Rev. and dear Sir,

Yours respectfully,

HENRY B. STEINHAUR.

Christian Guardian, 17 October 1849, p 206

▶ Peter Jacobs (1805-90), or Pahtaysagay, 'Come/Arrive Shining,' was an Ojibwa Methodist minister who laboured among the Indian tribes of Lake Superior and the Hudson's Bay territory to the west. At one time he was probably the best known Indian on the continent. A natural orator, he drew large crowds wherever he spoke, lecturing in Canada, the United States, and England on the manners and customs of Indian people. These extracts from his *Journal*, written on a trip from Rice Lake, Ontario, to the North-West in 1852, reveal his powers of keen observation and his straightforward, factual style. On 8 May Jacobs saw Niagara Falls for the first time.

... I went down to see the greatest fall in the world. The cataract is indeed awfully grand; and it appeared to me as if an angry God was dwelling beneath it, for my whole frame shook as a leaf while I was viewing these mighty angry Falls. Now 'tis no wonder that my forefathers, in by-gone days, should offer up sacrifices at the foot of these Falls; they used to come and pray to the God of the fall to bless them in their hunt and to prolong their life and that of their children; for every Indian believed that a God dwelt under this mighty sheet of water ...

On 28 May he saw Kakabeka Falls.

After an early breakfast, the men began to pole up against a strong current or rapid, somewhere about fifteen miles in length. The banks of the river are high, dry and sandy, the principal timber being birch, poplar, and small stunted pine. The north bank is inclining to be like a prairie, where, in the month of July, an abundance of blue berries (whortleberries) are to be found. I and eight men got out of the canoes and walked on the north bank of the river for the distance of some miles, and then got into the canoes again. After an hour's paddling, we came to a place where the men were obliged to make a half portage, by taking out part of the baggage, the current being too strong, so that when the canoe is thus discharged the men pulled them by a cord line about thirty fathoms long. After another hour's pull we came to a dead water, that is where the current was strong, and apparently no current at all. This was about two miles in length; and at the upper end of this we dined on a fine open space or plain cleared by former fires. After this, I and eight men crossed over to the south side of the river, and followed an Indian trail or path for about three miles, which brought us to the foot of the mountain Portage; and after waiting about fifteen minutes, the canoes arrived ... The stone composing this mountain is of the slate appearance. The portage itself is about a mile in length. At this place is one of the grandest falls of water to be seen at any of all the many noble rivers of America, and is second in grandeur to the greatest of cataracts, that of Niagara ...

He was at Rainy Lake on 25 September.

... It blew very hard, but the wind was in our favor. In two hours we passed the Nahmakaun, or Sturgeon Lake. When we reached the entrance of the Nahmakaun River, it blew a hurricane; we were glad that we were not wind-bound; we congratulated ourselves that we were in a narrow river at this time. We pulled up stream, and made several portages during the day. Nothing worth relating occurred to-day, but I will relate what occurred at the second portage from Nahmakaun in one of my former voyages. The fall is four feet high, and is nearly perpendicular. The surface of the water where it begins to fall is quite smooth. The fall is so large that voyagers dare not shoot over, as they do in smaller falls. I and my men were coming from Fort William, Lake Superior, with a load of flour, for the use of my family at Fort Frances. I was not able that year to get flour from Red River, on account of the troops being there. We had intended to go near the pitch of the rapids, in order to save ourselves much labor and trouble, and to make a short portage of thirty feet. But in approaching the desired place just above the pitch, we accidentally touched a stone under our canoe, which was immediately whirled round; as there was a strong current besides, the canoe became ungovernable. I was steersman at the time. The canoe was fast going down on her broad-side; our only alternative, therefore, was to go down the falls. It was too late to go back. Down we went. As we were going down, I cried out to my men, telling them to squat at the bottom of the canoe, while I did the same at the same moment. Plash we went; every one of us, without knowing it at the time, lost his paddle. By this time our canoe was half full of water. For a few minutes we were senseless. There was our luggage floating about, the flour-bags were quite wet. My men, as I said before, lost all their paddles, and as I also lost my steering paddle, our canoe was now at the mercy of the rocks below, to be dashed to pieces on striking them. At this critical moment kind Providence sent up my paddle to my hand, that is, by the motion of the water about a whirlpool, my paddle was forced up erect near me, and I laid hold of it, and steered the canoe, so that we evaded the projecting rocks that threatened to break our canoe to pieces, and went to an eddy, where my men luckily got their paddles. We soon went down all right again, as if nothing had happened ...

September 27. – Early this morning we started, and made two portages and two lakes. We had our breakfast at Ogoncekahning Lake. After breakfast the clouds began to gather, and looked as if it was going to rain or snow. At twelve o'clock the snow fell fast and thick; soon it was perceivable lying on the ground. At two o'clock in the afternoon we arrived at the French portage ...

In making this long portage, I never suffered so much in these cold regions for the whole term of twelve years that I was in them, as I did at this time. It snowed very much, and the wind was strong. We had to follow a narrow path, on each side of which were pine bushes and other evergreens covered with wet snow. It was impossible to walk on without touching these; consequently our clothes were quite wet from the snow melting on them. We were drenched to the skin, and felt very cold by the time we reached the other end of the portage. My men nearly cried from the cold. I was not in a much better state. Our teeth were chattering from the cold. O how glad we were when we kindled a large blazing fire, and partook of a hearty supper.

Journal of the Reverend Peter Jacobs, Indian Wesleyan Missionary, from Rice Lake to the Hudson's Bay Territory, and Returning, Commencing May, 1852, with a Brief Account of his life, and a Short History of the Wesleyan Mission in that Country (New York 1858) 9-10, 24-5, 83-5

Peter Jacobs' gift for oratory and his sense of humour can be seen in this address delivered at the annual meeting of the Wesleyan Methodist Missionary Society held at Exeter Hall, London, England, in 1851.

Mr. Chairman, I expect that a good many of my friends here are accustomed to hear of my long speeches; but I know that an Englishman always looks about four or five o'clock for his dinner, and as it is now past four, I do not intend to keep you from your dinner this afternoon. (Laughter). However, I shall occupy your attention for a few moments, while I endeavour to impress on your minds some very important truths. Poor North America has very small say in this great assemblage, although you know, that North America would put your England into one of her inland seas, Lake-Huron, Lake-Superior, or Lake-Ontario. I only tell you this, to show what a tremendous large country it is. I am only twenty years of age, – in Christianity, I mean. (Cheers). Twenty years ago, or thereabouts, I was, with my countrymen, a worshipper of the sun and moon. When your Missionaries came to us, and preached Christ, and Him crucified, I was led, by the preaching of the Missionaries, to come and pray to God through Christ. Formerly, my prayers were something like this: [the speaker, having repeated the prayer in his native language, translated it as follows:] – 'O god, the moon, – O god, the sun, – direct my steps through the woods in the direction where the deer are feeding, that I may kill him, and have something to eat.' This was all the prayer we could utter; and then we were all very wicked. We had no Lawyers, and there were no law-suits; we settled all our affairs by the force of the tomahawk; and, as regards our women, we did not use them with that civility that we now use them. In all Heathen countries, women stand in a very low class. Now, never send a Missionary into a Heathen country

without his wife. If you send a Missionary who is a single man, he is
only half a Missionary. When you send him with his wife, he is a whole
Missionary. (Laughter and cheering). We men look to the Missionaries
and respect them; but how are our females to be advanced, unless you
send Missionaries' wives? Now, then, the Missionary is respected by the
men, and the Missionary's wife is respected by our females; and that
excellent woman, the Missionary's wife, teaches our females not to be
tramped down as we did tramp them down when we were Heathens.
They teach them to be respected more. They say, 'Come up, come up,
and they are up. (Cheers). Why, there was a time when a poor woman
could not say any thing against her lord, for fear of the tomahawk. Now,
I expect, we have been so much Christianized and civilized, that I shall,
when I go home, hear at my ear a voice telling me that I have been very
many months away. But I shall be very deaf, that is all. (Cheering and
laughter). I have told you in what state we were. Now, at Alderville,
there are beautiful buildings; there is an academy, and a large house
where the whole of these young men go; and there is a house for the
Missionaries, erected partly by the industry of the Indians, partly by your
aid, and partly by the aid of the Government ... The Rev. Dr. [Egerton]
Ryerson [Superintendent of Education in Upper Canada] knew the time
when we did not raise a grain of wheat; we raised nothing but our Indian
corn and potatoes; but now, through all Canada, what do the Indians
raise? They raise fields of wheat, fields of rye, fields of oats, and fields of
Indian corn. There are Indians with fine houses, their horses, their oxen,
their cows, their sheep, and their pigs; all this you have done, you, the
supporters of the Mission cause. (Loud cheers.) Take another Mission
(which he named). I knew when they were poor people, and we used to
give them our old clothing. They do not want our old clothes now. They
can get new clothing for themselves, and they have fine houses. Not only
have they fine houses, but they have a large academy and chapels, and
schools, all over Canada West. In that academy, called 'Lord Elgin's Academy,' there are something like fifty boys as well as girls ... I have seen an
Indian Chief take the Chair at the Missionary Meeting. What a change!
The Chief who used to lead on the battle with his men is now the Minister of peace. (Cheers). The tomahawk and the scalping-knife have been
broken; and the Bible and the Hymn-Book are now his only weapons.
And these Chiefs are now taking the Chair to support the glorious cause
of Missions. (Cheers). You have done wonders in Canada West. Then
there is Hudson's-Bay Territory; that is also a large country. I have been
about there for the last twelve years. We have been preaching the Gospel

to those warriors. They are still using the tomahawk on the plains and
Rocky Mountains; but, as your Missionaries have gone on, the tomahawk
has been thrown away. Now, what we want you to do is, to help the
great cause in that country, until every tomahawk, all over the Rocky
Mountains, shall be thrown away, as has been done in Canada West. In
Hudson's-Bay Territories we have met with success. I could tell you,
again and again, what we have done. There is now a splendid Mission at
Norway-House. The people can read and write in their own tongue; and
there is printing-house, and so on. There is another station at Oxford-
House; and at Oxford-House there is a school-house and a Mission-house
built, and the people are all ready assembled; but they have no Missionary. A few days ago I was pleading their cause, that a Missionary might
be sent to them. It has been said, as you have heard to-day, that India
must be supported. If India has its millions, we have our thousands in
North America. So the poor Red North-American Indian is not to be
thought of! Is this Christianity? I hope not. (Hear, hear). The poor Red
North-American Indian has got a soul, and has got a soul to save, and
that soul cost the precious blood of Christ, when He bled on the cross,
and when He sweated the great drops of blood to save – who? To save
me! Yes. (Loud cheers). When I prayed, not to the sun and moon; but
when I said, [the speaker here uttered a prayer in his native language, and
proceeded,] when I cried, 'O my heavenly Father, have mercy upon me, a
poor Indian lad! let now the precious blood of Christ be applied to my
heart, that my sins may depart!' praying in faith, I found the forgiveness
of my sins; and, when I found Christ was precious to me, it moved me to
preach the Gospel to my countrymen; and I am ready again, after visiting
you, after my spirit has been filled with renewed love and renewed
energy, and more faith, I am ready to go home to my work cheerfully in
that hard country, that very hard country, that cold country, among the
savages who, every now and then, attempt to take my life. It is a freezing
country, where the people freeze to death. But is that any reason why I
should not go there again? No, brethren; I love that country, because that
is the country where I see the work does go on, although it goes on
slowly; but we cannot expect that it should become a whole world in a
day. (Hear, hear) ... I know that what you have given, year after year,
towards this good cause, will be a source of great joy to you, especially
when you know, as I have seen many times, poor John Curlyhead, in the
Hudson's-Bay Territories, who was a very faithful man. By and by poor
John got very sick, and I went to see John. I say, 'John, I see you are
dying; how do you feel now in this dreadful hour of death? How is thy

faith in Christ?' 'My faith in Christ,' he says, 'is as firm as a rock; I am immovable; I have nothing here on earth but Christ; I have nothing in heaven but Christ'; and he says, in closing his eyes, 'O Jesus! sweet Saviour! come now, take me away to those mansions above.' John closed his eyes in death; and he has gone to heaven. What did I feel? Pressing my hand to my heart, I said, 'My heavenly Father, help me, by the assistance of thy Holy Spirit, to walk in the right way, in that narrow path, during life; so that, when I die, I may join the spirit of poor John, which has gone to sing praises with the Redeemer at the right hand of the Father!' (Great cheering).

'Annual Meeting of the Society,' *The Wesleyan Missionary Notices*, n.s. IX (June/July 1851) 110-12

▶ Henry Budd (c. 1812-75), the son of an unknown Indian and a Métis woman, was a Hudson's Bay Company clerk, farmer, teacher, and the first Anglican minister of Indian origin in North America: he became a deacon in 1850 and was ordained as a priest in 1853. He was acknowledged to be one of the most dedicated missionaries in the North-West; contemporaries praised him as a 'good English scholar,' 'a fluent and forcible preacher,' who 'speaks English perfectly.' His 1852 diary provides a good example of pioneer missionary writing, giving useful information on the spiritual and secular activities of the members of his congregation.

Oct. 3: Lord's-day – We held the morning service at the usual place. The small room was quite full: all the people of the Fort, and our own, formed a little band. A few of the women among the Indians were present. After the service was over, the old man Mahnsuk followed us to our tent. I took the opportunity of speaking to him about breaking the Sabbath: how God made the world in six days, and rested on the seventh day, and sanctified it for His own worship; how very wrong it must be to rob God of that one day in seven, when all we have comes from Him. On telling him how man first sinned against God, he interrupted me by saying, that during his lifetime he nearly did one sin – 'I was persuaded by another man to consent to poison a woman with bad medicine; but when my mother knew what I intended to do, she made me leave it off, and I did not do it. Now,' said the old man, 'if I had hurt or poisoned the woman I should have done sin once in my whole life.' As much as to say, that since he did not hurt the woman he had not committed even one sin! Such is the state of the Indian! He is utterly blind as to his sinfulness; and, strange to say, the term sin, as we understand it, is not used by the

heathen Indians; it is made use of by the Christian Indians only. Astonished at the reply of the old man, I asked him 'What do you call sin?
When an Indian murders another do you call that sin?' He said, 'Yes.'
'But when an Indian steals, and speaks bad words, is that not sin?' He
said, 'No; we say of such a man, "nummaheyinneseu," "he is not wise,"
but we do not call that sinning.' When I told him that every thing that
the Indian does which breaks the holy law of God, and hurts his neighbour in any wise, is sin, and that all mankind, as well as the Indian, have
broken the law of God times without number, and committed more sins
than the hair upon their heads, he did not reply, but looked quite astonished, wondering how he could be such a sinner.

'The Nepowewin Station,' *Church Mission Magazine*, April 1854, p 96

▶ Allan Salt (1818-1911) was an early graduate of the Toronto Normal School
and for some years was a school-teacher. In 1853 he entered the Methodist
ministry and became a missionary in the North-West. The following is a
portion of a journal Salt kept during his stay in the Rainy River region.

Wed, Sept 20/54 Early this morning another band of Indians came to this
Fort to get their winter supplies. I endeavored to show them the evil of
drinking rum, for they as bands invariably call for it to take along with
them when they go to their places of locality, but they are not allowed to
drink it near the Fort. In the evening a chief of Lac-La-Pluie arrived from
Red lake the American Territory where he has been to visit the grave of
his wife. He was telling the Indians in the Fort that The Ojibways and
the Sioux are constantly killing one another, and also the wife of a
teacher among the Ojibways was shot through while sitting before a light
in her house. After he got through with his stories we got started on
other subjects, till we come to the subject of religion. One of the Indians
said that the reason that these Indians do not embrace Christianity is
because of a story told among them of an Indian who had embraced
Christianity and who died and came to life again.

When the Christian died he came to the God of the white man and
was asked are you an Indian that embraced the white man's religion? Yes,
said the Indian. Well this place is not for you it is only for the white
man, I gave the white man his religion and it brings him to and I gave
the Indian His religion and it takes him to another place, but not here, so
go away. so he came to the place of the Indians, but met the same recep-
tion as before, for as he had dropt the religion of the Indian and embraced
another, he could not enter into the place of the indian. So the soul

wandered about until it came to the body, and revived. I said to them, as you have just told me that this story came from the East and I am from the east but never heard of it so that it is very probable that someone who hated Christianity invented it. I also informed them that the British nation was once a heathen nation, but the Gospel was preached to them and you see and hear what that nation is at the present time, Its wisdom, commerce, greatness and power, the sun is always seen by that nation ...

Sunday [September] 24th, We had service as usual in the large room, two Roman Catholics with their children augmented our congregation. In the afternoon I visited the Indians on the portage and talked to them on the subject of eternity. They would attempt to laugh it off, one of them said to me, 'when we Indians speak to God we speak only twice for fear He would get out of patience with us, but you have been talking about him now for a long time, He must be getting out of patience with you' I said to him God is not as we are &, He said no more. An old woman who had been listening, said, 'we are too foolish to be taught your religion, but said I, you remember what was told you many years ago and still remember those things, that shows you that you can learn if you are willing to be taught the word of God.' She said no more but listened. Surely they are degraded and stubborn.

Monday [February] 5th [1855] Maskokonuya and Kichigauk were in Mr P's room while teaching a few of the children and after I had dismissed the school; the chief asked questions about the English, so I spoke about their steam boats, railroads, telegraphs and galvanism. he seemed very much surprised. The next thing he asked was about the great guns. Mr P, readily explained to him pictures of battles in the time of the Duke of Wellington. After which we entered upon other subjects, during which Kichigauk said. the pheasants have an easier way of getting their living than we have. T took Mr P's place and read the 6th chap, of Matt in the Indian, I was not interupted, I think the Indian paid attention to the reading.

Wed. 13 June 55. The Indians on the portage collected themselves into a long tent erected for the purpose of feasting and of practising their customs. Those who were initiated presented their offerings of cloth, calico, traps and guns; these were distributed among the metas who revealed all the secret injunctions to the initiated. The next performance was drumming singing and dancing. The last was their pretentions in supernatural agency with their fellow metas, as I told some of them the next day without any contradiction from them, for I stood close enough with those who were acted upon with the medicine bags without feeling any great effect

104

upon myself, their pretensions of being over powered was all pretense, for when one did not see the actor with the medicine bag he fell not, nor screammed, till one of his fellows whispered something in his ear. Men, women and children joined in the custom. In the evening I observed in some of them acts of obscenity. I left when it was dark, I heard them continuing until it was late at night ...

Thur, June 19/55 The Indians came into the fort naked making the war-whoop, their bodies variously painted with vermillion and mud mixed with oxide of iron, they had guns, war clubs and tomahawks in their hands. They performed the war dance in the fort yard and now and then the war whoop. The women sang and a couple of men beat the half drums.

I asked some of the principal ones what they were going to do? 'Nothing said one, merely to perform one of our customs' Mr S.L. and his son presented to the actors two kettles full of provisions then they retired. There was more than two hundred Indians in the fort young and old. As Mr James McKenzie and I were conversing I observed an Indian filling a redstone pipe, the stem of which was decorated with colored quills and feathers. The Indian made a ceremony of the pipe by turning it around several times in the course of the sun and after putting fire into it he held it out toward the interpreter Mr S.L. and after he had taken two or three puffs he handed it to me, but I declined saying I did not understand it. He withdrew without saying anything and so passed it to all the Indian men in the fort yard. I saw no rudeness when they were in the fort.

Teusday, Aug. 7/55 We passed the Long Sault this morning, the plain is more extensive than the Munidō. the soil is excellent. the corn and pota-toes are looking well, but there are no Indians, there are several old mounds here. It shows that the Indians were once numerous and the pre-sent race of Indians know very little about those times. They say that many years ago they were swept away with small pox, and but few chil-dren survived. In these mounds human skulls and bones are dug out by the dogs undecayed. There is also a good fishery at these rapids. A few miles below this there is another vestige of an old encampment about a mile long on the bank of the river and about 40 or fifty rods wide free of trees the soil is good. The sturgeon are constantly jumping up to the sur-face of the water. We arrived at the mouth of the river before dark, and here we found three families of the river Indians camping on the sandy beach. It was raining the oilcloth was thrown over some willows and under that my little boy Enoch (five years old) and I sheltered ourselves from the rain and wind on the Lake of the Woods.

Wed, Aug,8/55 The rain and the wind on the Lake of the Woods kept us from going on the plantation Island. In the afternoon it ceased to rain. The Indians sat around the fire in front of my oilcloth and asked me questions about astronomy ...

United Church of Canada Archives, Victoria University, Toronto, Allan Salt's personal papers, Journal 1854-5, pp 14-15, 31, 42-3, 47-8

▶ George Copway (1818-69) was an Ojibwa Methodist minister who later converted to Roman Catholicism. Lecturer, preacher, author, and herbal doctor,
he was the first Canadian Indian to publish a book in English, *The life, history, and travels of Kah-ge-ga-gah-bowh (George Copway), a young Indian
chief of the Ojibwa Nation*, in Philadelphia in 1847. So successful was the
book that it went through six editions by the end of the year, and was re-
published in 1851 as *Recollections of a Forest Life*. The book's success
brought Copway international recognition and he toured the United States
and Europe as a celebrity. He wrote a compelling and vigorous prose: contemporaries praised his 'biting satire,' 'pungent anecdote,' 'strokes of wit and
humour,' and 'touches of pathos.' This account of his birth reveals his pride
of race and love of nature.

I was born in *Nature's wide domain!* The trees were all that sheltered my
infant limbs – the blue heavens all that covered me. I am one of Nature's
children; I have always admired her; she shall be my glory; her features –
her robes, and the wreath about her brow – the seasons – her stately oaks,
and the evergreen – her hair, ringlets over the earth – all contribute to my
enduring love of her; and wherever I see her, emotions of pleasure roll in
my breast, and swell and burst like waves on the shores of the ocean, in
prayer and praise to Him who has placed me in her hand. It is thought
great to be born in palaces, surrounded with wealth – but to be born in
Nature's wide domain is greater still!

I was born sometime in the fall of 1818, near the mouth of the river
Trent, called in our language, Sah-ge-dah-we-ge-wah-noong, while my
father and mother were attending the annual distribution of the presents
from the Government to the Indians. I was the third of our family; a
brother and sister being older, both of whom died. My brother died without the knowledge of the Saviour, but my sister experienced the power of
the loving grace of God. One brother, and two step-brothers, are still
alive.

I remember the tall trees, and the dark woods – the swamp just by,
where the little wren sang so melodiously after the going down of the sun

in the west – the current of the broad river Trent – the skipping of the fish, and the noise of the rapids a little above. It was here I first saw the light; a little fallen down shelter, made of evergreens, and a few dead embers, the remains of the last fire that shed its genial warmth around, were all that marked the spot. When I last visited it, nothing but fur poles stuck in the ground, and they were leaning on account of decay. Is this dear spot, made green by the tears of memory, any less enticing and hallowed than the palaces where princes are born? I would much more glory in this birthplace, with the broad canopy of heaven above me, and the giant arms of the forest trees for my shelter, than to be born in palaces of marble, studded with pillars of gold! Nature will be Nature still, while palaces shall decay and fall in ruins. Yes, Niagara will be Niagara a thousand years hence! The rainbow, a wreath over her brow, shall continue as long as the sun, and the flowing of the river – while the work of art, however impregnable, shall in atoms fall!

Recollections of a Forest Life: or, the Life and Travels of Kah-ge-ga-gah-bowh, or,
George Copway, Chief of the Ojibway Nation (London 1851; Toronto: Canadiana House 1970)
10-12

George Copway was immensely proud of the Ojibwa language. 'A person might have travelled nearly one thousand miles from the head of Lake Superior, and yet not journey from the sound of this dialect,' he declared. He praised the musical qualities of the language and cited Henry Schoolcraft, who had observed that the language possessed 'a force of expression with music in its words and poetry in their meaning.'

... I cannot express fully the beauty of the [Ojibway] language ... After reading the English language, I have found words in the Indian combining more expressiveness. There are many Indian words which when translated into English lose their force, and do not convey so much meaning in one sentence as the original does in one word.

It would require an almost infinitude of English words to describe a thunder-storm, and after all you would have but a feeble idea of it. In the Ojibway language, we say 'Be-wah-sam-moog.' In this we convey the idea of a continual glare of lightning, noise, confusion – an awful whirl of clouds, and much more. Observe the smoothness of its words:

Ah-nung-o-kah   The starry heavens
Bah-bah-me-tum   Obedience
Che-baum   Soul
De-goo-wah-skah   The rippling wave

E-nah-kay-yah	The way
Gah-gah-geeh	Raven
How-wah-do-seh	Stone carrier (fish)
Ish-peming	Heaven
Jeen-quon	Earthquake
Kah-ke-nah	All
Mah-nah-ta-nis	Sheep
Nah-nah-gum-moo	Singing
O-nah-ne-quod	Pleasant weather
Pah-pah-say	Woodpecker
Quah-nauge	Pretty
Sah-se-je-won	Rapids
Tah-que-shin	He or she comes
Wah-be-goo-ne	Lily
Yah-no-tum	Unbelief
Ze-bee-won	Streams

Upon examination it will be found that there are several letters not sounded, to wit: F, L, R, V, X, ... We have none of the mouthing as of the thick sound of the letter L, nor any of gutteral accompaniments of the letter R. To the contrary, all the softness of the vowels are sounded without many of the harsh notes of the consonants, and this produces that musical flow of words for which the language is distinguished.

It is a natural language. The pronunciation of the names of animals, birds and trees are the very sounds these produce; for instance, hoot owl, *o-o-me-seh*; owl, *koo-koo-ko-ooh*; river, *see-be*, rapids, *sah se-je-won*. *'See'* is the sound of the waters on the rocks – *'Sah-see'* the commotion of waters, and from its sound occurs its name.

The softness of the language is caused ... by the peculiar sounding of all the vowels; though there is but little poetic precision in the formation of verse, owing to the want of a fine discriminating taste by those who speak it.

A language, derived, as this is, from the peculiarities of the country in which it is spoken, must, necessarily, partake of its nature. Our orators have filled the forest with the music of their voices, loud as the roar of a waterfall, yet soft and wooing as the gentle murmur of a mountain stream. We have had warriors who have stood on the banks of lakes and rivers, and addressed with words of irresistible and persuasive eloquence their companions in arms ...

When I was young I was taught [picture writing used in medicine and hunting songs], and while singing I could, in imagination, see the enemy, though none were within a hundred miles.

Spirit. Tree. Old tree. Rain, cloudy.

Medicine Lodge. Trees, woods. Storm, windy.

Worship, medicine, pure. War. Wounded water god.

Bad. Hemlock. Bad spirit under earth.

Islands. Duck, water birds. Deer, Moose.

Spirits above. Cold, snow. Fire.

Great. Night. Fight-man, bad spirit.

In their war-songs, animals are likewise represented in various attitudes. A rattle is made of deer's hoofs which is shook during the singing.

This rattle was sometimes used for the purpose of transmitting news from one nation to another; but in most cases shells were used for this purpose. I have been present in Canada when a string of beads has been received from the head waters of Lake Superior. A profound silence ensued, then followed a revelation of the message, and at its close a prolonged grunting sound from the vast assembly signified the people's assent ...

These are some of the figures used by us in writing. With these, and from others of a similar class, the Ojibways can write their war and hunting songs.

An Indian well versed in these can send a communication to another Indian, and by them make himself as well understood as a pale face can by letter.

There are over two hundred figures in general use for all the purposes of correspondence. Material things are represented by pictures (p 109) ...

George Copway, *The Traditional History and Characteristic Sketches of the Ojibway Nation* (London 1850; Toronto: Coles Canadiana 1972) 124-35

▶ Catherine Sonego Sutton (1824-65), or Nahnebahwequay, 'Upright Woman,' accompanied her Aunt Elizabeth, the English-born wife of her uncle, Peter Jones, to England in 1837, and was present at Queen Victoria's coronation. Throughout her life she was an indefatigable worker for the rights of her people, one of the few Indian women of her time to do so publicly. Through the financial support of a group of New York Quakers, she travelled to England in 1860 to petition the Queen on behalf of her family and the Port Credit Indian people, not as a subject appealing to a sovereign but as an Indian princess, as one royal person to another. The Queen noted in her private journal: 'She speaks English quite well, and is come on behalf of her Tribe to petition against some grievance as regards land.' This letter, sent to her uncle and grandfather on 29 June 1860, describes her visit to Buckingham Palace.

... So you see I have seen the Queen. The Duke [of Newcastle] went before us, and he made two bows, and then I was left in the presence of the Queen; she came forward to meet me, and held out her hand for me to kiss, but I forgot to kiss it, and only shook hands with her. – The Queen asked me many questions, and was very kind in her manners and very friendly to me. Then my Quaker friend [Mrs Christina R. Alsop] spoke to the Duke, and said 'I suppose the Queen knows for what purpose my friend has come?' The Duke said, 'All my papers have been explained and laid before Her Majesty, and I have Her Majesty's commands to investigate the Indian affairs when I go to Canada with the Prince of Wales.' Then the Queen bowed to me and said, 'I am happy to promise you my aid and protection,' and asked me my name. The Queen then looked at her husband, who stood at her left side, and smiled. She received me with so much kindness as to astonish me, when I saw her come smiling and so good to poor Indian. My Quaker friend has been in the habit of visiting the Royal family for ten years back.

I expect to return home in Sept., if all be well. May God bless us all. My love to you all.

C.B. Sutton

County of Grey Owen Sound Museum

▶ And royalty did come to Canada that year. In September 1860 the Prince of Wales, later Edward VII, visited London and Sarnia, and several Indian chiefs participated in the welcoming ceremonies and a torchlight parade. Ogishta, an Ojibwa chief from Garden Island near Sault Ste Marie, made the following speech, which was translated by 'a missionary chief.' As had long been the custom on such occasions, silver medals were then distributed by the prince among the chiefs.

Brother – Great Brother – The sky beautiful. It was with the wish of the Great Spirit that we should meet in this place. My heart is glad that the Queen has sent her eldest son to see her Indian subjects. I am happy to see you here this day. I hope the sky will continue to look fine, to give happiness both to the whites and the Indians.

Great Brother – When you were a little child your parents told you that there were such people as Indians in Canada and now since you have come to Canada yourself, you see them. I am one of the Ojibway Chiefs and represent the tribe here assembled to welcome their great Brother.

Great Brother – You see the Indians are around; they have heard that at some future day you will put on the British crown and sit on the British throne. It is the earnest desire that you will always remember them.

Canadian Free Press, London, 15 September 1860

▶ Sara Riel (1848-83), sister of Louis Riel, the Métis leader in the west, was the first Métisse missionary nun in Canada. A member of the Congregation of Grey Nuns of St Boniface, she wrote this letter to her brother.

111

December 14th, 1860

My beloved brother:

Oh, that this may be a day painful to any feeling heart! What sad memories it leaves in my soul! If there are sorrows that one can scarcely stand, there aren't among them any as piercing as that of seeing one's benefactors suffer, those benefactors to whom we owe so much. To see them suffer and not to be able to help them in any way. This sorrow so acute is the one that today weighs upon the inhabitants of Red River. But, then, what is the cause of so much suffering? Oh! do you see that mount of ashes, those ruins still smoking. They are the only remains left of a church which was dear to us all. Rightly so it is the parish church, full of memories to all of us. It is the cathedral where the beauty of ceremonies, while showing us the greatness of our Holy Religion, made us desire Heaven, a stay of peace and happiness which will never end. Only a few days had passed since we celebrated with such pomp the lovely feast of the Immaculate Conception. Altars were ornamented with their most beautiful objects; music lent its harmonies to hymns consecrated to Mary. Hardly had eight days passed and everything has disappeared. We hurried to take out of its niche the statue of Mary, our Good Mother. Today cries, tears, and weeping have replaced joyful hymns. If you glance at the rectory of the Reverend Fathers you will see it a victim of the flames. Monsignor Taché, who is not here, ignores this misfortune, but what a terrible blow it will be to his paternal heart when he discovers that his dear missionaries have been reduced to not having a house where they may rest. How is it possible not to cry after that? However, one thought consoles us, and that is the knowledge that nothing happens without the Good Lord's will, since a single hair does not fall from our head without his design, and those other words 'Let all those who suffer come unto Me, for they shall find consolation.' Let us submit to God's divine will, who, we hope, does not send us this tribulation in anger but in a merciful vein.

All the inhabitants of Red River were living happily and peacefully when suddenly a terrible misfortune pulled them out of their peace.

On December 14th, a Friday, towards ten o'clock at night, fire broke out in the kitchen of the Saint Boniface Bishopric, and here is how it happened: the girls were busy melting the fat in order to make candles which were destined to embellish the lovely feast of Christmas, which we wanted to celebrate with pomp. However, God had other plans: the girls had put too much fat in the pot. As the fat melted it spilled over, spreading all over the stove. Flames appeared almost instantly. The girls, trying to extinguish them, threw water on them. But the flames increased in size, and, in an instant, the kitchen floor was all on fire. The wooden floor, which was very dry, burned quickly. Thus, in a few moments, the fire had entered all the rooms. Seeing the speed at which the fire was spreading, the girls could only save themselves, carrying with them only whatever they found handy.

An old blind man, who had found in the rectory a shelter to spend his old age, was at that moment near the pot, unaware of the danger that enveloped him. Since there was no one to warn him, he remained sitting quietly on his chair. A young man in the Bishop's service ran immediately to save the old man when he saw the flames.

It is rather difficult to find the right words to express my feelings when I saw the bells tumble through the floor and hit the ground ...

Sara Riel

Mary Jordan, *De ta soeur, Sara Riel* (St-Boniface, Manitoba: Editions des Plaines 1980) 29-31 (my translation)

▶ Prior to 1871, when British Columbia entered Confederation, Indian education was provided entirely by the missionaries. This fragment of a journal kept by a Tsimshian boy illustrates the difficulties of learning English as well as the confusion and uncertainty caused by the attempt to adopt Christianity.

Tuesday, April 4th, 1860. – If will die my father, then will very poor my heart 4 my brother all die: only one Shooquanahts save, and two my uncle save. I will try to make all things. I want to be good, and I want to much work hard. When we have done work, then will please, Sir, Mr. Duncan, will you give me a little any thing when you come back.
April 17: School, Fort Simpson. – Shooquanahts not two hearts – always one heart. Some boys always two hearts. Only one Shooquanahts – not two heart, no. If I steal any thing then God will see. Bad people no care about Son of God: when will come troubled hearts, foolish people. Then he will very much cry. What good cry? Nothing. No care about our Saviour; always forget. By and by will understand about the Son of God.
May 17. – I do not understand some prayers, only few prayers I understand; not all I understand, no. I wish to understand all prayers. When I understand all prayers, then I always prayer our Saviour Jesus Christ. I want to learn to prayer to Jesus Christ our Saviour: by and by I understand all about our Saviour Christ: when I understand all what about our Saviour, then I will happy when I die. If I do not learn about our Saviour Jesus, then I will very troubled my heart when I die. It is good for us

when we learn about our Saviour Jesus. When I understand about our
Saviour Jesus, then I will very happy when I die.

[Eugene Stock], *Metlakahtla and the North Pacific Mission of the Church Missionary Society*
(London: Church Missionary House 1880) 31-2

► David Sallosalton (1853-72) was a young Chilliwack Indian who worked as
a Methodist missionary in the Fraser River region of British Columbia. At
the age of seventeen he gave his stirring 'Steamboat Whistle Sermon' at a
Chilliwack camp meeting. The Rev. Thomas Crosby claimed that he was
'one of the greatest natural orators he had ever heard.'

My dear white friends ... you look at our Indian people here, you hear
them cry very much and you say, 'What they make all that noise for,
what make them feel so bad?' Well, I tell you, my dear people just heard
about Jesus now, and they all want to find him, and love him, and get
sins pardoned and live for him. You heard long time ago, some of you;
you find Jesus long time; you love him. It all same as steamboat on this
river ... When she going to start she whistle one whistle, then she whistle
another, and if you don't get your things very quick and run, she whistle
last time ... and she go off and leave you behind, and you very sorry
because you too late. Now Jesus like that; He whistle, He call, He
whistle, and whistle, and if you don't get on board Jesus' Salvation Ship
you be too late. I think some my people get on board before some of you,
because they not afraid to repent and come on board. Now, my white
friends, you hurry up, have all your things packed up, be quick and get
on board or you be too late. I think some of this poor Indian people go
into heaven and you left out. Oh, come on board quick, come on board,
come to Jesus now! This a very good ship, room for all you people, and
Indian people, too, black and white; come now, all come.

Rev. Thomas Crosby, *David Sallosalton* (Toronto: Methodist Church, Canada,
Department of Missionary Literature 1906) 27-9

► Sister Marie-Josephine Nebraska (1861-94) was the first Sioux nun in Canada. After her father had been killed by the Saulteaux about 1864, her
mother took refuge with the Grey Nuns at St-Boniface, where the young
girl was raised and received an education in French. She entered the
novitiate in 1884 and became professed three years later. During a visit of
the Earl of Dufferin, the governor-general of Canada, and the Countess of
Dufferin on 9 August 1877, she read the following address of welcome.

To their Excellencies, the Lord and Lady Dufferin.
May it please your Excellencies.

This is a great day for the orphanage of St-Boniface for we have the great honour of receiving the representative of our august Sovereign.

We are poor children, given a home by charity; we cannot pretend to honours, but accustomed to receiving favours we wish you to know that we appreciate them. Therefore, I beseech your Excellencies to allow us to say that this day will live in our most cherished memories.

Carrying out your numerous and important tasks in the performance of your duties in this vast and powerful land of Canada, naturally requires all your time, my Lord, and yet your kind presence permits the orphans the comfort of seeing you and of expressing their admiration. Furthermore, the remarkable virtues that distinguish the Lady Dufferin help us to appreciate, more than we can ever say, the honourable favour of seeing her in our midst.

The purpose of all the care we receive here is to guide us in the true path of virtue. This visit, your Excellencies, can only help us appreciate more the noble motto that you uphold so well: PER VIAS RECTAS.

Your Excellencies have before you a unique assembly of young girls. I, who have the honour to address you in the name of my companions, am of the Sioux nation. On my right you have the Saulteaux, on my left a Maskegon. While our ancestors fought each other with unrelenting hatred, religion opened its arms to us with equal charity and we have become sisters.

Members from eight other nations share our good fortune, and you see in this haven of peace and charity children from eleven different nationalities. We are all, I repeat, sisters, and all of us, my Lord, learn here to venerate and love, as our sovereign, the noble lady who entrusted you with the government of a part of her vast British empire. We pray that your Excellencies will not scorn our welcome, which we offer in the different languages spoken by our ancestors.

It is true that we are treated here with a maternal tenderness. However, the hearts of the orphans would like to express this wish – that your children, my Lord and my Lady, will never become orphans. We shall add a prayer to those we offer every day to heaven for those who work to improve our lot.

Thank you, your Excellencies, for the happiness your visit has brought us, and accept the deep respect and humble allegiance of the orphans of St-Boniface.

Archives of the Grey Nuns, St-Boniface, Manitoba (my translation)

▶ Henry P. Chase (c.1816-1900), or Pahtahquahong, 'Coming Thunder,' was an hereditary chief of his Ojibwa tribe who in 1864 was ordained to the priesthood of the Church of England. He visited Britain and the Continent on several occasions, giving drawing-room lectures during the week and preaching in the churches on Sunday. He reported from Muncey, Ontario, in the Diocese of Huron, in 1883.

There is no special outpouring of the Spirit of God to report, no extraordinary movement in our congregations, but steady progress towards heaven.

I am glad to be able to state that the people greatly appreciate the means of grace.

During the past quarter we have lost five adult members, and I believe all were fully ripe for their eternal reward, – three Oneida women, one Ojibwa chief, and also one Muncey Indian.

At the time of burials we generally improve the occasions by preaching funeral sermons for the benefit of the mourners and their friends. The church is filled upon such occasions. The solemnity of the service acts as a light for the living.

The Oneida church is crowded every Sunday; the members are beginning to talk about enlarging it before very long.

The Oneida school teacher has resigned, and we have engaged Adam Sickles as the new teacher. He is doing well thus far, and he appears very much interested with the children. He works as though he desired to give satisfaction, and to set a good example to the children under his charge.

The old chief, Ojibwa Nahwahgwa, who died a weeks since, was a great sufferer; for many months he was prevented from attending the Sunday services in the church. He was most remarkably patient and was very happy. At one occasion, after having administered the Sacrament, he would express to me 'Megwatch, megwatch' ('Thank you, thank you'). I then directed his attention to give the thanks to God for the Holy Communion. 'I am only a humble servant to administer to you the bread and wine, to your own comfort.' He replied, 'Kagate sah, kagate sah' ('Very correct, very correct'). The chief exclaimed, 'I am not afraid to die.' His eyes filled with tears of joy and gratitude for having had brought before him the Gospel light, by which he has been brought in the way, to find the true religion before his death. At his death all was calm and peaceful.

At the funeral sermon there was a great crowd in the church – a truly solemn service.

The old Muncey Indian, Taylor Logan, who was removed by death, was another true witness that there is power in the Christian religion. To us there

116

are great satisfactions to witness happy manifestations from those, while they were living, we direct their attention to look to God, to prepare them to live happy and to die happy when called to leave the world for heaven.

The above names mentioned were Pagans once, as their forefathers. To hear them bear testimony to the reality of Christ's religion, to myself, and the living who know them as true Christian men, to our own mind is an evidence enough to stimulate us to preach more earnestly the Holy Gospel of Jesus, who shall save His people from their sins.

The Annual Report of the Colonial and Continental Church Society,
late the Colonial Church and School Society (London: Society's House 1883) 37-8

▶ Education allowed the Indians to begin to write their own history. The Rev. James Settee (c. 1817-1902) was ordained an Anglican priest in the Red River in 1853 and became a missionary. When advised not to move from place to place about the North-West but to establish a permanent mission station in a favourable locality, he replied: 'But you know Mr. Archdeacon, we read that "Here we have no continuing city."' As a boy he attended the Anglican school for natives in Red River and it may have been there that he heard this account of the war between the Sioux and the Saulteaux, which he wrote down in April 1891.

Some years before the year 1784 a bad disease had depopulated the Country. Thousands upon thousands of the Indians died by the small pox, that ended the wars for a long time. The Sioux Indians threatened the Ojebways that if they attempt to come up and rob them of their Horses and buffalo they would scalp them. The Ojebways & Crees sent their compliments in return that if they came to Red River or its neighbourhood they would shoot them down – but murders was committed between the two partys – the Sioux, Black Feet & the Ojebway & the Cree on the autumn of 1822. One Ojebway Chief name Black Duck sent his Tobacco to all the tribes living in Lake Superior and up Country but would not ask the Crees to asist him. Pegwys was asked to join them. He had received tobacco but did not understand that he was asked to go to war. He was sorry he had taken the stem the pipe stem. When once a man takes the pipe stem and draws a little, he consents to the war. The reason that Pegwys was sorry in taking the stem, was the Cree Chief was not invited; the greatest warrior in the Great Plains. Invitation to all the Saulteauxs living in the Rainy River and neighbourhood and north of that Country towards Albany, James Bay – Great many Saulteauxs around the Shores of the Lake Winnipeg and from Manitoba Lake & Wannipagoos.

In the Spring of 1823 report reached Red River as it was then called in those day, that the war party on its way, and would pass through our Settlement to ask for war implements and provision. The warriors began to make their appearance. The high road was litterally full with Indians – they passed through the road for one whole week travelling up to Pembina where the whole body of them was to meet. I remember the Indians had passed day after day and nights –

When on Sunday morning which was now the seventh day since the Indians had begun the warpath when four Indian Chiefs called to see our minister the Revd. David Thos. Jones to speak to him and to ask him to pray for their success. Mr Jones told them, that it would be wrong to him to pray for the destruction of his fellow men. He told them he would ask God to convert their hearts and change them by his good Spirit, that they might forgive their enemies and love them as their brethren. The Chief Black Duck stared at the Minister. Mr Jones said to the chiefs 'You hear the Bell at the Church I am calling for my children to come and hear the Great Book, God words that they might be made wise unto salvation through faith which is in Christ Jesus, and thus secure the salvation of their souls.' Black Duck answered that he never heard such a Lecture so foolish, to hear a book and to listen to it, when Keche Manito spoke to him almost every night. Mr Jones advised him to recall his followers & select a nice spot of land & plant a Church and a school and teach his people to read the word of God and to make farms. The old Chiefs laughed at Mr Jones advice. Old Pegwys came he was the last. he only took out his body-guard about one hundred men. Away they went about 50 canoes going up stream they were to go no further than Pembina about sixty-nine above our mission station. At Pembina a Large Camp was made waiting for warriors who was to join. They had to come from all parts. The Cree Indians was not invited. The Saulteauxs thought they were able to cope with Plain tribes alone.

Chief Pegwys joined them, he had been detained by the Officers of the Hudson Bay Company, not to join, but Pegwys had accept the Pipe of peace with the Chiefs, so he was bound to follow, but promised he would only go about fifty miles south of Pembina – which is now called Dakota. When Chief's Flagg made its appearance the very place ringed with the shouts of hundreds of Indians, during their stay at Pembina for the rest of their party, the days were employed in feasting and dancing and all night at their conjurations two weeks was spent in this way. Black Duck assured the Indians that the warfare about to take place would result to the favour of the Saulteauxs & destruction to Dakotas or the Sioux tribes.

A number of women & children who had followed so far was to remained at Pembina about one hundred women with their children hundreds of wives with the children had been left at different parts from whence the warriors came. Three or four men were left behind to watch over the children & their mothers.

The warriors moved out a large body of Indians they kept together in one body. The first camp, the General Black Duck made his prophecies by telling the Indians that at a place called gods Lake. the enemy had made their camp there and that the whole camp was given to him by the gods – very few of his band would fall, and that the whole plains was one flame of fire, nothing escaped the fire. The second evening the night was employed to ask the conjurers how the warfare would end, success, success, was the reply by many. Chief Pegwys told the conjurers that he did not see the enemies' camps in his conjurations nothing whatever. The third day they came to the gods Lake, no sign of the Sioux to have visited the place. Black Duck was greatly put out at the non fulfillment of his prophecy.

Chief Pegwys saw that the old Black Duck was labouring under a false delusion, and would assuredly lead many fellow Indians to destruction. On the fourth day old Pegwys assembled all the Chiefs and Captains. He told them he wanted to tell them, that did not intend breaking his word or the promise he made to the Officers of the Hudsons Bay Company and to the Minister at St. John's, now Winnipeg, but would return from the gods Lake. The rest of the Chiefs, that it was cowardice that made him return, but Pegwys never broke his word he was most conspicuous for this. Pegwys ordered his Band to return. The young fellows was sorry they wanted to see the fun.

The following evening Black Duck's followers discovered a camp of the the Siouxs to the number of 300 lodges an attack was to be made on fifth day. The warriors examined the situation of the ground and how the camp was laid out. at mid-night they approached the camp and laid wait until at dawn as soon as they could see distinctly an hundred yards the signal was given every man rushed for the tents. in twenty minutes every man women was scalped two young men escaped and ran to a large camp that was near and told the fate of their friends. In less than an hour had passed while they were gathering the spoil. The saw thousand of horse men coming flying like the birds of the air. A young man son of Black Duck. He raised his hands & pointed his weapon to the Sun and he said, 'Sun you told me last night that you would allow me to accompany you to mid-day.' 'Comrades, now is the day that you have longed stand firm, led world know that you are the Ojebways that never turned your backs from the enemy.'

The Ojebways took their position into square The Sioux tried to break their rank, but it was impossible. The Ojebway pouring in volley after volley among the Sioux and shooting them down by hundreds every shot. The young man the Black Duck's son got of the ranks with three companions. Those four made lively times among the Sioux. They felled every man that came in their way and they kept near together. The young warrior calling out – 'Sun stay a little' and the Siouxs sometimes rushing for him and at times fleeing by hundreds before him. while thousands of Siouxs was adding every minute and still thousand of the Sioux rushing to the war. at the very commencement of the second attack, Black Duck was disabled by a bullet that fell on his knee and broke his leg. but he still fought of his knee, He was a splendid shot. he shot down more twenty Sioux. he called for his son at times, he was told four of them where playing a beautiful game with the Siouxs. about eleven o'clock Black Duck fell over a stray bullet fell on his head. The Ojebways was furious. They swore by the god of the Sun and the god of Thunder, they would avenge the death of their leader and lay their bones besides Black Duck. The young man heard Black Duck's son that his father had fallen. He said, 'Thanks to the gods that the father shall not weep for the son, nor the son for the father. I will join to you.' He spoke as if speaking to his father. The Ojebways looking at the sun Young Duck would fall there was twenty Indians at him constantly, but he brought down so many every minute at last he fought with the butt of his gun breaking the skulls of Sioux, shouting, 'Hurrah Ojebways play the men. The rest of the Ojebways scattered among the Siouxs fighting hand to hand but the Ojebways killing them. At 12 o'clock the Young Duck fell the whole battle ground was filled with shouts by the Sioux the other three men an hour after. The Siouxs continued pouring in to the battle but the Ojibways had no reservation to fall upon. but they did not care. it is the glory of the Indian to die in the battle field. Towards evening the Ojebways rank was dwindling down a small body, but they still shouted, the battle raging as fierce as ever. Gunpowder was exhausted the Ojebways fought with the butt end of their guns – the Siouxs with their bows – the weight of a bow is light, but a blow from a gun is no joke, the Siouxs skulls felt the weight of the gun, in that way the Ojebway maintained their ground obstinately.

Before sun-down six Ojebways and one woman made up their minds to escape from the battle field. The Siouxs determined not to allow one

Ojebway to get away, but these six men and one woman declared pub-lickly that they would have their power to escape. These seven persons broke through a large body of the Siouxs while hundred arrows was flying after them, and horsemen with their spears. No, the men fought and now began to load their guns & shooting at the enemy by that means – they kept off the Siouxs when night came upon them the Ojebways got off and one woman. The Sioux Indians told their people, that the six men and the woman could run opposite any horse in the plains. Out of that multitude of Ojebways only six men and one woman escaped to relate the destruction of that tribe.

On the latter part of August we heard voices above the river, we thought some people were singing but it was the cries of the widows and orphans who had waited for their people at Pembina. They related that only one man had come to relate the state account of Black Duck and his warriors. the others who had made their escape had gone respectively their hunting lands where their friends would remain. It was most dis-tressing scene to see so many widows and orphans and not able to give them help, except something to eat.

One could hear cries through the settlement for many families were connected with the Ojebways by marriage. Pegwys made a great lamenta-tion for his tribe. Mechat kee-yew-up was extremely sorry that he had not been invited. Pegwys knew the mistake it had been made when the Crees were excluded. but it showed afterwards to the Saulteauxs that the Cree was able to cope with any tribe in the land. A decree then went forth that a Battle was prohibited that is on such large number without the consent of the White man unless another tribe invades another to take his land from him. This battle was fought in the summer 1824 – the largest Indian war in my day. If the Ojibways had invited the Half-breeds, they would have prevail against them. But our missionary the Rev Mr Jones would never have given consent to it.

Public Archives of Canada, Bell Papers, MG 29, B-15, vol. 33,

Rev. James Settee, 'Wars between the Sioux and Saulteaux,' April 1891

Francis Assikinack   Louis Jackson

John Brant-Sero

Pauline Johnson

Edward Ahenakew

Dan Kennedy

James Gladstone

4 'There is song in everything'

'The sky blesses me; the earth blesses me.
Up in the skies I cause the spirits to dance.
On the earth, the people I cause to dance.'

Fine Day (1847-1941), Cree song of the Round Dance,
Saskatoon Star-Phoenix, 9 January 1941

The Origin of Song

Oh some got them in their dreams, but mostly we got them from things around us. We would get a song from the whistling of the trees when the wind was blowing, from the rippling of the stream upon the mountain sides or from the roaring, dashing waves on the great salt seashore, from the great storm or tempest or from the singing of birds and the voices of different kinds of animals. There is song in everything.

Me-dee-kes, Tsimshian, in Rev. Thomas Crosby, *Up and Down the North Pacific Coast by Canoe and Mission Ship* (Toronto: Missionary Society of the Methodist Church 1914) 381

For thousands of years before they were written down, Indian legends and tales were told by the elders around countless campfires. Myths are the oldest and most popular form of Indian literature. Though representative specimens appeared earlier, it was not until the late nineteenth century that they were copied down in earnest by both Indians and whites, in large part a response to such notions as Peter Dooyentate Clarke's claim in 1870 that Indians were a 'doomed race.' At least it was realized that a great deal of the oral tradition was being lost, and ethnologists and folklorists set out to rescue what they could by collecting and publishing Indian tales and legends as well as ancient songs.

Indians were becoming increasingly aware of their physical and spiritual roots in North American soil. Essayists like Francis Assikinack and platform speakers like John Brant-Sero described the history and ancient customs of their people. The contemporary poet Pauline Johnson, who wrote very much in the late Victorian style of her day, nevertheless reached far back into her Indian heritage to find themes and subject matter. In the first half of the twentieth century, men like Dan Kennedy and Walter Wright told stories and legends of the Indian past.

Many Indians were travelling abroad, some to lecture, some to be involved in foreign wars. In 1885 Louis Jackson recounted his extraordinary adventures in Egypt as a non-combatant in the British expeditionary force. And in the early twentieth century many Indians joined their compatriots to fight in the Great War in Europe. The Rev. Edward Ahenakew, in 1920, paid tribute to the Indian men from across Canada who had fought and lost their lives overseas, and he spoke also of a new sense of brotherhood, a new spirit, that was uniting Indians from different nations in all parts of the country.

But all was not well, as can be seen in the speech Deskaheh gave in exile in 1925; many Indians in the first half of the twentieth century felt they were in danger of losing their rights and their culture, and that they were second-class citizens in a land that had once been theirs.

This chapter is far-reaching: ending with a Canadian senator's maiden speech in the 1950s, it begins with an ancient legend of the creation of a new world.

▶   Buhkwujjenene, or 'Man of the Wild' (c. 1815-1900), an Ojibwa chief and son of Shinguaconse, visited England in 1878; at a garden party in London, putting on feathers and ornaments, he became 'at once the centre of attraction' as he narrated this legend about creation.

Nanaboozhoo ... had a son. He loved his son. He told his son never to go near the water lest evil should come to him. The son disobeyed his father, he went out in a canoe and was never seen or heard of more. Nanaboozhoo then vowed vengeance against the gods of the water who had destroyed his son. There were two of these gods and one day they lay sleeping on the shore. Nanaboozhoo was looking everywhere for them, determined to kill them. A loon offered to show him where they were sleeping. He followed the loon till he found them, and then he made short work of them with his tomahawk and his war-club. But lo, and behold no sooner were the gods dead than the waters of the great lake rose up in vengeance; they pursued Nanaboozhoo up on to the dry land, and he had to run for his life. He sought the highest mountain and climbed to the top of the highest pine tree. Still the waters pursued him. They rose higher and higher. What could he do! He broke off a few of the topmost branches, and made a raft upon which he got and saved himself. He saved also a number of the animals that were kicking and struggling in the water all around him. At length he bethought himself of making a new world. How should he do it? Could he but procure a little of the old world he might manage it. He selected the beaver from among the animals, and sent it to dive after some earth. When it came up it was dead. He sent the otter, but it died also. At length he tried the muskrat. The muskrat dived. When it came up it was dead. But in its claws was clenched a little earth. Nanaboozhoo carefully took this earth, rubbed it in his fingers till it was dry, then placed it in the palm of his hand, and blew it gently over the surface of the water. A new world was thus formed, and Nanaboozhoo and all the animals landed. Nanaboozhoo sent out a wolf to see how big the world was. He was gone a month. Again he sent him out and he was gone a year. Then he sent out a very young wolf. This young wolf died of old age before it could get back. So Nanaboozhoo said the world was big enough, and might stop growing.

The Algoma Missionary News and Shingwauk Journal, 1 March 1879, pp 20-1

▶   In 1892, Father A.G. Morice, an Oblate priest, recorded the following Déné myth of the 'Origin of Water.'

... men had no water and were thirsty. As the old man who alone possessed it would not share it with them, OEstas (the legendary hero of the Carriers) who was very smart decided to snatch it away from him.

The old man had a daughter, a virgin. One day as she was on the point of drinking she saw on the surface of the water the frond of a coniferous tree which she cast away to the ground. Bending to drink she again perceived in the same place that very frond which she again threw out of the barrel in which the water was kept. But as she [bent] to apply her lips to the water, there again she found the frond.

After having repeatedly cast it out as it was always to be found in her way, she finally swallowed it, out of patience with the water. Immediately she became pregnant and a short time afterwards she bore a son who was no other than the wily OEstas, who had transformed himself into a coniferous frond.

He grew up in a wonderfully short time and as soon as he began to walk on all fours, he used while his mother was sewing in the house, to play with the barrel of water invariably rolling it in the direction of the door. His mother would then take it back in its place in the house. Soon becoming stronger and able to walk as a boy he would thus carry it out some distance from the door with the usual result of his mother taking it back to the house. One day as he had grown to be a man, he rolled it so far out, that he suddenly sprang away with it and sprinkled water all over the surface of the earth. What he spread with his hand formed the lakes of our days, and rivers resulted from the sprinkling of water with his index. In his precipitation he stumbled where Lake Français now is, thereby spilling out part of the barrel's contents which accounts for the size of that lake. Finally he burst away the barrel by dashing it to the ground with what was left of water thereby causing the sea to spring into existence.

Thus it was that *OEstas* gave water to men.

Public Archives of Canada, Bell Papers, MG29, B-15, vol. 32, folder A

▶ A Micmac legend, 'Uktce-bal-lok,' which appeared in *Acadiensis*, had been found among the papers of Dr Silas Tertius Rand, a Baptist minister who had worked among the Micmacs, translating much of the Bible into their language and compiling a Micmac grammar and dictionary. Jeremiah S. Clark, of Prince Edward Island, who sent the legend to the journal on 6 May 1903, described it as of 'a splendid conception, and well worthy of a place in Acadian literature.'

Uktce-bal-lok, the great 'Spirit of the Air,' lives in his wigwam somewhere far away in the blue vault above; he is sometimes seen by mortals, sitting in the forks of a tree, but many have been struck blind until sunset by looking at him. Once, a long time ago, an *ulnoo* (red-man) tried to shoot him, but in an instant, before he had time to take aim, the Spirit of the Air swooped down and flew off with him, carrying him above the clouds, and leaving him on the top of a lofty mountain, from which it took him months to find his way back to his tribe.

Uktce-bal-lok has no real body as men have, only a heart with wings to cover it, a large head with enormous cheeks, and very long legs. Though he does not either eat nor drink, yet he is tremendously powerful, being the only one whom Glooscap fears; indeed there is power enough in his *mas-kwel-a-mil* (shriek) to paralyze and kill outright any mortal who hears it. He has fought many battles with *mid-o-lin* (witches), and with *ke-wa-kwe* (giants with hearts of ice) and on every occasion has come off victorious.

Once the great *Oo-tcou-sun* (hurricane) went to visit him, and said: 'I have often heard of you but never had time to come and see you before.' To which *Uktce-bal-lok* replied: '*Moosooms* (grandfather), you are the first and only one who has ever dared come to see me, and I like you well, though I have one fault to find with you, – you move your wings too fast for me: sometimes I have to fly out of my wigwam, fearing it will be blown down upon me and kill me, it trembles so.'

'Well,' replied *Oo-tcou-sun*, the only thing for you to do is to move away from here, for you are a little too near me; in fact you are the nearest neighbour I have; besides, I cannot stop flapping my wings, – if I should do so my people would all die.' 'I will not move,' retorted *Uktce-bal-lok*, 'that is one thing I will not do.' 'Ha! ha!' laughed *Oo-tcou-sun*. 'Glooscap will defend me and my people!'

'There you are mistaken, for Glooscap does not fight with me,' proudly answered *Uktce-bal-lok*. 'He is afraid to do so, and, let me tell you, sir, he does not like the flapping of your wings any too well; for he says that often he dares not go sailing in his *kwedun* (canoe) your wings move so fast; moreover, did not Glooscap once go to see you, and throw you down?'

'Yes he did,' said *Oo-tcou-sun*, 'but he was glad to hurry back and set me up again, for the water in the rivers and lakes all became thick with slime, and the fish and game died on every hand from the scum that rose to the surface. He was only too glad to have my wings move freely again. You and I, too, had better be friends and keep our places.' And so it happened that after much wind blowing back and forth between the Hurricane *Oo-tcou-sun*, and *Uktce-bal-lok*, the great Spirit of the Air, the two agreed to live at peace for many moons, each following his own inclinations and in his own territory.

▶ The following Loucheux tale about 'The Man in the Moon' was collected in 1905 by Charles Camsell, a geologist with the Geological Survey of Canada, and was prepared for publication by Marius Barbeau. Camsell was told the story by Peter Ross, a Loucheux at Fort McPherson, in the Mackenzie Valley inside the Arctic Circle.

Once, a long time ago, a child asked his parents to let him make some 'medicine' for deer-hunting, so that his father might kill a great many fat deer whenever he wanted to; but he was so young that he could barely walk as yet, and his father did not want him to do so, thinking that the medicine would not be strong enough. The boy implored him; and, being again refused permission, he began to cry. Day and night he cried, until the Indians in the neighborhood were concerned, and inquired from the hunter about the cause of all these tears. But when they were told the reason why, they were satisfied that the boy was too small to prepare a 'medicine.' So disturbed were they by the cries, however, that in the end they persuaded the hunter to humor his son. So the boy made some medicine, and said to the people, 'You shall now kill as many deer as you wish, but you must always give the fattest animals to my father.'

Now, then, they went out hunting, and killed a great number of deer, many of which were very fat. Instead of complying with their promise, however, some Indians kept the fattest game for themselves, and gave only the next choice to the child's father; and from this time on the hunters failed to kill any deer. Soon the people began to starve. The boy again made a 'medicine'; for he and his father, like the others, had no longer anything to eat. 'You must take a fine and clean deer-skin,' said he to his father, 'and make it into a bag. When it is done, lay it on your sledge, outside of the lodge. Then take a deer's shoulder, cut all the meat off it, and, when only the clean bone is left, put it along with a bit of blood into the bag on the sledge.' So it was done; and the next morning, as the hunter looked at the bones in the pouch, he found them covered with flesh. Day after day the same thing happened, the bones being found with new flesh every day, in the morning. So the boy and his father had enough to eat, while, as long as the famine lasted, the other Indians were starving.

One day the boy spoke to his father, saying, 'Father, I should like to go to the moon on a visit.' But the old man replied, 'What is the use, my son, as you could not get there?' – 'Never mind!' said the child, 'if I suddenly disappear some day, you will know that I have gone to the moon.'

When, soon after, the hunter got up in the morning, he could not find his son. His calls remained without an answer. Searching for the child, he only found one leg of his trousers hanging at the top of the lodge-pole, in the smoke-hole. This reminded him of what the boy had said about going to the moon. So when the moon rose that night, he looked up, and, sure enough, the boy was standing in it with one leg of his trousers torn off. That is why ever since the man in the moon has one of his legs bare.

'Loucheux Myths,' *Journal of American Folk-Lore*, XXVIII (1915) 254-5

▶ Truth is sometimes stranger than fiction. A Blood chief visited eastern Ontario in the late nineteenth century. Upon his return he was called upon by his band to tell what he had seen in the land of the white man.

That is a wonderful country. I went to the towns of the white men and saw the houses made of stone. The white men live upon each other's heads, for there is not room for them to make stone lodges for every man. One of the white chiefs gave me a paper, and when I was hungry I showed my paper at the white man's trading post, and they gave me all I wanted to eat for nothing. Whenever I wished to go anywhere I showed a man my paper, and he took me in his waggon for nothing. I went into a trading-post, and then got into a small house, which went up and up, when it stopped, and I got out. I saw so many fine things after I got out! I then went into another little house, and it went down and down. Ugh! I thought I was going down to the place where the white men say there is a great big fire, but it stopped, and then I got out. I went into a house which sat on wheels, and it ran away. Some birds came along and tried to run a race with it, but it beat the birds. There are as many white people down there as there are blades of grass upon the prairies!

Stop! said one of the chiefs. There have been some white medicine men down there, and they have been beating upon the medicine drums. They have made strong medicine and blinded your eyes, that you could not see. We do not believe you.

John MacLean, *Canadian Savage Folk: The Native Tribes of Canada*
(1896; Toronto: Coles Canadiana 1971) 64-6

▶ Francis Assikinack, or 'Blackbird' (1824-63), attended Upper Canada College in Toronto. He taught school for a while, and at the time of his death was employed as chief clerk in the Indian Department. He wrote three essays for the *Canadian Journal* in 1858; this extract, from the second one, describes the training of young people among the Ottawa Indians.

Some time after the birth of a child, the parents, or rather grandparents prepared a feast, to which the principal men of the tribe were invited. At the commencement of the banquet one of the old warriors was requested to name the child, upon which he left his seat and began to sing as he danced slowly round the fire-place in front of the guests, and when he arrived at the door he called out the name he intended to give the child. On hearing the name the guests gave a hearty cheer in token of their approbation. During the performance of the dance round the hearth some of the party busied themselves in giving the appropriate responses, while others uttered encouraging words with becoming gravity.

With regard to the manner of bringing up Indian children nothing can be more erroneous than to suppose that the young were allowed to grow up without any sort of discipline. So far from this having been the case, in addition to the ordinary way of correcting children, there were many other restraints imposed upon the young. The Indians knew in their primitive state, apparently as well as civilized communities, that children too much humored and neglected in moral training when young, as they grow up are apt to become turbulent and bad members of society. As one of the most effective means for training and forming the character of the Indian youth, fasting seems to have been established and practised from time immemorial, and prevailed, I am led to believe, universally among the Indian tribes of this continent. As soon as children were thought capable of reasoning they were required to practise fasting, until they were married. Besides their regularly abstaining from food for so many days successively, at different parts of the year, they were obliged to fast before they were allowed to take any of the wild fruits of the earth, at the different seasons as they became ripe. The same rule was observed with regard to the produce of the farm.

The Indians were most exact in enforcing their rules of fasting. With young children it lasted the whole day, and if a child put anything in his mouth during the day, as, for instance, snow or a piece of icicle, – which children are very apt to do when playing in the open air in winter, – that day went for nothing, the child was then permitted to eat, with strict injunctions to renew his fast the next day. It was also imposed as a punishment upon those children who manifested a disposition to be disobedient and disrespectful; and was found an excellent means of discipline to make children sensible of their duties, and exercised a wholesome restraint upon the youth. With young men from sixteen to twenty-five years of age it was no longer necessary to remind them of the practice. It was looked upon as a duty by every young man, who had too much honourable feeling to submit to the sneers of his companions as a worthless glutton. They, moreover, believed gluttony to be highly displeasing to the Great Spirit; and that, in order to obtain special favors from him, it was absolutely necessary to restrain the appetite. The young men frequently spent one or two months during the winter in fasting, taking only one meal in the day after sunset. In summer less time was spent, but the fast was more severe; it lasted from two to four and even five days, according to the strength of the individual. On these occasions it was usual for the young men to withdraw from the family residence to a retired spot, under the shade of a tree, where they passed their time in fasting and contemplation. To this spot the mother sometimes repaired with a small bunch of wild, unripe berries, which she suspended from a twig about a foot and a half from the ground, so that the young man might have the poor consolation of fixing his eyes occasionally upon them. The sight of these berries had the effect of watering the mouth in the same way as we feel before tasting any unripe fruit, especially when we have reason to suspect its being sour. The dreams of the last night which terminated their regular fasting days at any time of the year, were considered the most important, and were carefully studied as revelations from the Great Spirit. In the evening small wigwams were put up at a little distance from the family residence, each just big enough for the accommodation of one person. The youths who were practising the rite of fasting had to take up their quarters in these lodges for the night using, if possible, only new furniture. Next morning it was the duty of the grandmother, or some other elderly female, to visit the young fasters by daylight. The first thing she did was to make a very thin corn soup, or some kind of broth, after which she went to ask them one by one of their dreams. She congratulated those who had favorable dreams upon their good fortune; but for those who had unlucky dreams she threw a piece of fur of some animal on the fire, in order to avert the consequences of such ill-omened visions. The longest fast practised among the Indians lasted ten days, during which time it was indispensable that the candidates for the special honours which it secured should neither taste anything nor sleep. They were made to dance every night, and sometimes were put in small cribs suspended from the ground, which were moved sideways, like a cradle, for the purpose of inducing sleep. Those who yielded, and fell asleep, were dismissed forthwith as unworthy. Most frequently all the candidates failed; but on some rare occasions one or two succeeded in completing the time. Even with these, however, this severe undertaking seems to have exceeded the powers of nature, as those who were successfull – though regarded ever after with a certain degree of superstitious veneration – never fully recovered from the effects of it. Besides fasting, the young people had to abstain from certain kinds of animal food, and from certain parts of animals, for instance, the head, the meat near the bone, and the marrow. They were also strictly prohibited from eating blood until after they were married, when they were no longer subject to restraint. Girls were considered marriageable at fifteen, but it was customary for a young man to remain single until he was twenty-five years of age, after which he might take a wife if he liked, or rather if his parents chose.

Young girls when fasting rubbed clay on their temples, whilst the young men partially blackened their faces, or occasionally painted them with one or two other colors ... Like the Jews ... the Indians regarded several animals as unfit to be eaten; in fact, they had strong prejudices against their flesh. Among the feathered tribes, I may mention the raven, the crow, the blue jay, the owl, and many others, and amongst quadrupeds the fox, the mink, the wolf, &c.

With regard to matrimonial affairs it may be remarked that the Indians do not seem to have much appreciated what is called 'keeping company' nowadays, as the choice of a wife was entirely left to the parents. The young bridegroom may never have seen, spoken to, or been acquainted with the girl until she was introduced to him as his bride. Generally speaking, when the eldest brother died, his younger brother was required to marry his widow; in all other cases it was not thought lucky for a young man to marry a widow; and in case the woman should die first her younger sister had to supply her place, provided the parties were not already married. The degrees of relationship extended a great way among the Indians; and it was prohibited by custom to contract marriage within the forbidden bounds ...

Another discipline to which the young people are subjected, in addition to that of fasting, constituted a useful training for future life. They were required to bathe at daybreak every morning for about a month in the spring, whilst the water was cold. This was done with a view to render them hardy, robust, and capable of standing all sorts of weather. Unhappily the ancient discipline by which the Indian youths were thus trained to hardihood and self-denial, is no longer practised. It is a matter of regret that the young Indians of the present day have almost entirely lost the virtues of sobriety and self-respect practised by their predecessors. Self-indulgence of the grossest kind has taken the place of self-denial. Too often they frequent the low grog-shop, where they lose all sense of shame, and are rendered mean and beggarly, as well as useless members of society. It is scarcely necessary to remark that there were good speakers among the Indians formerly; but I have too much reason to believe, that there are no such speakers to be found among them at the present day. In my opinion it was chiefly owing to their deep contemplation in their silent retreats in the days of youth, that the old Indian orators acquired the habit of carefully arranging their thoughts; when, instead of the shoutings of drunken companions, they listened to the warbling of birds, whilst the grandeur and the beauties of the forest, the majestic clouds, which appear like mountains of granite floating in the air, the golden tints of a summer evening sky, and all the changes of nature, which then possessed a mysterious significance, combined to furnish ample matter for reflection to the contemplating youth.

Francis Assikinack, 'Social and Warlike Customs of the Odahwah Indians,'
Canadian Journal, n.s. III (1858) 297-301

▶ Indians in the late nineteenth century were being asked to speak on a variety of subjects, ranging from their ideas of white society to their own customs. Gabriel Acquin (1810-1901), or Sachem Gabe as he was affectionately called, a renowned hunter, trapper, guide, and story-teller, was a Malecite Indian of the St Mary's Band in New Brunswick, 'who could converse with equal fluency in the English, Milicite, Micmac and Penobscot tongues.' In March 1885 his views on several topics were given in an interview and published in the newspaper.

Talking about moose-hunting ... do you know in fifty years I believe like the Indians they will all be gone. Like the Frenchman's pork they last very quick. Lumberers and settlers kill them in the deep snows in the winter. Moose chiefly feed on greenwoods, those that taste bitter, such as maple, moosewood, green hemlock and cedar. That is the reason they cannot live if you try to tame them. They want their own food and if it is cut for them it does not seem to do them so much good as if they browse for themselves. The
BEST PLACE FOR MOOSE
is between the Salmon and Washademoak rivers. The calling season is about the full moon in September, and that is the time to hunt for them if you want good heads. Every year they have a new crop of horns. They begin to sprout out the first of April and increase in size until August. Up to that time they carry the velvet horns. In August the fur commences to peel off and then the calling season sets in. About the 1st of November they begin to shed their horns. These horns you sometimes see six feet across are only of one season's growth. After the running season is over a joint grows on the horns and they drop off without any trouble. Before

that time they are so firmly fastened on the head that you could only get them off by sawing them. The horns of a moose are just like a flower; they sprout in the spring, blossom in the summer, and in the fall the leaves die and drop to the ground.

Can you tell the age of a moose by his horns?

From two to four years old they carry more branches. As they get older less branches grow, until after a while their horns become almost straight like a goat's. You can tell whether a moose is young or old, but not his exact age.

Are many moose killed out of season?

Hundreds of them every year. The killing season commences the first of August and ends the last of January, but they are shot at all times by persons who catch them in the deep snow.

CARIBOU INCREASING

What about caribou?

Getting more plentiful every year. We find them between Gaspereaux river and Pleasant brook and on both branches of the Salmon river, where there is a large tract of barren country almost like a prairie. They are also found at Cain's river and Penniac, but you cannot depend on them. After the Saxby gale a fire came and burnt up all their feed at Penniac and Bull Pasture, and they left. They are very often driven off their grounds by fire, because their favorite food, white moss, will flame up like paraffine. It is very dry and there is no taste to it. It is said that it would make the best alcohol in the world. The season for shooting caribou is from the first of August till the last of February, and then you have six more days to haul them in. Caribou and deer act exactly the same as the moose in the running season, and their habits are very much the same. There are not many red deer in the province now. About 45 years ago, near Fredericton junction, I killed 60 deer in a fortnight. They came from Canada and were followed by wolves, which killed a great many of them. Deer are more plentiful now than for several years past. We find them at Magaguadavic lake, Oromocto lake, etc.

And bears?

Bears are increasing all the time. They are the most shy and cunning of all the animals we meet. They will even double back on their tracks for half a mile until they see a good chance to jump out. A great deal of 'rot' is printed about bears. I have seen more wild animals than any one else, and they will all run away from a man unless they are badly cornered.

And the Indian devil?

I do not believe there are any in the province now. Some years ago I

killed one of them myself. They are the same as the [panther] or cata-
mount of New England. People say they hear them in the woods, but I
never heard them, except the different notes of owls ...

GLOSCAP CAME FROM THE SPIRIT WORLD

to redress the wrongs of the red people. He persuaded them to live at
peace, told them how to hunt and fish, and what they should kill for
food. He passed from tribe to tribe, rebuked them for their bad habits and
advised them to live on their own lands and respect the property of their
neighbors. All the animal kingdom were brought before him and taught
submission to them. None rebelled against the decision except the red
squirrel which flew furiously at a stump and tore it in pieces as a sign of
its hatred. The squirrel was then one of the largest of the animals and
seeing that he was dangerous Gloscap decreed that he should be reduced
to his present size. At the present site of the St. John river falls was then
an immense beaver dam. The

BEAVERS WERE AS LARGE AS WHALES,

and seeing that they were dangerous Gloscap pried out the dam with a
red pine tree. At the Narrows, Boar's Head ... the head of the spirit can
still be seen on the rock, that the red men may never forget his words
and works. At present the Spirit resides at the southern end of the world
where his cross is hung in the sky. When the red man prays to him he
always grants the request.

Have you ever seen the spirit?
No; but I have seen lots of the signs he has left about in the world. I see
that he opened the St. John river falls, for part of the river used to run
into Courtenay Bay. What you call Split Rock is where he rested his
handspike. Another place where I see his works is between Eastport and
Portland, where he killed a big moose. There the antlers and inner parts
of the moose, even to the liver and fat, are turned to stone, and may be
clearly seen ...

*You know the common belief is that man originated in the eastern
part of the world. How do you account for the Indians being here?*
Look at the animals, the flowers and the trees. They came here just the
same as anywhere else. Why not men? ... What puzzles me ... is how the
Indians in old times cut these flint stones. I know they used to skin animals with beaver's teeth, but they could not cut this flint.

New Brunswick Museum, *Saint John Daily Telegraph*, 12 March 1885

▶ Louis Jackson, born about 1843, was foreman of a select group of Caughnawaga canoe-men who in 1885 led the British Boat Expedition for the

relief of Khartoum in the Sudan up the cataracts of the Nile. This passage, taken from his booklet *Our Caughnawagas in Egypt*, reveals his keen eye for detail.

... We found the Nile river water of good taste but muddy and we generally left it standing for an hour to settle. A funny sight was presented by a cow and a small camel harnessed to a plough. A stick crooked suitably by nature was laid over both necks and tied round each and a native rope was run from the yoke to a stick, also crooked to suit the purpose by nature, used as plough, scratching about two inches deep and three inches wide, at a speed as I judged of one acre per week. Another unusual thing was to see the crops in several stages of growth at the same time in adjoining patches, from sowing to quarter grown half grown and ripe crops. This is one of the consequences of the Nubians depending upon the over flow of the Nile to fertilize their soil. Directly the river begins to fall they commence to sow their seed in the mud it leaves behind, and as the water recedes they follow it up with the sowing. The crop farthest from the river of course gets the start.

The next novel sight was the irrigation of the fields. To lift the water from the river, a frame is made by putting some cornstalks into the ground and putting clay round them to make posts, which are placed about six feet apart; the posts suppport a small stick, across which is laid a crooked pole, with about a dozen bends in it, that balances a mud basket on one end against a leather bucket on the other. The bucket holds about as much as our common well bucket. A man is continually filling from the river and emptying into a mud spout between the posts. The water is led off in a small mud conduit over the farm which is divided into sections, when one section is filled with water the stream is turned into another one. These waterworks are kept going day and night. Once in a while one may see cattle power used for irrigation of the following old fashioned kind, the yoke is hitched to a primitive cog-wheel of about twelve feet in diameter, which works into a smaller wheel placed underneath it, the cattle walking over a bridge. The cogs are simply pins driven into the outside of each wheel. The shaft of the smaller wheel runs out over a ditch cut from the river and carries a large reel about eighteen feet in diameter over which two native ropes are laid to which are attached about forty earthen jars. The cattle here are about the same size as ours, but they have a lump on their back and their horns run straight back. The colour of most of these cattle is blueish. Where the fertile strip of land is wide, canals are dug in curves to bring the water back near, to the sand mountains. The cattle feed along the river bank, which is left uncultivated for about twenty feet from the water, and I have seen a number of them of all kinds, feeding on this poor strip and never touch the rich crops alongside, although left to themselves and I was told that they were taught that way. The sheep look like dogs dragging long tails on the ground and the dogs look much like the Esquimaux dogs I have seen in Manitoba.

Louis Jackson, *Our Caughnawagas in Egypt* (Montreal: W. Drysdale & Co. 1885) 10-11

▶   One of the more flamboyant Indians of the late Victorian era was John Ojijatekha Brant-Sero, born in 1867, a Mohawk poet, dramatist, and historian from the Six Nations Reserve, descended from Joseph Brant, who gave lectures and concerts before the public in Canada and abroad. He once recited passages from *Othello* in English and Mohawk on a stage in Chicago, and on another occasion, in 1908, won third prize in a 'big male beauty show' in Folkestone, England. This paper on 'the unwritten constitutional law and government of the Caniengahakas [Mohawks], as given to them by De-ka-na-wi-deh,' was delivered before the British Association in 1901.

It is an important story: the basic principles of this ancient system of government being still in use by the Six Nations of Canada, with slight modifications in detail. It would not be wise nor yet safe to say how many centuries the system has been in practical use. The confederacy of the Five Nations, the people of the United Long House, has always impressed me with the fact that it existed a very long time before the Europeans reached the shores of America. Haiwatha (Ayonhwadha, commonly, but wrongly called Hiawatha) founded the confederacy; but the government of the confederacy is an exact counterpart of the system formulated by Dekanawideh probably ages before the era of Haiwatha.

How long the Mohawks existed in a deplorable condition before the Law-giver, whose name and memory even the Indians themselves have never heard – save a few, and those from the lips of the aged – it is beyond my province to conjecture. Lacking a suitable form of organisation, chaos, misery, and war threatened the annihilation of a great people. A long transitory period of 'thinking' ensued, pondering how the lives of the people might be preserved. Malice in its most deadly form became rampant. Warriors ceased from their war-like expeditions to stay around and defend their women and children. That did not prove effective, for the families murdered one another with impunity. In the confusion the people became more infuriated than the beasts of the woods. Their minds darkened even in the glare of the hot sun; night served to awaken the horrors of bestial slaughter; children alone were spared. The earth and the beautiful world, with its abundance of fruit, foliage, streams of glistening waters, followed their allotted pace without murmur, summer and winter. The 'People of the Flint,' the mightiest in the land, alone amongst humanity were troubled and anxious.

Dekanawideh, the determined man, 'setting his teeth together,' as his name would indicate, vowing to master himself and save his people from destruction, wandered from the crowd, and reached the side of a smooth clear-running stream, transparent and full of fishes. He sat down, reclining on the sloping bank, gazing intently into the waters (ohondon), watching the fishes playing about in complete harmony: they had their sports and pastime which he did not understand. The sun's ray reflected its warmth upon him. He rose, dipping his hollowed hand into the water, drank freely, and sauntered quietly towards the spreading branches of a tree which stood near – a tall pine tree. He was deep in thought and did not notice, perched on the top-most point of the pinery, the Great White Eagle – a national totemic emblem. The tree was very high; no brave had yet been able to make and handle a bow and arrow which would send the arrow over the lofty position of the king of birds. Under the bird's keen eyed scouting protection Dekanawideh's 'great idea' evolved itself into specific form. Drafting a plan as he sat upon the grass, trusting merely to his memory did not prove satisfactory.

Taking an eagle feather, placing it upon the ground, 'That,' he said, 'shall represent the great idea.' He placed many articles side by side to represent the 'lesser ideas,' the details of a great plan. These articles, he thought, would help to command attention to his 'ideas' and receive consideration from his people.

Over and over again did he rearrange the various light articles which acted in lieu of letters. At last it was finished. His joy was great. He felt inclined to yell with delight. However, the Great White Eagle, perched on high, as if anticipating the result, gave a loud, triumphant scream. The first real American statesman was startled, and while he looked cautiously about him, a gust of wind playfully performed a whirlwind dance and circulated his great policy in all directions. The primitive record, though not the system, was lost.

A lively little woodpecker alighted on an old tattered hollow pine stump, mockingly singing his limited song, pecking for food between the notes. In a revengeful moment Dekanawideh grabbed his bow and arrow, and sent a swift arrow, pinning the bird to the stump. Leisurely he brought the bird and arrow down. Dekanawideh standing erect, bird in hand, carefully examined his plumage. Looking up to the lofty position occupied by the Great White Eagle, it drew from him a sigh of lofty admiration. 'The Great Idea,' said he, 'will one day occupy a position in the affairs of men as lofty as the Great Eagle holds among the feathered kind.' The incentive awakened and urged him on as if the 'Ruler of All' had prompted Dekanawideh to finish the 'task.'

Once more he sat upon the grass, still examining the little bird's feathers. Suddenly, there was a pause, a new discovery, another idea. Small white discs marked the feathers. The little white round marks would help to diffuse knowledge. One by one, feathers were plucked and stuck into the ground. In this manner the whole scheme was rehearsed, and securely tied the previous feathers together. A new era opened. Dekanawideh rose and slowly wandered back to his people, mingled with them awhile, then secretly laid his plan before the principal men and mothers of the nation. The scheme was approved by them, and on its presentation to the people it was adopted unanimously.

Such is the story handed down for ages, not from father to son, but from mother to children. I am reminded by my people that it has never been told to Europeans.

John Brant-Sero, 'Dekanawideh: The Law-Giver of the Caniengahakas,' *Man* (1901) 166-7

▶ Emily Pauline Johnson (1861-1913), or Tekahionwake, 'Smoky haze of Indian summer,' was one of the most renowned Canadian poets of her day. Born in Brantford, Ontario, the daughter of a Mohawk chief and an English Quaker mother, 'The Mohawk Princess' toured Canada, Great Britain, and the United States for sixteen years as a platform recitalist, popularizing her stories and poems. Although she usually followed the typical Victorian models in thought, topic, and imagery, her poems on Indian life reveal the depth of her native roots and her passion and loyalty to her Mohawk blood.

Lullaby of the Iroquois

Little brown baby-bird, lapped in your nest,
    Wrapped in your nest,
    Strapped in your nest,
Your straight little cradle-board rocks you to rest;
    Its hands are your nest,

Its bands are your nest;
It swings from the down-bending branch of the oak;
You watch the camp flame, and the curling grey smoke;
But, oh, for your pretty black eyes sleep is best, –
Little brown baby of mine, go to rest.

Little brown baby-bird swinging to sleep,
   Winging to sleep,
   Singing to sleep,
Your wonder-black eyes that so wide open keep,
   Shielding their sleep,
   Unyielding to sleep,
The heron is homing, the plover is still,
The night-owl calls from his haunt on the hill,
Afar the fox barks, afar the stars peep, –
Little brown baby of mine, go to sleep.

As Red Men Die

CAPTIVE! Is there a hell to him like this?
A taunt more galling than the Huron's hiss?
He – proud and scornful, he – who laughed at law,
He – scion of the deadly Iroquois,
He – the bloodthirsty, he – the Mohawk chief,
He – who despises pain and sneers at grief,
Here in the hated Huron's vicious clutch,
That even captive he disdains to touch!

Captive! But *never* conquered; Mohawk brave
Stoops not to be to *any* man a slave;
Least, to the puny tribe his soul abhors,
The tribe whose wigwams sprinkle Simcoe's shores.
With scowling brow he stands and courage high,
Watching with haughty and defiant eye
His captors, as they council o'er his fate,
Or strive his boldness to intimidate.
Then fling they unto him the choice;

'Wilt thou
Walk o'er the bed of fire that waits thee now –
Walk with uncovered feet upon the coals,
Until thou reach the ghostly Land of Souls,
And, with thy Mohawk death-song please our ear?
Or wilt thou with the women rest thee here?'
His eyes flash like an eagle's, and his hands
Clench at the insult. Like a god he stands.
'Prepare the fire!' he scornfully demands.

He knoweth not that this same jeering band
Will bite the dust – will lick the Mohawk's hand;
Will kneel and cower at the Mohawk's feet;
Will shrink when Mohawk war drums wildly beat.

His death will be avenged with hideous hate
By Iroquois, swift to annihilate
His vile detested captors, that now flaunt
Their war clubs in his face with sneer and taunt,
Not thinking, soon that reeking, red, and raw,
Their scalps will deck the belts of Iroquois.

The path of coals outstretches, white with heat,
A forest fir's length – ready for his feet.
Unflinching as a rock he steps along
The burning mass, and sings his wild war song,
Sings, as he sang when once he used to roam
Throughout the forests of his southern home,
Where, down the Genesee, the water roars,
Where gentle Mohawk purls between its shores,
Songs, that of exploit and of prowess tell;
Songs of the Iroquois invincible.

Up the long trail of fire he boasting goes,
Dancing a war dance to defy his foes.
His flesh is scorched, his muscles burn and shrink,
But still he dances to death's awful brink.

The eagle plume that crests his haughty head
Will *never* droop until his heart be dead.

Slower and slower yet his footstep swings,
Wilder and wilder still his death-song rings,
Fiercer and fiercer thro' the forest bounds
His voice that leaps to Happier Hunting Grounds.
One savage yell –

        Then loyal to his race,
He bends to death – but *never* to disgrace.

E. Pauline Johnson, *Flint and Feather* (Toronto: Musson Book Company 1917) 94, 6-8

▶ Khalserten Sepass, or 'Lord of the waterfalls' (c.1840-1945), was a Chilliwack chief who decided to make public the ancient secret songs that belonged to him before they became lost forever. From 1911 to 1915 he recited 'The Songs of Y-Ail-Myhth,' a cycle of sixteen songs sacred to his people, to Eloise Street, who, as editor of *Indian Time*, published them much later. This song is the first of the series.

The Beginning of the World

Long, long ago,
Before anything was,
Saving only the heavens,
From the seat of his golden throne,
The Sun-god looked out on the Moon-goddess,
And found her beautiful.

Hour after hour,
With hopeless love,
He watched the spot where, at evening,
She would sometimes come out to wander
Through her silver garden
In the cool of the dusk.

Far he sent his gaze across the heavens
Until the time came, one day,
When she returned his look of love
And she, too, sat lonely,
Turning eyes of wistful longing
Toward her distant lover.

Then their thoughts of love and longing,
Seeking each other,
Met half way,
Mingled,
Hung suspended in space ...
Thus: the beginning of the world.

Sat they long in loneliness,
The great void of eternal space
Closing in upon them.
Despair hung heavy in their hearts.
Gone was the splendor of the golden throne;
Gone was the beauty of the silver garden;
Their souls burned with a white flame of longing.

Up leaped the Sun-god,
Chanting his love song,
The words of his love thoughts:
    My heart wings its way to you,
    O daughter of the Moon!
    My heart wings its way to you,
    Where you stand,
    In your silver garden,
    Your white face turned toward me.
    You will receive a gift,
    O daughter of the Moon!
    A gift of my great love
    For you only;
    You will receive a gift of my love
    This day, ere the dusk falls.

He seized his knife
And with swift slashes,
Tore a strip of bark
From a great tree.
Still he chanted his songs
Of love and longing,
As he wrote on the birch bark
In the speech of springtime,
The language of lovers.

Then,
From his place at the gate of the Sun,
He, the Sun-god,
Raised his arm high
And cast his message
Far into the sky.

Swift it flew,
Following an unerring course
Toward the distant garden
Where sat the Moon-goddess.

But what of the message?
Alas! It wavers in its flight;
Drops;
Falls on the embryo world;
Thus: the land.

Far across the heavens,
In her silver garden,
The Moon-goddess wept bitterly.
A tear was borne by the wind;
Fell on the half-formed world;
Thus: the water.

There from the love thoughts,
Longings and love words,
Sprang beautiful trees and flowers.
Little streams gurgled through the forests;
Leeping waterfalls foamed;
Great rivers flowed to the sea;
Fish abounded;
Buffalo roamed the plains
And through the wood-paths
Sped all the wild things
Of a new world.

The Sun-god left the seat of his golden throne;
Swung wide the gate of the Sun!
A ringing shout cleft the heavens!

The Moon-goddess,
From her silver garden,
Heard the cry;
Stood,
And answered.

He of the Sun,
She of the Moon,
Stood they
With arms outstretched
A moment
Silent.
Then, in the first shadow of evenfall,
They leaped into space;
Came to rest
On the new world of their love;
Thus: the first man and woman.

Queen's University Archives, Kingston, Lorne Pierce Manuscript Collection, 'Sepass Poems as told to Eloise Street,' *Indian Time* (October 1955) 1-3

► On 15 February 1913, H.R.H. the Duke of Connaught, governor-general of Canada from 1911 to 1916, visited the Six Nation Council House and was welcomed by Chief Da-qu-nea-da-rich Asdawenserontha (A.G. Smith).

May it please your Royal Highness; your brother chiefs of the Six Nations Indians in conformity with the ancient customs of their league or Confederacy, beg, upon this auspicious occasion to tender to your Royal Highness a most sincere and hearty welcome to this their native land and to their Council Chamber, and cordially invite you to be seated in your place in their midst, so that they may hold conference with you during a short season of their council meeting today.

Your brother chiefs are thankful to the Great Spirit for having guarded and protected you from all danger throughout all your long journey, and for having safely brought you to visit them in good health and strength and free from all bodily harm.

Ka-rah-kon-tye, (Flying Sun) while modern civilization and education, with their wonderful and useful inventions, have changed conditions and customs, your Royal Highness will, they hope, pardon their continued use of their ancestors figurative phrases as follows:

You have come a long distance to pay your brother chiefs a visit, and must in consequence be wearied and footsore from your journey.

Your brother chiefs therefore hasten to extract every thorn that may have pierced your moccasins and marred your feet; and gently bathe them in pure spring water, wipe them and apply to them soothing balms, so that you may again be free from weariness and pain, and be fully refreshed.

They now, also, wash off the dust that may have impaired your vision, so that you may again see with clear and unobstructed sight.

They moreover take a fine, soft feather, with which to clear your ears of all foreign substances that may have found lodgement therein, so that you may hear distinctly what your brother chiefs have to say to you.

And finally they now give you a draught of pure clear cold spring water, with which to quench your thirst and clear your throat, so that you may be able to speak with clear enunciation, all that you may have to say to your brother chiefs ...

A. Leon Hatzan, *The True Story of Hiawatha* (Toronto: McClelland and Stewart 1925) 291-3

► In August 1914 the Great War broke out in Europe. A year and a half later, Joseph C. Cope (1858-1951), a prominent Micmac whose father had conferred with Queen Victoria before Confederation, wrote to H. Piers, curator of the Provincial Museum in Halifax, offering this contribution to the war effort.

Mossman's Grant,
Lunenburg Co., N.S.
Mar. 7, 1916.

Mr. Piers.
Sir: – I am sending you a crude drawing of an aerial device I have been studying for sometime past, which I'd like you to see, and to show to some of your Military gentleman friends, and also to find out if the like device is not already employed in aerial war-fare.

As the cruel Huns resort to all kind of schemes in their work of destruction, why can't we do all we can too to defend ourselves.

I am one of your Halifax Mic-Mac Indians, unfortunately too old to shoulder musket to defend my King and Country, but if my idea or invention is of any use, I will gladly offer it to my King and Country free of charge.

The Origin of the idea.

In reading accounts of aeroplane warfare, it appeared to me that aeroplanes were obliged to fly direct above the enemy, and from that dangerous position or distance, drop their bombs, and I asked myself this question. 'Why can't a device be made to lessen all that danger?' 'Why can't a device be made that can carry bombs almost any angle downward from aeroplanes, distance according to the height they are. What do you think of that for an old indian?

I have a sample in wooden frame 3½ feet long in workable order requiring couple or three yards of light cotton for wings to complete it.

The device is collapsible. The weight lever or bomb holder controls every part, as you will notice in the accompanying illustration.

Keep it away from German spys.

My skin is dark, let my name be the same before the public for awhile.

Humbly,

Yours truly,

(Signed) Joe C. Cope

Indian.

Nova Scotia Museum, Printed matter file, Cope to Piers, 7 March 1916

▶ Edward Ahenakew (1885-1961), a Cree from Saskatchewan, grand-nephew of Poundmaker, and an Anglican clergyman, was prominent in religious and educational circles in western Canada. On 16 June 1920 he delivered an address at the annual meeting of the Woman's Auxiliary of Prince Albert, in which he paid tribute to the Indians who fought in the First World War.

Now that peace has been declared, the Indians of Canada may look with just pride upon the part played by them in the Great War, both at home and on the field of battle. They have well and nobly upheld the loyal tradition of their gallant ancestors who rendered invaluable service to the British cause in 1775 and 1812 and have added thereto a heritage of deathless honor which is an example and an inspiration for their descendants.

Before the settlement of the Indians in the reservations, the idea of death, sudden and violent, was always in their minds. The times were such that no one could ever lie down to sleep with any feeling of security. Any night the enemy may surprise and attack, so that lasting vigilance was necessary. By night and by day somebody had to be ever on the watch. The blow fell usually quickly, suddenly and effectively. A deadly feud had arisen between the Blackfoot Confederacy and the Crees, some time in the darkness of the past, that Indian past from which no light penetrates to the present and about which we know nothing concerning the Great North-Western land. The human abhorrence for the snake was no worse than the hate that resulted from the feud. No quarter, no mercy was ever asked for nor given between them; each tribe was bent on exterminating the other. Each year ambitious young men stole away from their camps and secretly travelled across the hundreds of miles of prairie for the purpose of stealing the swiftest horses of the enemy and killing them if possible. It was a repetition of the old-time raids between the English and the Scotch. It is easy to see how living such a life would in time breed into the Indians warlike sentiments and enable them to obtain a certain amount of knowledge regarding military strategy. Much has been written about their warlike character, bravery and skill; some few have given a different opinion of them, but we may well judge from the conduct of our young men during their participation in the Great War as to what their ancestors must have been.

The news of the outbreak of war fell with a numbing thud upon our hearts, as it did upon yours. Owing to the ignorance of many of our people, it seemed far more terrible to many of us than it did to you perhaps. Your knowledge of geography at least shewed you the distance you were from danger, but for many of us there was no such comfort. As an example, one of our headmen from a northern reserve sent to ask me if it was true that the fighting was taking place just east of Battleford. Fighting in the air and under water is just a scientific matter with you; for many of our more ignorant people these things take on a semi-supernatural aspect.

After a little while, however, things began to take shape in the confused minds of the Indians. Our old men who had seen fighting in the old days were very much against our nation joining in it. They did all they could possibly do to discourage enlistment of their young men, not because they were disloyal, but because they shrank from seeing a thing happen which never happened before, or that an Indian should go and lay his bones to mingle with a soil that is not Canadian. Furthermore, it did not seem to them as if it were altogether England's quarrel, and much less did they think it was Canada's quarrel. England was only helping other nations and not fighting for her own life. 'If our own land were attacked,' they said, 'it would then be up to every man of us to go, but not to this one.'

Their gospel of discretion went to the winds. Youth is youth the world around ... The fine record of the Indians in the Great War appears in a peculiarly favourable light when it is remembered that their services were absolutely voluntary, as they were specially exempted from the operation of the Military Service Act, and that they were prepared to give their lives for their country without being compelled to do so or even the fear of compulsion. Furthermore it must be borne in mind that a large part of the Indian population is located in remote and inaccessible locations, are unacquainted with the English language and were therefore not in a position to understand the character of the war, its cause and effect. It is therefore a remarkable fact that the percentage of enlistments among them is fully equal to that among other sections of the community and indeed far above the average in a number of instances. As an inevitable result of the large enlistments among them and of their share in the thick of the fighting the casualties among them were very heavy, and the Indians, in common with their fellow countrymen of the white race, must mourn the loss of their most promising young men ...

The one section of warfare in which the Indians distinguished themselves most was sniping. Naturally taking to the use of the gun, they proved expert and deadly marksmen. It is said that they were unexcelled in this branch of fighting. It is claimed that they did much towards demoralising the entire enemy system of sniping. They displayed their old-time patience and self-control when engaged in this work, and would sit hour by hour at a vantage point waiting the appearance of the enemy at his sniping post. These Indian snipers recorded their prowess by the old-time picturesque method of notching their rifles for every observed hit ...

... For the first time since the Treaty of 1876 the Indian has stood side by side with the white man upon the same plane and with equal chances. When death confronts, man stands with man as man, and if he be brave and efficient his name will be made. The war supplied this opportunity. The Indian feels that he has done a man's work and he will never again be content to stand aside, giving no voice to matters that affect him. The spirit of unrest has taken hold of him; it has stirred up in him desires he never felt before. He chafes under the circumstances which render him dumb before the public; from the Atlantic to the Pacific a feeling of brotherhood and the need of union has arisen among all the scattered Indian people. Tribes far removed from each other, unknown to each other and uninterested in each other now correspond and exchange opinions.

... At last I see that which I have always longed for, to see my race dissatisfied with themselves and the conditions under which they live. It pained me to see the stoical indifference, the lethargy, the masklike countenance with which they viewed their condition. I longed to see the flicker of the old spirit, the spark of the old-time flint and the breakneck speed of the chase and the battle.

150

A sleeping nation is a hard nation to help. The awakening has come; the war has done its work.

Not in vain did our young men die in a strange land; not in vain are our Indian bones mingled with the soil of a foreign land for the first time since the world began; not in vain did the Indian fathers and mothers see their son march away to face what to them were ununderstandable dangers; the unseen tears of Indian mothers in many isolated Indian reserves have watered the seeds from which may spring those desires and efforts and aspirations which will enable us to reach sooner the stage when we will take our place side by side with the white people, doing our share of productive work and gladly shouldering the responsibilities of citizens in this our country.

Saskatchewan Archives Board, Regina, Ruth Matheson Buck Papers, Coll. R-20, file no II.3

▶   Deskaheh (1873-1925), or Hi-wyi-iss, Levi General, was a Cayuga chief of the Younger Bear Clan of the Six Nations Indians. In 1923 the government was taking steps to replace the traditional Six Nations government at the Grand River with an 'Indian Act' elective system; Deskaheh, who opposed the change, travelled to London and Geneva to make his case before the British government and the League of Nations. Returning to Canada he felt his freedom was threatened, and he therefore spent the rest of his days in exile south of the border. His last speech, part of which follows, was made over the radio in Rochester, New York, on 10 March 1925.

Nearly everyone who is listening to me is a pale face I suppose. I am not. My skin is not red but that is what my people are called by others. My skin is brown, light brown, but our cheeks have a little flush and that is why we are called redskins. We don't mind that. There is no difference between us, under the skins, that any expert with a carving knife has ever discovered.

My home is on the Grand River. Until we sold off a large part, our country extended down to Lake Erie, where, 140 winters ago, we had a little sea-shore of our own and a birch-bark navy. You would call it Canada. We do not. We call the little ten-miles square we have left the 'Grand River Country.' We have the right to do that. It is ours. We have the written pledge of George III that we should have it forever as against him or his successors and he promised to protect us in it. We didn't think we would ever live long enough to find that a British promise was not good. An enemy's foot is on our country and George V knows it for I told him so but he will not lift his finger to protect us nor will any of his ministers ...

In some respects we are just like you. We like to tell our troubles. You do that. You told us you were in great trouble a few winters ago because a great big giant with a big stick was after you. We helped you whip him. Many of our young men volunteered and many gave their lives for you. You were willing to let them fight in the front ranks in France. Now we want to tell our troubles to you – I do not mean that we are calling on your governments. We are tired of calling on the governments of pale-faced peoples in America and Europe. We have tried that and found it was no use. They deal only in fine words ... We have a little territory left – just enough to live and die on. Don't you think your governments ought to be ashamed to take that away from us by pretending it is part of theirs? You ought to be ashamed if you let them. Before it is all gone we mean to let you know what your governments are doing. If you are a free people you can have your own way. The governments at Washington and Ottawa have a silent partnership of policy. It is aimed to break up every tribe of Red-men so as to dominate every acre of their territory. Your high officials are the nomads today – not the Red People. Your officials won't stay at home. Over in Ottawa they call that policy 'Indian Advancement.' Over in Washington they call it 'Assimilation.' We, who would be the help-less victims, say it is tyranny ...

We want none of your laws or customs that we have not willingly adopted for ourselves. We have adopted many. You have adopted some of ours – votes for women for instance – We are as well behaved as you and you would think so if you knew us better. We would be happier today, if left alone, than you who call yourselves Canadians and Americans. We have no jails and do not need them. You have many jails, but do they hold all the criminals you convict? And do you convict or prosecute all your violators of the thousands of laws you have?

Your governments have lately resorted to new practices in their Indian policies. In the old days they often bribed our chiefs to sign treaties to get our lands. Now they know that our remaining territory can easily be got-ten away from us by first taking our political rights away in forcing us into your citizenship, so they give jobs in their Indian offices to the bright young people among us who will take them and who, to earn their pay, say that our people wish to become citizens with you and that we are ready to have our tribal life destroyed and want your governments to do it. But that is not true. Your governments of today learned that method from the British. The British have long practiced it on weaker peoples in carrying out their policy of subjugating the world, if they can, to British Imperialism. Under cover of it, your law-makers now assume to govern other peoples too weak to resist your courts. There is no three mile limits or twelve mile limits to strong governments who wish to do that. About three winters ago the Canadian government set out to take mortgages on farms of our returned soldiers to secure loans made to them intending to use Canadian courts to enforce those mortgages in the name of Canadian authority within our country. When Ottawa tried that our people resented it. We knew that would mean the end of our own government. Because we did so the Canadian government began to enforce all sorts of Dominion and Provincial laws over us and quartered armed men among us to enforce Canadian laws and customs upon us. We appealed to Ottawa in the name of our right as a separate people and by right of our treaties and the door was closed in our faces. We then went to London with our treaty and asked for the protection it promised and got no attention. Then we went to the League of Nations at Geneva with its covenant to protect little peoples and to enforce respect for treaties by its members and we spent a whole year patiently waiting but got no hearing.

To punish us for trying to preserve our rights, the Canadian government has now pretended to abolish our government by Royal Proclamation and has pretended to set up a Canadian-made government over us, composed of the few traitors among us who are willing to accept pay from Ottawa and do its bidding. Finally Ottawa officials, under pretence of a friendly visit, asked to inspect our precious wampum belts, made by our Fathers centuries ago as records of our history, and when shown to them those false-faced officials seized and carried away those belts as bandits take your precious belongings ... The Ottawa government thought that with no wampum belts to read in the opening of our Six Nations Councils, we would give up our home rule and self-government, the victims of superstition. Any superstition of which the Grand River People have been victims are not in reverence for wampum belts but in their trust in the honor of governments who boast of a higher civilization ...

We are not as dependent in some ways as we were in the early days. We do not need interpreters now. We know your language and can understand your words for ourselves and we have learned to decide for ourselves what is good for us. It is bad for any people to take the advice of an alien people as to that.

You Mothers, I hear, have a good deal to say about your government. Our Mothers have always had a hand in ours. Maybe you can do something to help us now. If you white mothers are hard-hearted and will not, perhaps you boys and girls who are listening and who have loved to read stories about our people – the true ones, I mean – will help us when you grow up if there are any of us left then to be helped. If you are bound to treat us as though we were citizens under your government then those of your people who are land hungry will get our farms away from us by hooks and crooks under your property laws and in your courts that we do not understand and do not wish to learn. We would then be homeless and have to drift into your big cities to work for wages, to buy bread and have to pay rent, as you call it, to live on this earth and to live in little rooms in which we would suffocate. We would then be scattered and lost to each other and lost among so many of you. Our boys and girls would then have to intermarry with you or not at all. If consumption took us off or if we brought no children into the world or our children mixed with the ocean of your blood then there would be no Iroquois left ... Boys – think this over. Do it before your minds lose the power to grasp the idea that there are other peoples in this world beside your own and with an equal right to be here. You see that a people as strong as yours is a great danger to other peoples near you. Already your will comes pretty near being law in this world where no one can whip you, think then what it will mean if you grow up with a will to be unjust to other peoples; to believe that whatever your government does to other peoples is no crime however wicked. I hope the Irish-Americans hear that and will think about it – they used to when that shoe pinched their foot.

This is the story of the Mohawks, the story of the Oneidas, of the Cayugas – I am a Cayuga – of the Onondagas, the Senecas and the Tuscaroras. They are the Iroquois. Tell it to those who have not been listening. Maybe I will be stopped from telling it. But if I am prevented from telling it over, as I hope to do, the story will not be lost. I have already told it to thousands of listeners in Europe – it has gone into the records where your children can find it when I may be dead or be in jail for daring to tell the truth – I have told this story in Switzerland. They have free speech in little Switzerland. One can tell the truth over there in public even if it is uncomfortable for some great people.

This story comes straight from Des-ka-heh, one of the Chiefs of the Cayugas. I am the speaker of the Council of the Six Nations, the oldest League of Nations now existing. It was founded by Hiawatha. It is a League which is still alive and intends, as best it can, to defend the rights of the Iroquois to live under their own laws in their own little countries now left to them; to worship their Great Spirit in their own way and to enjoy the rights which are as surely theirs as the white man's rights are his own ...

'The Last Speech of Des-ka-heh,' *Ontario Indian*, III, 11 (November 1980) 34-8

►   Dan Kennedy (1877-1973), or Ochankugahe, was an Assiniboine Indian from Saskatchewan. The following excerpts are taken from an address he delivered to students at the Normal School in Saskatoon on 12 April 1939.

Mr. Chairman, Members of the Staff and Students:

The English name under which I have just been introduced was given to me at one of the Government schools I attended, when I received a thin veneer of sophistication.

OCHANKUGAHE is my original name – translated into English – means 'Pathmaker.' It was given to me by my grandfather in commemoration of his exploit of leading a war-path across the trackless wastes of snow in winter, thereby tracing his death warrant to counter war parties of the enemy tribes ...

I will ask you to be indulgent with me. I may be fluent in my mother tongue but I am greatly handicapped by the impediments of your language. It is next to impossible to articulate some of your words. Now let me give you an illustration of my difficulties by asking how many of you can pronounce my Indian name OCHANKUGAHE. It comes very easily from my lips, but probably difficult for yours.

Do you remember the song 'I Was Born Four Thousand Years Ago?' This little song has a strange meaning for me. It brings back the memories of my boyhood days in what you might term the stone age. Visualize to yourself a little fellow with his face powdered with Indian red, sporting two black braids of hair, wearing a little buckskin jerkin, leggings, loin cloth and moccasin-footed, who lived with the rest of his tribe, in a buffalo-skin lodge winter and summer, whose only conveyance was the *travois*; his weapons, the bow and arrows and other primitive contrivances, and you will understand the conflicting emotions and reactions obsessing my mental faculties.

I have lived the life of your forefathers, the ancient Britons, as Caesar found them when he invaded their country 54 B.C., with all their mystic rites of the dark ages, before Christianity dawned on your people.

With this brief introduction let us now explore that field seldom revealed to the whiteman – the inner sanctum of the Redman's soul. The most sacred of his rites is vested in the PIPE OF CHIEFS. To the Redman the Pipe of Chiefs symbolizes what the Magna Carta and the Ark of the Covenant stand for with other races. The Pipe is the medium and poetry of the Redman's plea to the Great Manitou. Over burning Sweet Grass the Pipe is incensed before it is proferred to the Manitou by the suppliant. As Moses of Biblical times received the Ten Commandments on the sacred tablets, so has the Redman the sacred Pipe as the symbol of the Manitou's Covenant.

His moral, social and religious structure, his traditions, ceremonies and sacred rites are all deeply rooted in the ennobling influences of the Pipe.

'Take this Pipe,' the Redman was commanded by the Great Manitou, 'and with this Pipe you shall grow into nationhood. You will return to your people by the white path across the firmaments, the backbone of the skies (the Milky Way) ...

In conclusion I will tell a short old time prairie tale of my people, but before I proceed, I will ask you to think for a moment and speculate on what your mental reactions would be, if you were to go to sleep like Rip Van Winkle not merely for the lapse of twenty years or so, but for a thousand years, and found on waking up, that the world has been transformed by revolutionary changes, and inhabited by super men with giant intellects who have unlocked the secret of atomic energy and harnessed other hidden forces of nature, that baffle our present day scientists. We were confronted by such paralyzing reactions – by our impact with civilization, as the following little amusing story will reveal.

The Liar's Adventures with the Windigo

'The Liar' died about ten years ago, at the age of 103 years. He was the grand-dad of our Reserve [Carry-the-Kettle] – a few years before he died, he told me of a near-encounter he had had with the Windigo, the legendary ogre that roamed the northern forests, living on human beings. It is claimed that the mighty voice of the Windigo will paralyze the hearer with fright and he could then capture the victim at his leisure.

At the time this story took place, there were no modern means of communications, and the Canadian Pacific Railways was in the course of construction. The Indians on the Plains heard vague rumours of a fantastic monster belching forth smoke and fire, as it was wending its way westward towards the great Rockies. I will now tell the story in The Liar's own words. 'My grandson,' he commenced, 'you must have heard of my near-encounter with the Windigo many years ago.'

I answered in the affirmative, 'how,' and then he proceeded.

'I was among a party of Assiniboines, who were heading for the trading post at Fort Qu'Appelle. On the evening of the fourth day of our journey, we reached this place, where our present Reserve is situated. The women were pitching camp and we men were tending to the ponies, when suddenly there roared the challenging cry of the dreaded Windigo, from that direction,' pointing northward toward the forest. 'The women and the children shivered with fright. The children started to whimper. We had to break camp at once, and started on a long detour westward, hoping to evade the monster in the darkness. We pushed our tired ponies all through the night and towards morning, we were in the vicinity of where South Qu'Appelle is now located, when out of the darkness, there came again, that dreadful voice, this time quite near and directly ahead of us. It would have been foolhardy not to heed this second warning cry of the Windigo. We had to leave the Windigo's domain at once if we wanted to save our women and children. Reluctantly we had to abandon our trading trip, although we were sorely in need of tobacco, tea and other things, and returned south to the Plains.

'Your own grandfather "Panapin" and others of his time, believed my story, but the present generation have been voicing doubts about the truth of my adventure, and some of these mischievous tongues have the temerity to point out that the whiteman's "fire waggon," the locomotive, was "The Liar's Windigo," and some of the bolder among them insinuated that I did not stop running until the Missouri River in Montana stopped me.'

Saskatchewan Archives Board, Regina, 'Address by Dan Kennedy to Normal Students,' 12 April 1939, SHS file no 30

On another occasion Dan Kennedy related the adventures of Inktome in the 'glacial age.'

In the pre-reservation days, when the freedom of the boundless plains was ours to roam, and the countless teeming herds of buffalo guaranteed our economic security, we did not have the written word nor the books with which to wile away the long winter nights, but we had Tribal story-tellers that were a delight to us youngsters.

I still retain vivid recollections of those boyhood days or rather of those nights – waiting in breathless anticipation and excitement for our storyteller to commence his tales of the fascinating and thrilling adventures of 'Inktome,' a legendary character in our mythology.

Inktome is an Assiniboine word, which means The Liar or the Deceiver.

The Crees named this mythical character 'Weesakeja' or 'Nenapoosh.' He was the counterpart version of your famous Baron Munchausen and then some.

In some of the stories he is depicted as an artful deceiver, in others as a roaming rollicking minister of mirth, again in others as a sage, invested

157

with the knowledge and wisdom of the ages, and to cap it all, he was credited with the attributes of the omnipotence.

According to tradition, the telling of the adventures of Inktome is tabu during the summer months or in the daytime.

We were admonished that if we violated the tabu, its dire consequences would catch up with us and that sooner or later we would be hopelessly lost in the wilderness. Now it will be obvious that these story-tellers were extremely popular and were much in demand around our winter camp-fires. We youngsters had to be tucked in snugly in our buffalo robe beds and be very quiet before he would commence his narrative.

Sometimes the adventures of Inktome would take us into the land of the Colossus, the nitwit giants with empty craniums, who prey on humans, or perhaps into the land of the midgets who hunted and stalked the snowshoe rabbit with their tiny bow and arrows, as we ourselves did the big game.

Then again on other nights our story-teller subjected us to night-marish tales of the mammoth age, painting vivid word pictures of the loathsome monster reptiles, the avowed foes of the thunder bird, the benevolent manitu of the clouds.

Though versatile in his wide range of subjects and eloquent as only a professional Tribal story-teller could be, none the less often times some of these tales left our young minds mystified and bewildered.

Throughout my life my mind has been haunted by the unanswerable mysteries of where we were originated and how we acquired the knowl-edge of the earth's history ...

Let me tell you one of the adventures of Inktome, which will take us back to that remote period in the earth's history, the glacial age.

The legend begins in a great Tribal encampment, where a new baby was born to a young couple. The child drove his mother and grandparents frantic by his incessant crying babbling mnoketu, mnoketu, mnoketu, which means summer, summer, summer.

The child would not be pacified despite all their efforts. They consulted the medicine men and sought advice from every source without obtaining any palliative.

They were driven desperate by the child's ceaseless crying, until someone told them that Inktome was in the camp and advised them to consult him.

When Inktome heard the story of the dilemma and the child's babbling of strange incoherent words – he asked them to repeat the words and they complied and repeated mnoketu, mnoketu, mnoketu – summer, summer, summer, which incidentally was meaningless to them at the time. They had never heard the word before.

'Now isn't that strange' Inktome told them and then went on – 'This child was born wise, there is such a wonderful thing as summer the exact opposite to this perpetual snow and ice in which you are now living. Summer is a season in which these trees now standing lifeless and stark naked are transformed with beautiful living foliage and instead of the snow and ice covering the earth, it is carpeted in green. The snow and ice are changed into running waters that form the rivers and the lakes and man, beasts and the birds bask in the warmth of the sun.' 'But where is this phenomenon you have described as summer, and how would we procure it,' they persisted.

Inktome saw how he had inadvertently commited himself by the revelation of the existence of summer, so he summoned a war Council, to which the beasts and the birds were invited to take part.

Incidentally, our story-teller would have us believe, that in those far-off days the animals and the birds were able to converse with men.

To this strange incongruous and gregarious assembly of the denizens of icy Keewatin's domain, Inktome related the story of a powerful Tribe living far away to the south, who have in their possession the magic bundle of summer but warned that it was strongly guarded and a constant vigil was kept over it by day and by nights.

'Not by the blandishments of ferocious teeth and sharp claws, nor by resort to force could the magic bundle be wrested from its guardians,' Inktome cautioned, 'but, only by crafty and subtle strategy.'

He then presented a comprehensive outline of the projected warpath he had in mind, comprised of a system of relay posts, stretching across the frozen wastes of snow and ice to their objective.

'Now then little brothers, I have spoken, and what have you to say,' he concluded.

Again at this point of the narrative our story-teller went on to explain that this big brother role was a prerogative of Inktome, by which he addressed himself to all living beings, and even to inanimate objects.

A demonstration clamouring for a raiding party to proceed immediately for the purpose of abducting the magic bundle from its custodians was the answer.

The monarchs of the artic regions and the lords of the air vied with one another vaunting their powers and skill, to further their claims to a leading role in the forthcoming adventure.

Among the aspirants for the honours was the little tinted grey owl, the tiniest of the owl family, whose impertinent insistence provoked the rebuke from Inktome.

'What could you do little brother?' to which the little impudence answered, 'It takes keen eyes to detect my presence and besides being small, I blend well and harmonize in any surrounding, and my wings are noiseless.'

Inktome was quick to appraise the significant merits of the little claiment and assigned him to the most hazardous job, the job of snatching the magic bundle of summer from the lodge, where it was kept.

To sparrow hawk the swift, he designated the significant honour of winging it across the sky on the first lap of the home-bound race, but cautioned him to be on deck and on the alert, to relieve tiny owl of the precious bundle the moment he appeared with it.

He then entrusted to the swift winged birds the first half of the relay posts and the latter to the fleetfooted animals, reserving for himself the honour of bringing the magic bundle to the encampment.

Following fast upon the heels of the war council, the war-path sped its way southward, bent upon the great adventure, posting relays to their respective positions as they went, until only sparrow hawk and tiny owl were left to proceed with the mission, upon which depended the success of the undertaking.

As soon as it was dusk, tiny owl vanished into the enemy camp, leaving sparrow hawk to watch and await his reappearance. He spotted his objective in the dark without any difficulty, knowing instinctively the lodge of the magic bundle would occupy a prominent place in the enemy encampment.

He flew noiselessly to a tree, which stood near by and lit on one of its limbs, waiting patiently for a momentary diversion or distraction of the guards that would give him the desired opportunity.

But the sharp eyes of one of the guards thought he detected something that should not have been on that tree. To satisfy himself he took a burning ember and held it against tiny owl's beak, but the brave little owl never flinched, convincing the guard that there was no cause for alarm. Reassured, the guard dismissed the incident from his mind and left little impudence unmolested.

Thus our little friend scored the first round in the game of wits. A momentary distraction of the guards, gave him the opening and in a flash he swooped down between the lodge poles and before the astonished guards recovered from their surprise, he snatched the much coveted magic bundle of summer and was off.

Sparrow hawk met him and caught the magic bundle in midair and darted across the horizon, hotly pursued by his adversaries, intent upon recapturing their precious treasure.

So the chase continued, streaming across the sky like a meteor, as from each relay post rose a new challenger, fresh and eager for the race.

First it was borne through the sky lanes by the lords of the air – then skimming over the snow and ice by the fleet-footed animals and lastly Inktome made the touch down, when he brought the magic bundle of summer to the encampment.

Inktome hastily summoned another council in which the victors and vanquished were invited. He offered to mediate for both contenders on a compromise of alternating custody of the magic bundle.

A battle of words ensued around the council fires. Some advocated lop-sided seasons and others openly refused to share summer with the vanquished.

Little froggie who sat near the doorway, a seat usually relegated to the 'no bodys,' was heckling the council at the top of his voice croaking seven moons, seven moons without a break, holding his seven tiny fingers outstretched to further emphasize his point.

One of the important councillors, a polar bear, who had been advocating ten moons of winter was particularly annoyed and peeved by the impertinence of our little friend's behaviour, that he threw a piece of wood at him, knocking the poor froggie out. His seven tiny fingers were outstretched in convulsions even as he passed out.

Inktome who sat in judgement at the council of the inhabitants of the earth, clothed in the wisdom of the ages, was deeply moved by the tragic climax and forthwith made his pronouncement. 'Our brave little brother has paid the price of his conviction with his life, so it shall be seven moons of winter' ...

Saskatchewan Archives Board, Regina, 'Inktome – The Adventurer,'
Clippings file Indians of North America – article by Dan Kennedy

▶ In 1935-6 Walter Wright, chief of the Kitselas Band of Tsimshians on the Middle Skeena River, told Will Robinson the history of the legendary city of Tum-L-Hama and the migration westward of his people to the Kitselas Canyon in British Columbia. Robinson later published the history as *Men of Medeek*; this is number eight of the series.

The Grizzly Bears

Great disasters are the landmarks of a people who are wise.
   They mark the ending of a time of error.
   They set a starting point for a better mode of life.

So in the days that followed the visitation of Medeek, the giant grizzly bear, Wise Men pondered long over what had come to pass.

To them the situation became clear.

Once again Gyamk, the Sun God, had been offended.

The dancing maidens, decked with trout bones, had violated the Law; they had desecrated His beings.

And the Spirit of the Trout People, taking the form of Medeek, had been sent to exact recompense; an awful retribution from the men who had failed to train their children in the ways of wisdom.

In due course Neas Hiwas called a Council.

Many things had to be done. New Chiefs had to be raised up in the place of those who had been slain.

New laws, governing the proper training of children, had to be made.

In that Council Neas Hiwas brought to memory the gift of The Goat Crown.

Here was a like instance.

'From this day,' he announced, 'I take as my head-dress the head of Medeek, the Grizzly Bear. It is the Law that when men die in a great disaster those who follow after them have the right to take unto themselves the name of the destroyer. Thus, from this day on, I take the name of Medeek. It shall be the crest of my Totem.'

Months passed and spun themselves into years. Years waxed and waned.

After many years the Spirit of Neas Hiwas passed from his body.

In the funeral rites that followed a new chant was sung. A funeral chant that has come down through the ages, and is still sung when a Chief of The Grizzly Bear Totem dies:

Leig yu hou – dis caan caana yu haw law aw hee hee
The trees fall all ways when the grizzly comes on.

ee-ya haw law ya haw law ah hee hee.
Will guik koi dex me dee-k yu haw law aw hee hee.
Here comes the Grizzly Bear out of the lake.

ee-ya haw law ya haw law ah hee hee.
Gis see ya guehth me dee-k yu haw law aw hee hee Tum-L-Hama.
The Grizzly Bear comes down through the town of Tum-L-Hama.

162

Will wahl-da yu haw law as hee hee.
Ee-ya haw law ya haw law ah hee hee.

Will Robinson, *Men of Medeek* (Kitimat: Northern Sentinel Press 1962) 20-1

▶ Alexandre de Laronde, or Sosop Lolo (1862-1944), graduated from the Collège de Saint-Boniface with a Bachelor of Arts degree in 1887 and entered a teaching career.

Death Chant of the Last Blackfoot

Where are my meadows of flowers, my lush forests?
Where are my thick woods, sombre, silent?
Where are my lakes of azure, my solitary paths?
Where are my people who traversed these –
All is pain, alas, where are my brothers?
Where are those whom I have loved, those who were so dear?
Wake up now noble warrior race.
Listen to my voice, revive my roots.

Annette Saint-Pierre, *Au pays des Bois-Brûlés*
(Collège Universitaire de St-Boniface, February 1977) 13 (my translation)

▶ James Gladstone (1887-1971), or Akay-Na-Muka, 'Many Guns,' was a Blood Indian of the Blackfoot Confederacy in Alberta. He was a successful rancher and farmer and a prominent Indian leader in Canada. In 1958 he was appointed to the Senate, the first Indian to be so honoured. The following excerpts are from his maiden speech in the Senate on 13 August 1958.

Honourable senators, this amendment [Bill C-24, to amend the Indian Act] has a great deal of importance attached to it by myself personally and by many other treaty Indians in this country. Not only does it remove from the Indian Act certain clauses which are objectionable, but it is a reassurance to the Indians of Canada that their treaty rights are not being endangered.

During the weeks that I have listened to the debates here I have heard two languages spoken – English and French. To me, and to other native Canadians, these are foreign tongues. Therefore I should like to place in the official Debates a few words in the language of my own people, the Blackfoot Indians, as a recognition of the first Canadians.

Eekoh-kinay-tam-etakee-kunay-apee un-ohk-ohtayts-tseeh-pee mukiy-sitsip suko-moh-kee unok-see awk-aw-kee-tsee-maks. Nitowat-simoyee-nukohk-okomot-ayhpo-wat-omohsah-ow.

My words, translated into English, were these:

The Indians of Canada are very happy to know they have someone in Ottawa to represent them in the Government of Canada. I pray that I will be able to speak the right words for them.

As this is my first address to the honourable members of this august chamber, I will take the opportunity to bring before you some of the history and problems of the people I have the honour to represent.

It is a great honour to me personally to be chosen to speak for my people. It is also an honour to my own nation, the Bloods, Peigans and Blackfeet. In the few months since my appointment to the Senate I have visited many Indians, in Alberta, Saskatchewan, Manitoba, British Columbia and the Yukon, and everywhere I have been overwhelmed by the friendly feeling of the Indians who have received me. The great regard these people have for the Prime Minister [John Diefenbaker] for carrying out his pledge of appointing a member of their race to the Senate was said by some to be the biggest moment of their lives. Now they look forward to seeing some of the things which were promised to us by our great mother, Queen Victoria.

In this brief time, I cannot begin to tell you all about the history of my people. There are more than 165,000 at the present time, speaking about 50 different languages. Some people think that if a man knows one Indian language he knows them all. But this is not true. For a Blackfoot to understand an Iroquois would be the same as an Eskimo understanding an Arab. Each of our languages is separate, and their grammars are often more complicated than English.

Besides speaking different languages, my people have different problems. Some signed treaties with the French or English, those on the Prairies signed with the Canadian Government, and some have no treaties at all. In each case they were given different promises or were governed under different rules before the Indian Act came into being.

Now, in this modern world, some live by farming or ranching, some by fishing, logging, trapping or hunting. Some have mixed very well with their white neighbours and work off their reserves; others have never been more than a few miles away from their homes.

These are the people I must speak for and their problems I must learn. It would be easy if we could find one answer for everyone's problems, but what is good for one tribe might be a hardship on another. Tribal customs, treaties, and local needs all have to be taken into consideration.

On my own reserve we have had many problems over the years in dealing with farming and also in holding onto our reserve, which, by the way, is the largest in Canada. When we were given our reserve, in 1883, our head chief, Red Crow, asked for the land between the Belly and Old-man Rivers on one side and the St. Mary on the other, from their confluence back to the mountains. The Government surveyed the land at five persons to a square mile, but the Indians didn't have any idea of what a square mile was. All they could understand were the natural boundaries like rivers and mountains. Since that time, many of my people have felt that the reserve should have gone right to the mountains, instead of being cut off 15 miles from the United States boundary. It is things like this which have caused suspicion and misunderstanding between the Government and the Indians.

Since they were given the reserve, the Bloods have never surrendered any of it, although we were often under great pressure from the Government and other people to do so. I remember our head chief, when approached some years ago about surrendering his reserve, replied in this way. He bent down and plucked a handful of grass and, handing it over, said: 'This you can use.' Then, bending down with his right hand, he picked a handful of earth and pressed it to his heart and said: 'This is mine and will always be mine for my children of the future' ...

Honourable senators, may I sum up what I have already said. The Indian people have an innate sense of pride, self-respect and love of this beautiful country of Canada. As the original inhabitants they want not the patronage or tolerance of their fellows, but rather their understanding and help – so that they may materially improve their lot and status in the months and years to come, and so that 'equality of opportunity' and 'equal status' will mean something in the future. If we in Canada can freely grant aid, comfort and recognition to under-developed and distressed people all over the world, at the public expense, we can well afford to have a careful and continuous regard to the fulfilment of the legitimate, and indeed, humble, aspirations of our native population. We must give encouragement and provide economic, and in particular educational, aid to the thousands of our own people who need it, and who, in a specially Canadian sense, deserve it.

I say this in a completely non-partisan spirit. The Indian people need the understanding and support and deserve the confidence of all Canadians, regardless of party, race or creed. This co-operation I now earnestly solicit in the hope and expectation that it will be freely granted.

Canada, *Debates of the Senate* (*Hansard*) 13 August 1958

Alanis Obomsawin

Dan George

Jim Morris

Lenore Keeshig-Tobias

Walter Currie

5 'Walk in our moccasins'

'Walk in our moccasins the trail of our past.
Live with us in the here and now.
Talk with us by the fires of the days to come.'

Indians of Canada Pavilion, Expo 67

I am a chief, but my power to make war
is gone, and the only weapon left to me
is speech. It is only with tongue and speech
that I can fight my people's war.

———

Already signs of new life are arising
among my people after our sad winter
has passed. We have discarded our broken
arrows and our empty quivers, for we know
what served us in the past can never serve
us again.

Chief Dan George, *My Heart Soars*, 91, 78

'A people without history is like wind on the buffalo grass.'

Sioux proverb

Indians writing in Canada today have a long and unique heritage on which to build. They have an oral literary tradition that reaches into the distant past, and they have been speaking and writing in English and French for more than three centuries.

Since the coming of the written word, there have been several significant stages of development: translation of Indian words and thoughts into European languages, early attempts to speak and write in difficult foreign tongues, imitation of European literary models, and, increasingly, original creative writing in English (as well as in French and in the native languages themselves, generally outside the scope of this book). At every stage in its evolution, Indian literature has drawn on its heritage of myths, legends, songs, and tales passed down through the generations, on its rich imagery and habit of metaphorical thought, on a reverence for mother earth and a belief in the sacredness of life.

In the past twenty years there has been a bursting forth of Indian creativity. There is a trend towards a pan-Indian approach, with less focus on tribal affiliation and increased concentration on a common native identity; at the same time, perhaps paradoxically but also indicative of maturity, there is a shift from emphasis on the shared experience of the group to the single experiences of the individual. There is greater diversification of literary genres: poetry, drama, short stories, historical and autobiographical writing, and political rhetoric and oratory worthy of the forefathers. Finally, there is a resurgence of interest in the past, the use of native background as material for characters, plot, setting, and the evocation of ancient beliefs and values for inspiration, providing a sense of historical continuity.

Contemporary Indian writers are nourished by ancestral voices. The few included in this chapter, and many more across the country, give evidence of a promising future.

▶   Dr Walter Currie, a Potawatomi Ojibwa, was born in Chatham, Ontario, and is now a professor in the Department of Native Studies at the University of Saskatchewan. The following speech was given in Thunder Bay, on 20 August 1969, as the keynote address at a luncheon during a conference on the Mid-Canada Development Corridor.

As an Ojibwa Indian, one of the many Indian peoples of Canada, one of this country's three founding races, I would like on behalf of my people to officially welcome you to our shores. We hope and expect that your stay here will be pleasant and memorable, that while you are here you will not only take note of our customs and beliefs but will respect and honour them. In turn, we will not try in any manner to impose upon you our ways, nor to change yours.

You smile when I say these words, and yet, over the past few hundred years, my forefathers by word and deed expressed these feelings to your predecessors. As a matter of fact, examine the writings of those early explorers along either coastline, and you will find that my people greeted the newcomers graciously and made them welcome; that in no case were my people hostile. That did not come until later, until after sad experience taught us that all newcomers were not worthy of trust and brotherhood.

Further to this, it was our forefathers who taught the European how to survive and how to live in this land. Now it is true, the Indians accepted and adopted some of the technical advantages of your culture – the killing stick, the iron pot, the steel blade, the steel traps, the blankets, the geegaws, the liquor – but only to improve upon their physical way of living. It was the Indians' way of life – which animals to kill and how to kill; which plants, fruits and nuts to eat; which herbs for medicinal purposes; how to build a shelter to keep out the cold of winter; how to make clothing from the skins of animals for warmth, comfort, and beauty; how to use and build the canoe to travel great distances, to make portages easily, to explore around the next bend in the river – it was the Indians' way of life that made it possible for those first Europeans to survive and prosper.

It was the generosity of our forefathers who ensured the survival of many of the first white settlements. As Captain John Smith wrote 'It pleased God (in our extremity) to move the Indians to bring us Corne, to refresh us, when we rather expected they would destroy us.' Further writings show that when the Indians were starving and the people of Jamestown had corn, the English governor traded 400 bushels for 'a mortgage on their whole countries.'

In our nation's yesterdays, the Indian was a true resource to the newcomer. It was he who ensured the survival of the settlements, he who gathered the furs upon which a great industry with great riches was founded, he who provided the balance of power in the great border wars between the warring European nations, he who guided the explorers along the waterways, across the prairies, and through the mountains to the sea, he who was the majority – and look how he treated his white immigrant minority! Yet it was he who found himself crowded off his lands and eventually compressed onto reserves when he was no longer of any use to the 'coat-wearing people.' Under the Indian Act today, my people exist on some 2,200 reserves across Canada in abject poverty, poorly housed, with limited health services and less than satisfactory educational opportunities. The Department of Indian Affairs reports that there are 237,490 registered Indians in Canada as of 1968 – a 3-per-cent increase over 1967 – despite an infant mortality rate of 51 in every 1,000 compared with a national average of 22 in every 1,000. At the same time six out of 10 Indian homes have three rooms or less; nine out of 10 Indian homes have outdoor plumbing, with the water supply a pump, a creek or a lake; four out of 10 Indian families are on welfare; three out of four Indian families earn less than $2,000 a year.

My people are a young people. More than half the total registered Indian population is of school age – under 17. And yet, in this, 'the Province of Opportunity,' of 14,000 registered Indian children in school, one quarter of this province's Indian population, there are only 35 students in Grade 13. In this whole nation, there are only 186 Indians in university.

We must know and understand what facts and causes, what successes and failures of yesterday, brought about the good and bad of today. Too often our agencies, both political and private, have failed to examine with objectivity their efforts and results, and have perpetuated the headaches they seek to remove. For example, education given to the Indian by the Department of Indian Affairs has been an annual repetition of the same program ensuring the same poor results. Nationally, only one in eight of the Indian children continues beyond Grade 8, and yet the methods and programs have not fundamentally changed; these methods have persisted in preparing the Indian child 'to take his place in our society.' You businessmen, you mining people, you labour people – where are your Indian foremen? Your Indian field bosses? Have you made efforts to ensure the use and growth of native Canadian people in your plants? I give you Coppermine and Thompson, Manitoba, as two of several examples of failure to do this. What is needed is new thinking economically, socially and politically to cure these problems. In some cases, maybe thinking for the first time.

In the yesterdays of my people, we were three major groups – those who lived between the Rockies and the Pacific, those who moved across the plains, and those of the forests and streams. The nations had their varied languages, their customs, their beliefs, their ways of living. Unlike the arriving white man with his peasant ethos, the Indians of North America followed a hunter ethos. He lived – and lives – within his environment; he was a part of the land and what it yields. He took only what he needed. He had no need either to command or to obey another's wishes. Time and work had not been invented; acquisition of property was unknown. Group interest was paramount to self interest: When I eat you eat; when you go hungry I go hungry.

The European – with his peasant ethos of competition for the acquisition of private property; his saving for tomorrow when he would be too old to enjoy it; his 'time is money,' his emphasis on individualism and competition; and his command over others – found (and finds today) that there was a great communication gap, leading to little or no direct understanding between the two societies: 'These Indians are just too lazy to work; they lack ambition; they're undependable.' Eventually, the Indians were placed on reserves, where their way of living was to continue, protected. And yet, change was constantly thrust at the Indian, directly and indirectly. As the hinterland was filled by the ever-increasing numbers of arrivals, the game upon which the Indian relied disappeared. He could no longer provide food, clothing and shelter by his hunting skills. To overcome this, he would be made a farmer! And yet, for centuries before you came, the people of North America had known of farming and had obviously decided to remain hunters, even after the arrival of the white man. When this did not work, welfare was instituted, a further and continuing emasculation of the Indian male.

This was not and is not an answer. Involvement in the seeking of answers and the execution of the plans is the answer. Do it with, not for, the Indian.

What remains to the Indian today? His beliefs, his gods have been taken from him; the Indian's dress, this too is gone. His mobility is gone; his ability to provide for his family by hunting is gone; his customs and beliefs have been destroyed and replaced by Christianity. All that remains are his languages. And soon they, too, may disappear. The language of the classroom is French or English. The language of the child and his community is not used, nor even encouraged. True, the forbidding of the Indian child his right to use his native language in school has been repealed; but the damage has been done. I am not advocating the use of the native languages only; the Indian is wise enough to realize the realities of life. But do we have to give up everything? Must you practise cultural genocide?

The policy of the ruling powers has been, 'Use and then discard the native: banish him onto a reserve and he will disappear.' Unfortunately he has not disappeared but is growing in numbers; so a new policy, one of assimilation and integration, makes him into a brown-skinned white man. Unhappily for both the white man and the Indian especially, it is not working. I wonder what would happen if white Canada would accept us, would be aware of us as Indians, would accept us as a people, would share with us pride in our heritage – for it is Canada's heritage also. I wonder what would happen if you would stop trying to change us into something you think we ought to be?

By an Act of Parliament, we have been divided into two groups of people – the quarter of a million 'status' Indians who are registered as Indians (those of British Columbia, Quebec, the Atlantic Provinces, the Sioux) and those who are 'treaty' Indians because their forefathers signed a treaty with the Crown. The second group, equal in number to the first is made up of the Metis of the prairies and of those of native descent who like myself are not within the terms of the Act, but who choose to remain Indians.

Where are these half-million people? About 70 per-cent of the status Indians are still on the reserves. Many of the Metis are in their colonies, scattered across the prairies. Other non-status people are in small towns like McDiarmid, or on the edges of towns in non-incorporated areas. The remainder, like the other Canadians, have moved into the cities, pushed there by an exploding population, by an education that has divorced them from their parents, their friends, their communities, their culture. And yet, they find in the cities that their education has not prepared them; that they have little or no skills for hire; that they are even further down the economic totem pole; that they are again on welfare; that they are unprepared for urban living – living by the clock, paying rent, the impersonality, the high cost of living, the rush, the loss of freedom.

You can easily find these people in our cities. Go to the inner city ghettos, to the cheap bars and beverage rooms, where they are accepted despite their Indianness. Some remain in the inner city. A very few climb out of the inner city into a better world. The rest go back to the reserve. And this is an irony, in that the status Indian can go back to the reserve, whereas the non-status Indian, the Metis, has no place to go, no Department of Indian Affairs to help him. He is alone. In our cities they find it difficult to get a decent place to live, to find a job, to find a social life, to adjust to a new environment, to avoid the law, and to escape discrimination and prejudice.

And you say, 'so does every other migrant,' and I agree – except for one vital fact: These other migrants do not carry the burden of being an Indian in a non-Indian, white world.

We must look at people not things, humanity not material goods. What are their needs, wants, ambitions? Manitoba and the proposed flooding of South Indian Lake is a case in point. Too much and too often we forget

173

people, and how they may suffer for the sake of material or environmental change as dictated by big business. A spokesman for Manitoba hydro asks: 'For the sake of 77 Indian families at Southern Indian Lake, should we create a situation where hydro rates must be increased for the entire province?' And I say, 'yes, if we live in a democracy that recognizes the rights of the individual!' How dare anyone weigh the self-sufficiency, the freedom of happiness of 77 families, 650 people, against dollars! What is to be done must be done to serve people. While we plan for tomorrow, we must cure the ills of today. You men of business, of mining, of labour – What are your attitudes towards my people? Are we irresponsible, lazy, too dumb to learn? Or are you too impatient, too unconcerned about people to invest the time and finances to incorporate the native people into your operations? Why not compel companies to hire, train and use the indigenous population? My fathers were patient and generous with yours. Can you not be patient and helpful with us?

If we cannot cure the ills of today, Heaven help us tomorrow. We spend millions enforcing the laws of society to protect society from crime. Why don't we spend as much enforcing the laws of human rights to protect society from slums, poor housing, unemployment, limited medical care, discrimination, prejudice? Why don't we do it now? You cannot talk to the Indian of the bright new tomorrow, when right now he is hungry, on welfare, poorly housed, a second-class citizen. He wants and needs those things corrected today. If it isn't done with asking it may have to be done with force.

Whatever happens in curing today's problems and preventing tomorrow's ills, you must involve Canada's native people – the Indians and the Eskimos. Indian organizations do exist, nationally and provincially. They are trying to organize their people, trying to learn and hear their needs, trying to create a voice to help them be heard and recognized. You men of industry and financial resources, can help these struggling organizations to become viable and effective by offering them dollar assistance.

You must involve them wholeheartedly and significantly in all aspects of the Mid-Canada Development Corridor, of any development. Do not perform lip service and merely use us on advisory committees. Use us creatively with responsibility and involvement. Will tomorrow in the Corridor and elsewhere in Canada be no better than yesterday or today for my people? Or will we be invited as equal partners to participate in determining our futures? This may be the last asking. What will be your answer?

Bulletin no 201 Anglican Church of Canada (1970) 35-9

► Dan George (1899-1981), a hereditary chief of the Coast Salish Indians, was born on the Burrard Reserve in North Vancouver, and was a logger, a long-shoreman, and an entertainer; he appeared on radio and television and in motion pictures as well as on the stage and on lecture tours. His lyrical response to life is seen in this excerpt from his prose poem collection, *My Heart Soars*.

The beauty of the trees,
the softness of the air,
the fragrance of the grass,
   speaks to me.

The summit of the mountain,
the thunder of the sky,
the rhythm of the sea,
   speaks to me.

The faintness of the stars,
the freshness of the morning,
the dew drop on the flower,
   speaks to me.

The strength of fire,
the taste of salmon,
the trail of the sun,
And the life that never goes away,
   They speak to me.

And my heart soars.

Chief Dan George and Helmut Hirnschall, *My Heart Soars*
(North Vancouver: Hancock House Publishers 1974) 83

► Duke Redbird, born on the Saugeen Reserve near Owen Sound, Ontario, has been publishing poetry for more than fifteen years; the first collection of his poetry, *Loveshine and Red Wine*, was published in 1981.

I am the Redman

I am the Redman
   Son of the forest, mountain and lake

What use have I of the asphalt
What use have I of the brick and concrete
What use have I of the automobile
Think you these gifts divine
That I should be humbly grateful.

I am the Redman
Son of the tree, hill and stream
What use have I of china and crystal
What use have I of diamonds and gold
What use have I of money
Think you these from heaven sent
That I should be eager to accept.

I am the Redman
Son of the earth, water and sky
What use have I of silk and velvet
What use have I of nylon and plastic
What use have I of your religion
Think you these be holy and sacred
That I should kneel in awe.

I am the Redman
I look at you White Brother
And I ask you
Save not me from sin and evil
Save yourself.

Duke Redbird, *Loveshine and Red Wine* (Cutler, Ontario: Woodland Studios Publishing 1981)
58

Duke Redbird's 'I am a Canadian,' printed in a limited edition of two thousand copies, was presented to Queen Elizabeth II in Ottawa on 17 October 1977, on the occasion of her Silver Jubilee.

I am a Canadian

I'm a lobster fisherman in Newfoundland
I'm a clambake in P.E.I.
I'm a picnic, I'm a banquet
I'm mother's homemade pie

I'm a few drafts in a Legion hall in Fredericton
I'm a kite-flyer in a field in Moncton
I'm a nap on the porch after a hard day's work is done.
I'm a snowball fight in Truro, Nova Scotia
I'm small kids playing jacks and skipping rope
I'm a mother who lost a son in the last great war
And I'm a bride with a brand new ring
And a chest of hope
I'm an Easterner
I'm a Westerner
I'm from the North
And I'm from the South
I've swam in two big oceans
And I've loved them both
I'm a clown in Quebec during carnival
I'm a mass in the Cathedral of St. Paul
I'm a hockey game in the Forum
I'm Rocket Richard and Jean Beliveau
I'm a coach for little league Expos
I'm a baby-sitter for sleep-defying rascals
I'm a canoe trip down the Ottawa
I'm a holiday on the Trent
I'm a mortgage, I'm a loan
I'm last week's unpaid rent
I'm Yorkville after dark
I'm a walk in the park
I'm Winnipeg gold-eye
I'm a hand-made trout fly
I'm a wheat-field and a sunset
Under a prairie sky
I'm Sir John A. Macdonald
I'm Alexander Graham Bell
I'm a pow-wow dancer
And I'm Louis Riel
I'm the Calgary Stampede
I'm a feathered Sarcee
I'm Edmonton at night
I'm a bar-room fight
I'm a rigger, I'm a cat
I'm a ten-gallon hat

And an unnamed mountain in the interior of B.C.
I'm a maple tree and a totem pole
I'm sunshine showers
And fresh-cut flowers
I'm a ferry boat ride to the Island
I'm the Yukon
I'm the North-West Territories
I'm the Arctic Ocean and the Beaufort Sea
I'm the prairies, I'm the Great Lakes,
I'm the Rockies, I'm the Laurentians,
I am French
I am English
And I am Metis
But more than this
Above all this
I am a Canadian and proud to be free.

Duke Redbird, *I am a Canadian* (Toronto: Wacacro Productions Inc. 1977)

▶ Harold Cardinal was born in High Prairie, Alberta, and raised on the Sucker Creek Cree Reserve. His first book, *The Unjust Society: The Tragedy of Canada's Indians*, was published in 1969. The following extract is from *The Rebirth of Canada's Indians*, published in 1977.

What are the ingredients for our rebirth? Perhaps the most difficult aspect of Indian leadership today, is knowing that in the battles to come we have very little hope of being able to win an equitable accommodation for our people in a country that was once all theirs. It requires no little hope, and no little faith to latch on to the strong, rock-like belief of our elders that if we make the right decisions, keep true to our nationhood, then the losses that are coming will not be the end. That, in fact, in the long run, there is hope for the continuing survival, perhaps even a good life, for Indian nations in Canada.

Many of the situations that we face today, many of the changes we have seen over the past one hundred years, were prophesied by our people as much as two hundred years ago. As our young people delve into the essence of Indian nationhood, the parallel between our people and the Jewish people, with their steadfast belief in their nationhood, becomes much more striking. There is also a parallel between the Indian nations and their hopes and aspirations, and the liberation movements in third-world countries. There remains one fundamental difference – the liberation, the rebirth of the Indian people is not going to be achieved at the end of a gun barrel, but through their ability to maintain their laws and their relationship with their Creator.

Present-day Indian leaders and the qualities of Indian organizations, will not be judged in the future upon what programmes they have been able to win from provincial or federal governments, or from anyone else. Indian leaders and Indian organizations will instead be judged on their strength and determination in adhering to the principal basis of Indian nationhood. This basis comes most strongly through religious ceremonies that have, for century upon century, defined the reason for the existence of Indian nations in this country. Our people define themselves as Indians, because they believe that they, like all other human beings, were created by the Great Spirit. They believe that each race was given special responsibilities, special obligations, special work to do in the various parts of this globe.

Our sole reason for being here as Indians, as whites, as any race, is to recognize our responsibilities to our Creator; to raise our children in His image, according to the laws that He gave us, and to relate to all people and to all things around us within the framework of those laws. In that sense, if we talk about Indian identity or Indian nationhood, the troublesome problem of our relationship to others who live in Canada should be fairly easy to resolve.

With respect to the land and the resources contained within that land, what in essence Indian people must guard is their continued right to use all of those things that exist on and in this land in fulfilling our responsibilities to our Creator. If we continue to use wood for pipe-stems, grass for incense, stone for pipe-bowls in our religious ceremonies, then those are the things that we cannot sell, or sign away, or barter for dollars, or lose access to, or control over. In that same context, we, as a people, must take a long second look at, and seriously examine, the role that material wealth plays in taking us away from our responsibility to our Creator. In this rebirth, Indian people will undergo a process of de-brainwashing themselves from the stultifying century-long hold that the so-called Christian denominations have imposed upon them. The tremendous importance of our reserves is emphasized here, because it always has been the view of our elders that our reserves are the one place where we can hold to the responsibilities that we have to our Great Spirit.

For this rebirth to be meaningful, anything short of true independence and complete freedom will not be acceptable. Trimmed to the bare bone, this means that we must regain control over the basic decisions affecting our everyday lives, our communities, our children, our futures. Parents must regain the right to make decisions about the lives of their children; their education, the values they grow up with, their preparation for life. We are talking about the right to make the decisions that will allow our communities to flourish, the simple right to earn a living in the way we feel will best reflect our identity and our society.

We must have the right to reject the tug-of-war federal and provincial governments play with our children to control their formative years. We must have the right to reject the government's continued determination to hold our people in the thraldom of welfare.

The most important of all our rights, without which there can be no rebirth, is the right of our elders to define their centuries-old perception of our Creator, and to perform the centuries-old religious rituals from which all the true values of our Indian society stem. Only then is our right to follow the path shown to us by our Creator sacrosanct. Then, and only then, will our rebirth be complete.

Harold Cardinal, *The Rebirth of Canada's Indians* (Edmonton: Hurtig Publishers 1977) 220-2

▶ Jacob Nibènegenesábe, 'Slowstream,' is a Swampy Cree from the Lake Winnipeg region in Manitoba.

One time I wished myself in love.
I was the little squirrel
with dark stripes.
I climbed shaky limbs for fruit for her.
I even swam with the moon on the water
to reach her.
That was a time little troubled me.
I worked all day to gather food
and watched her sleep all night.
It is not the same way now
but my heart still sings
when I hear her
over the leaves.

There was a storm once.
That's when I wished myself

into a turtle.
But I meant on land!
The one that carries a hard tent
on his back.
I didn't want to be floating!
I wanted to pull everything inside
and dry.
Here comes the waves
shaking me,
and I'm getting sick in the insides.
I wanted to be the turtle
eating buds and flowers and berries.
I've got to wish things exactly!
That's the way it is
from now on.

The Wishing Bone Cycle, Narrative Poems from the Swampy Cree Indians,
gathered and translated by Howard A. Norman (New York: Stonehill Publishing Co. 1976) 8, 9

▶ Ben Abel, an Okanagan Indian, was born in Westbank, British Columbia.

A grizzly bear can only understand
Indian words,
'cause they have heard it
many times.
An Indian can talk his way out
of a fight with a grizzly.
If they can't
they wouldn't be alive to tell about it.
To an Indian,
the bear is closest.
When they kill a bear,
they cut off their feet,
and hang them on a branch
to say they're sorry
but can't help it.
Bears understand.

Ben Abel, *Wisdom of Indian Poetry* (Cobalt, Ontario: Highway Book Shop 1976) 17

▶ Basil Johnston, an Ojibwa, is a writer, teacher, and lecturer in the Department of Ethnology at the Royal Ontario Museum in Toronto. This short story, 'Cowboys and Indians,' is based on a story told to him by Benjamin Pease.

Hollywood grew fast and big. By the 1930s there were many studios employing many actors in the production of many motion pictures. Within the same few years as the studios got bigger, techniques improved; as techniques improved so did the quality of acting; and as acting got better, so did the range and variety of themes enlarge. And of course viewers' tastes became more refined and discriminating, requiring of Hollywood and the studios more authenticity and less artificiality in their productions.

And the studios were willing to oblige.

It was decided by the producer and director of a major studio planning a western picture with either Hoot Gibson, Tom Mix, or Ken Maynard as the principal star, to hire real Indians to take part in the production. With real Indians the advantages were obvious. Besides lending authenticity to the motion picture, Indians represented a substantial saving. Their natural pigmentation would reduce expenses in cosmetics and make-up artistics; their natural horsemanship would save time and expenses usually incurred in training greenhorns to ride; their possession of herds of ponies would save time and outlay in the rental and feeding of horses; and their natural talent for art would obviate the need for anthropologists to act as consultants in authenticating Indian art and design. The only expense to be incurred was the fee of $2.00 per day for movie extras.

Management calculated that 500 Indians along with 500 horses were needed for no more than two days to shoot an attack upon a wagon-train. The producer and the director also decided that there would be substantial savings by establishing the location of the filming near an Indian reservation somewhere in the west.

Inquiries, preliminary and cursory, made of historians and the Bureau of Indian Affairs in Washington indicated that the Crow Indians of Montana, having retained their traditions and still owning large herds of horses, would be best suited for a motion picture of the kind planned by the studio. Besides, the terrain in the area was genuine honest-to-goodness Indian country, excellent for camera work.

Negotiations with the Bureau of Indian Affairs for permission to treat with the Crows for their services as actors and for the provision of horses began at once. Permission was granted by Washington; and the Crows were more than willing to take part.

182

Crew and cast arrived by train in Billings, Montana. Anxious to get started and to finish shooting the siege of a wagon-train in as short a time as possible, the producer and director sent a limousine to the reservation to fetch the chief.

Over a meal with the chief and his retinue of councillors and hangers-on, the producer, portly and bald, beneath a cloud of smoke produced by a fat cigar, informed the chief that it was a great privilege to work with the Crows and that it was an honour and a distinction for his studio to set precedent in the entire industry by being the first to use real, live, honest-to-goodness Indians in a motion picture. For the Crows, it would mean fame and national recognition ... and money ... $2.00 a day for those taking part; $1.00 per day for those providing horses; and $1.00 per day for those providing art work and the loan of teepees.

An interpreter translated for the chief.

The producer smiled and blew a cloud of smoke out of the side of his mouth. The Crow responded 'How! How! How!'

'It shouldn't take long chief, three or four days ... no more. A day to get ready and two or three to film the scene. We don't want to interfere too much in your affairs, you've probably got a lot to do and ... we are working under a pretty tight schedule.'

The interpreter relayed this information to the chief.

'Now chief. We want 500 warriors; 500 horses; bows and arrows and ... maybe fifty or so rifles ... feathers, head-dresses, buckskin jackets, and ... buckskin leggings ... and four or five people who can paint designs on horses and put make-up on warriors.' The producer continued, 'The scene itself will be easy. The warriors will attack the wagon-train at daybreak. It shouldn't take more than half an hour. Very easy, really don't need any rehearsals. My colleague will tell you what to do. Probably the easiest two bucks you'll ever make ... cash, as soon as the scene's shot. Can you get all this stuff by tomorrow night, chief?' And the producer flicked ashes from his fat cigar.

The interpreter prattling in Crow to his chief and councillors pounded the table, slashed the air, shrugged his shoulders to emphasize his message to his listeners, who looked dumbfounded. Nevertheless they injected a 'How! How!' frequently enough into the discourse to intimate some understanding.

The chief said something.

'How many horses?'

'500, the producer might even settle for 450.'

The interpreter addressed his chief who shook his head grunting 'How!'

'Ain't got 500 horses,' the interpreter said sadly.

'450?'

'Ain't dat many on de reservation.'

'300?'

'No, not dat many: not like long time ago.'

'Well! How many have you got?' the producer asked, his face pinching into worried lines and his voice losing its cheer and vitality.

'Maybe 10 ... 20 ... an' not very good dem.'

Keeee ... rice ...!' And the producer bit a chunk of cigar, crushing the other end in the ashtray. 'Are there any horses around here?'

'Yeah. Ranchers and farmers got dem.'

To his assistant, the producer instructed 'Get 500 horses by tomorrow evening. We have to shoot that scene next morning with the Indians charging down the slope.'

The interpreter whispered to his chief who shook his head.

'Say, mister,' the interpreter addressed the producer, 'how about saddles?'

'Saddles!' the word errupted.

'Yeah, saddles.'

There was a moment of cosmic silence. 'Saddles!' the producer repeated mouthing the word in disbelief. 'What do you mean ... saddles! You're all going to ride bare-back. This film is going to be authentic ... who ever heard of Indians riding on saddles ... supposed to be the finest horsemen in the world.'

The interpreter stiffened in fright at the thought that he might be one of the warriors to ride bare-back, and he hung his head.

'Don't know how to ride ... us. Forgot how ... long time ago ... Need saddles ... might fall off an' git hurt ... us.'

'This is incredible! ... unbelievable! ... no horses! ... can't ride! ...' the producer gasped as he sank into the chair. 'Keeeeee-rice.'

Hope waning from his brow and voice, the producer tried 'You still got bows an' arrows?'

The interpreter slouched even lower 'No! Got none of dem t'ings, us.'

'Buckskin outfits?'

'No,' another shameful shrug.

'Moccasins?'

'Some,' a little brighter.

'Head-dresses?'

'Maybe two, three – very old dem.'

'Teepees?'

'No more – live in houses us.'

'Anyone know Indian designs ... you know – war paint for warriors ... and horses?'

'Don't t'ink so ... everybody forgot.'

The producer groaned. 'This is astounding ... I can't believe it ... No horses ... can't ride ... no teepees ... no buckskin ... no ... no moccasins ... no ... no head-dresses ... and ... probably not even loin-cloths ...' and he was quivering. 'It boggles the mind.'

'What do we do?' the director asked.

For several moments the producer assessed the circumstances, and possessing an analytical mind he stated what needed to be done.

'With all our crew and cast here, and with our wagon-train and canon and horses, we can't very well go back now. We'll have to train these Indians to ride. Now ... Adams,' the producer's assistant, 'I want you to get on the line right away. Get a guy who knows something about Indians, from the Bureau of Indian Affairs. I want you to get maybe a dozen chiefs' outfits; and 500 loin-cloths, bows an' arrows for everyone, about a dozen head-dresses and moccasins ... everything we need to make these Indians ... *Indians*. Is that clear? And get those horses by tomorrow night.'

'Yes sir!'

'In the meantime, I'll call the studio office for more money. Let's get movin'.'

The assistant went out.

'How long we gotta stay in this miserable God-forsaken cow-town?' Ken Maynard inquired.

'Coupla weeks ... maybe.'

Ken Maynard groaned.

'Now!' directing his cigar at the interpreter and his remarks to the chief, the producer said, 'Tell the chief to get 500 young men to learn to ride bare-back; an' to learn fast.'

The interpreter apprised his chief of the message. The chief responded.

'He say $2.00 a day!'

'Keeee-rice! Tell him, okay!'

Two mornings later, 500 horses borrowed and rented from the local ranchers were delivered to the Indian reservation. 500 Crows began practising the art of horsemanship at once, and in earnest. And while it is true that many Crows shied away from the horses, just as many horses shied away from the Crows, so that there was much anxious circling of horses around Indians and Indians around horses, pulling and jerking midst the clamour of pleas 'Whoa! Whoa! Steady there Nellie! Easy there!' all in Crow;

and the horses perhaps because they were unfamiliar with Crow refusing to 'whoa.' Eventually, horses and Crows overcame their mutual distrust and suspicions and animosities to enable the Indians to mount their beasts.

There were of course some casualties, a few broken legs, sprained ankles, cracked ribs, and bruised behinds suffered by the novices on the first day. But by the third day most of the young men, while not accomplished equestrians, were able to ride passably well; that is, they fell off their mounts less often.

With the arrival of the equipment, bows and arrows, head-dresses, moccasins, loin-cloths, shipped by express from Washington, one day was set aside for the Crow warriors to practise shooting arrows from bows, first from a standing position and then from horseback. There were a few more casualties but nothing serious.

Along with the equipment came twelve make-up artists accompanied by an anthropologist to advise the artists in war-paint designs and to instruct the Crow in war-whooping. Twelve immense pavilions were erected, outside of each bill boards bearing symbols and markings representative of warrior war-paint and horse-paint designs. Each Indian having selected the design that best suited his taste and his horse entered a pavilion where he and his steed were painted, emerging at the other end of the massive tent looking very fierce and ready for war.

The movie moguls decided that they would film the siege of the wagon-train at 5 a.m. regardless of the readiness of the Indians. 'So what if a few Red-skins fall off their horses ... be more realistic.'

As planned and according to script ten Crows, dressed in white buck-skin heavily beaded and wearing war-bonnets to represent leadership, along with 450 warriors wearing only loin-cloths and armed with bows and arrows were assembled in a shallow depression unseen from the wagon-train. The horses pawed the ground and snorted and whinnied, while the director, producer, assorted assistants, and camera-men waited for the sun to cast its beams upon the wagon-train. When that critical moment occurred, signalled by an assistant with a wave of an arm, the director shouted 'Action! Cameras roll!'

450 Indians on 450 horses erupted over the lip of the valley a 'hoopin' an' a hollerin', their savage war-cries splitting the air while 1800 hooves thundered down the slope, shaking the earth. Wagon-train passengers spilled out of covered-wagons, splashed up from blankets, seized rifles, yelling 'Injuns! Injuns!' and hurled themselves behind boxes and crates and barrels and began firing. At one end of the valley, Ken Maynard on

his white charger waited for his cue; at the other end fifty cavalrymen waited to charge to the rescue. Bang! Bang! Bang! The Crows, a 'hoopin' an' a hollerin' were riding round and round the wagon-train, firing their arrows into the covered wagon and into boxes and crates and barrels. Bang! Bang! Bang! Round and round rode the Crows.

'Cut! Cut! Cut!' everyone was shouting. 'Cut! Cut! Cut!' everyone was waving his arms. Cut! Cut! Cut! 450 Crows, yelling whoa! whoa! whoa! brought their steeds to a halt.

The director, also on a horse, was livid with rage. He almost choked 'Somebody's gotta die; when you're shot, you fall off your horse and die. Don't you understand?'

The Indians nodded and grunted 'How! How!'

The director in disgust rode off leaving the cast and crew to repair 3000 to 4000 punctures and perforations inflicted by arrows on the canvas of the covered wagons. Six members of the cast suffering injuries from stray arrows needed medical attention. The Indians, with the arrows they had recovered, retired to the reservation to mend their weapons.

Just before sun-up next day there was a final admonition. 'Get it done right this time!' The warriors responded 'How! How!'

At the hand signal, 'Action! Cameras roll!' were uttered.

450 Indians on 450 horses boiled over the lip of the valley, a 'hoopin' an' a hollerin', their savage war cries rending the peace, while 1800 hooves pounded down the slope convulsing the ground. Wagon-train patrons scurried out of covered wagons, sprang from blankets, seized their rifles, yelling 'Injuns! Injuns!' and dove behind boxes and crates and barrels and began firing. Bang! Bang! Bang!

Seventy-five of the Crows, a 'hoopin' an' a hollerin' fell off their horses. Bang! Bang! Bang! 200 more Crows, a 'hoopin' an' a hollerin' spun off their mounts. Bang! Bang! Bang! The rest pitched off their steeds who fled in all directions.

'Cut! Cut! Cut!' everyone was shouting. 450 Crows suspended their moanin' an' a groanin' an' a rollin' on the ground, even though many had sustained real injuries, to listen to and to watch the director.

There was a torrent of curses, sulphuric glares, which eventually subsided into mutterings, the gist of which was relayed by the interpreter to the chiefs and warriors 'that not everyone should have fallen off his horse.' To this the chief replied $2.00.

The scene was re-enacted the next day without incident. After the shooting there were hand-shakes all around; and expressions of admiration tendered by Ken Maynard to the Crows for the speed with which they had developed horsemanship, remarking that 'it must be in-bred.'

Crew and cast were celebrating over wine and whiskey, cheese and crackers, when the film editor summoned the director. 'Come here and look at these,' he said, thrusting a magnifying glass to his superior. The director held the film strip against the light; he applied the magnifying glass to the stills.

'Sun-glasses! Keeee-rice ... sun-glasses ... those damned Indians. Keeee-rice ... what next ...'

When told, the producer kicked a chair after hurling a bottle into a corner: for close to ten minutes he cursed Indians. But it was useless, the scene had to be shot again.

Horses and Indians had to be recalled and reassembled for retakes for which the good chief demanded $2.00 for his people. It took another week before the wagon-train siege was filmed to the satisfaction of the producer and his director. In the interim there were two days of rain, one filming aborted by several Crows wearing watches, an extra filming of a prairie fire ignited by Ken Maynard that miscarried because several Crow warriors, supposedly dead, moved to avoid getting burned during a critical segment of the filming. When the first real epic of 'Cowboys and Indians' was finally done, the Crows were jubilant, indebted to their chief for the prosperity and lasting renown that he exacted during difficult times. The producer and director, cast and crew, departed in disquiet over having exceeded their budget.

But whatever doubts the producer and the director might have entertained were more than vindicated by reviews of the film in which the horsemanship of the Crow was acclaimed and the genius of the producer for his vision and for his foresight in using Indians in motion pictures.

▶   George Kenny was raised on the Lac Seul Reserve in northwestern Ontario. His first book, *Indians Don't Cry*, a collection of short stories and poems, was published in 1977.

The Bull-frogs Got Theirs
(as now I do)

As a boy, I would go out with my friends
and spear bull-frogs.
It didn't matter if each frog might someday
be turned into a prince
by some little girl's magic capable mind,

nor did it matter if the bull frogs
had feelings to feel
our jack-knife sharpened stakes
through their hearts;
as boys will do without caring
for small animal life,
my friends and I would launch our wooden
spears, yelling
like the warriors we imagined
ourselves to be ...

And as I'm older now, often I see people
with word-spears cut me down.
It doesn't matter if someday I might
become a prince
by the power of some woman's love,
nor does it matter if I
have feelings to feel
their verbal spears sharply
through my heart;
as people will act without caring
about others,
people, even now, spit their word-
spears, sneering
like the gods they imagine
themselves to be.

George Kenny, *Indians Don't Cry* (Toronto: Chimo Publishing 1977) 18

▶ Wayne Keon, part Algonkin and part Iroquois, lives in Elliott Lake, Ontario;
his work has appeared in a number of periodicals.

the eye
of the raven
black upon black
speck in the face
of the sun
flies so high
flies so high
flies so high

and you have been tricked
for even tho i am raven
i am man
and even tho i am man
you have been tricked
and i do not fly so high
in the face
of the sun
and the great
mystery
flies so high
flies so high
flies so high

David Day and Marilyn Bowering, eds., *Many Voices* (Vancouver: J.J. Douglas Ltd. 1977) 72

▶ John Snow, chief of the Wesley Band of Stoney Indians and a United
Church minister, was born in Morley, Alberta. In his book, *These Mountains are our Sacred Places*, he writes about his people's culture and history.
He begins by describing a pilgrimage to the Annual Indian Ecumenical Conference in Morley in 1976.

The sun rises with a blood-red headdress of prairie clouds throwing fiery
colours to the mountains. Smoke rises lazily from the teepee fires. All the
living things awake around the Indian religious camp in the foothills. A
lonely eagle rides the air currents, almost out of sight. Half a mile away a
buffalo bull welcomes the day as he calls to his herd. A magpie announces
his arrival with his chatter as he teases an old dog lying beside the teepee
entrance. Below the huge teepee encampment, the rustling mountain
streams can be heard. A tethered horse whinnies and stamps his hooves,
and a grasshopper joins in the medley of sounds and activity of a new
day.

From out of a teepee an old man stoops, carrying his pipe bag carefully.
He calls out and is joined by four or five men as he walks to a small hill
overlooking the camp.

On the hill, the men arrange themselves in a circle. The old man offers
a prayer to the Creator, a daily thanksgiving for the glory of another summer day, as he lights the braided sweetgrass and prepares the pipe.

The mountains seem closer in the morning light, enclosing the whole
valley in a great cathedral which the Great Spirit built for Himself and

His people. The old man's prayer speaks of the Creator's love and His protection for His red children. The pipe, now lit, is passed from hand to hand, with *reverence*, speaking of the unity and brotherhood of all in the Great Spirit's creation. In each hand the pipestem is directed to the four winds, east, south, west, and north, acknowledging the dominion of the Creator, and only the Creator, over all things. In this way man acknowledges, with humility, that he is only a part of the Creation, that he is dependent, that he, too, must submit to the natural laws of the Creator. The herbs in the pipe are consumed, the ashes are knocked out, the pipe is returned to the bag, and the men stand and return to their families in their teepees to break their fast.

Ten thousand years ago? Perhaps a century? No! This occurred last summer and the summer before and each summer for the past six years ...

Nearly every morning I take my hunting dogs and go out and spend some time among the hills, the valleys, and the woodlands of Stoney country – my home. And, whenever I go out, be it during the colourful fall, on frosty winter mornings, in the fragrance of spring, or early during the sun-drenched days of summer, I am always conscious of the mountains on the horizon. These sacred rock monuments remind me that the Great Creator is timeless, while the refreshing mountain springs and the wildlife that inhabit His hills remind me that He is generous and loving.

The legends of long ago tell how close my people have always been to these mountains. They tell how our braves sojourned in them in search of their calling. They remind us that these mountains are our sacred places.

Yesterday the mountains were covered with snow, and the snows were red with the fires of dawn; today they are wrapped in a film of mist; tomorrow they will be dressed in another natural garment. Their appearance is always altering – yet their reality never changes. They remain as they were in their creation.

The whiteman has carved his roads and railways across them and stopped their waters with his hydro dams. Yet the mountains remain – they are immovable. In some areas our mountains have been left untouched as yet by technology, development, and the accompanying pollution. In those areas, spirits of long ago still remain; the mountains retain their sacred trust as the dwelling places of the spirits.

My people are like the mountains ...

So, as I run with my hunting dogs among the hills in the morning of a new day, the question comes ringing in my ears over and over again: 'How do we, as the Great Spirit's people, build a path into the next hun-

dred years?' And the answer comes loud and clear to me: 'The Great
Spirit has been our guide in the past, He is our guide today, and He will
be our guide into the future.' As I climb the hills and look over the
valleys and think of our heritage, I seem to get new strength and courage
as I look to the future.

As I stand on top of the hill which overlooks the beautiful Bow River
Valley, with the sacred shining mountains in the background as a refuge,
I am reminded of our proud heritage, the little babies in their moss bags,
the beautiful maidens, the brave warriors, the medicine women, the wise
elders, and the buffalo that roamed as monarch of the plains, the eagle
that guarded the skies. They all speak of brotherhood and oneness with
the universe.

As I look across the beautiful valley, it seems as if I am looking across
the next one hundred years. I am reassured about the future because I
have faith in the Great Spirit, the Creator, and I am reminded of the
words of the Hebrew prophet of old and I repeat:

They that wait upon the Great Spirit shall renew their strength,
They shall mount up with wings as eagles,
They shall run and not be weary,
They shall walk and not faint. [Is. 40:31].

The old path is a proven path to travel on, it has withstood the test of
time, not only over centuries, but over thousands of years. This is the path
my ancestors walked and it shall be the path my future generations will
walk on and on and on. It is the path of the Great Spirit, the Creator.

Our proud history is unequalled and unsurpassed on this Great Island.
Each of us can hold his or her head high, as one of the original people of
this beautiful land, and say, 'I am an Indian.' The Stoney philosophy of
living in harmony with nature and in accord with the creations of the
Great Spirit will be the theme of many peoples, cultures, and languages
who live on this Great Island in the future.

We are the Great Spirit's people! These mountains are our sacred places!

Chief John Snow, *These Mountains are our Sacred Places: The Story of the Stoney Indians*
(Toronto: Samuel Stevens 1977) 142, 152, 160

▶   Rita Joe, a Micmac, was born in Whycocomagh, Cape Breton Island.

When I was small
I used to help my father
Make axe handles.

Coming home from the wood with a bundle
Of maskwi, snawey, aqamoq,
My father would chip away,
Carving with a crooked knife,
Until a well-made handle appeared,
Ready to be sand-papered
By my brother.

When it was finished
We started another,
Sometimes working through the night
With me holding a lighted shaving
To light their way
When our kerosene lamp ran dry.

Then in the morning
My mother would be happy
That there would be food today
When my father sold our work.

———

Your buildings, tall, alien,
Cover the land;
Unfeeling concrete smothers,
    windows glint
Like water to the sun.
No breezes blow
Through standing trees;
No scent of pine lightens my burden.

I see your buildings rising skyward,
    majestic,
Over the trails where once men walked,
Significant rulers of this land
Who still hold the aboriginal title
In their hearts
By traditions known
Through eons of time.

Relearning our culture is not difficult,
Because those trails I remember
And their meaning I understand.

While skyscrapers hide the heavens,
They can fall.

Poems of Rita Joe (Halifax: Abanaki Press 1978) 17, 4

▶ Midnight Sun, a member of the Anishnawbeg nation (Ojibway), is a freelance writer living in Toronto.

windswept snow
dancing like tumbleweed,
snaking down the highway
in rippling waves
shadows in the distant
cloud my eyes

———

intertwined,
we the rose and the thorn
both beauty and strength

the thorn,
shielding, protecting
the soft petals

the delicate flower
deep red, blood red

our blood
mingling over the rocks
in the stream

▶ Daniel David Moses is a Delaware from Ohsweken on the Six Nations Reserve; his first collection of poems, *Delicate Bodies*, was published in 1980.

Falling Song

There was the sweet but reedy
honking of geese coming down
this morning with rain over
rush hour streets, coming
through like bells that celebrate.

I got right up, pushing up
close to the sooty window
pane. I peered out and up through
the weather, imagining
that that line of winged dots would

be shifting as if waves moved
easily through them, as if
waves floated them south. I wanted
to catch them riding, spots on
the wake of the wind, marking

the certain direction of
their migration. But I got
no satisfaction. Mist kept
them mysterious, quickly
dampening their call. Leaning

over the sill, I gaped at
a window shade dull sky, at
a hollow city, and felt
like I'd missed a parade I
would have wanted to follow.

A Visit in Mid-Summer

You now are little
more, Grand
father, than the blue wool
rumples of your blanket and the berry

blue veins threading
through the skin of your untanned
feet. You are not

fat enough. Your body's
receding, though your hands are still
the same size, and in your pillow
the same hollow is full
of your head with its dried
apple face and insistent
breath. In the dull after

noon of this upper
bedroom your glasses are clean
ponds your eyes rise
though, black as the eyes of
the God of All Frogs, so wise
they can take the whole
ceiling in. Your voice, an old

leaf, scratches the air. *You can't live
for ever*, it says. I pour you more
tea and through the window we
hear the maples and spruces are
sifting the gusts from the August
thick atmosphere. The sky is so much and
rushing, and soon it will rain here.

Daniel David Moses, *Delicate Bodies* (Vancouver: blewointmentpress 1980)

▶ Verna J. Kirkness, a Cree born on the Fisher River Indian Reserve in Manitoba, is assistant professor and supervisor of the Native Indian Teacher Education Program at the University of British Columbia. The following excerpts
are from a speech she gave at the World Assembly of First Nations Education
Conference in Regina, Saskatchewan, on 20 July 1982.

It is an honour for me to participate in this historic occasion of the World
Assembly of First Nations, the largest gathering of Indigenous people ever
held. It is also a privilege to have the opportunity to share educational

views and experiences with people of other First Nations of the World. I'm sure we all look forward to the outcome of this Conference designed to generate 'Agreements and Protocols' to be signed by the First Nations of our respective countries.

In the short time available, I will briefly outline the history of Indian Education in Canada. I will attempt to delineate the major problems and offer alternate actions that may be taken toward resolving the problems.

Education has been a part of the lives of Indian people of our country from time immemorial. Prior to the arrival of the European to this country, the Indian people provided their own form of education. The teaching was done by the family, parents, grandparents, aunts and uncles. Each had a unique part to play in the development of the child.

The most important aspect of traditional Indian education was that of spiritual learning. It is recorded that the Indian had the most spiritual civilization the world has ever known. His approach to all life and thought was spiritual.

Another aspect of traditional Indian education was that of behavioural learning. These teachings emphasized pride, humbleness, truthfulness, bravery, cleanliness and kindness; respect for the elderly; respect for nature; learning to share, to be co-operative; learning to be silent at times. Silence was regarded as the cornerstone of character. As Chief Wabasha stated, 'Guard your tongue in youth and in age you may mature a thought that will be of service to your people.'

Traditional Indian education was inextricably linked with economics. Learning was for living – for survival. Boys and girls were taught at an early age to utilize and cope with their environment. Independence and self-reliance were valued concepts of our forefathers. Boys and girls learned how to hunt, trap, fish and farm. They learned whatever livelihood their particular environment offered.

This was the traditional education of our people. This was an education where the community was the classroom and its members, its teachers. Each adult was responsible for each child, to see that he learned all that he needed to live a good life.

What was the effect of this type of education provided to Indian children? It was very positive and very relevant because it addressed itself to the times, to the total being, to the family, and to the total community. It held in high esteem, Indian culture, values and customs. This process contributed to the positive development of the child's potential as an individual in a society and to the image he had of himself as an Indian person.

Then came the change.

From the early seventeenth Century, Indian people were exposed to education designed and directed by missionaries and federal and provincial civil servants. The missionary approach was to 'civilize and Christianize.' This gave way in later years to the governments' approach of assimilation under the aegis of integration. These hundreds of years have been a dismal failure in terms of educating the masses of Indian people ... This failure has been attributed to several factors, namely: the absence of a clear philosophy of education with goals and objectives, failure to provide a meaningful program based on Indian reality, a lack of qualified teaching staff and inadequate facilities, and, most important, the absence of parental involvement in the education of their children ...

Indian people recognize education as the key to equal opportunity and to social and economic mobility. To make education meet Indian needs, there must be Indian input, Indian influence on the education process on reserves and in provincial and territorial schools. There must be improvement in the quality of education and in the creation of a learning environment which will give Indian children the chance to know and understand their own language, culture and history and to develop their unique talents to the maximum potential ...

There is some evidence that a new system is on the horizon that will enable us to report in ensuing years a totally improved education system for Indians in Canada. This must happen or Indians will be a vanishing race.

▶ Alanis Obomsawin, an Abenaki woman raised on the Odanak Reserve in Quebec and later in Trois-Rivières, now lives in Montreal and produces films for the National Film Board. She sings and tells stories in six Indian languages as well as in French and in English. In this article, she describes herself as 'A Bridge between Two Worlds.'

I don't know the exact place of my birth. I do know that I was born around Lebanon, New Hampshire. I lived there for six months, then my mother returned to her reservation in Canada. I'm from the Abenaki Nation. The word comes from Wamabenaki and means 'People of Sunrise.' We are eastern woodland Indians. Originally our land was all of New England. Groups of Abenaki people still live in Vermont and in Maine. On the reservation in Canada, I lived with my aunt who had six other children. We lived mainly outside, whether it was winter or summer. I was very fortunate to know my aunt and an old man that was my mother's cousin. He told me a lot about the history of our Nation. He also taught me many songs and stories. Those two people gave me something special and strong. It was my best time.

I left the reservation when I was nine. We settled in a small town in Canada. That's where all the problems started. We were the only Indian family there. It was bad. I remember sleep as being my best moments. I had such fantastic dreams about animals and birds. But it was the bad time of my life. I attended a French school in the town's slums. That's when they told me that I was poor, that I was dirty, and that we were savages. The tall lone savage in the back of the classroom. When I grew older, the same people who had beaten me up for years and years all of a sudden started flirting with me. It was strange. It took me a long time to lose the hate. I really had a lot of hate in me. Those memories are in my songs. I started collecting music and singing professionally about twenty-five years ago. I always used to sing. I remember rocking my rocking chair and singing all the time, as a young girl. Later I started singing for friends. But I never had any idea that I would go and sing on the stage in front of other people ...

I started writing songs about fifteen years ago. Mainly making sounds of what was happening. What I was seeing at the time, and of the visions and dreams I had. I put them into sounds for singing. I also sing traditional sounds and tell stories and legends. I make songs in Indian, in English and in French. It all depends on how it's speaking to me. I don't really think about the audience when I'm singing. I feel I have to sing what is real to me, through me. If they feed me something, it's not because I'm thinking of them. They're either giving me something or taking something from me and it makes me feel a certain way and that's what comes out. I'm very insecure until the last minute because I don't know what those people are. What they're going to make me say. I don't even make rules in terms of a message. It's experience of my life and intuition. I can only go by that. I have to admit that I'm a very emotional person. I live my life that way. So every word is like pulling a tooth out. It has to do with what happens around me, or in me.

... Sometimes I'm afraid because I don't know how to read or write music. I never will be able to be in that category. I don't follow those notes. I don't know how. Indian singing doesn't follow the same scales. At least that's what I've been told. My purpose is to preserve and maintain the history and culture of Native people. That's why I sing. That's why I make films.

I started making films about twelve years ago. I make mostly documentary films. I've produced several films for children because I feel that's where it all starts. I want our children to know their languages. To know who they are before anything else, before anybody else. If you know who you are, you can stand anywhere in the world and not be afraid. If you're always told that your parents were dirty, ugly and pagans, you know what the hell you think you're going to look like when you look at yourself in the mirror, because you are a reflection of what they told you; and it takes a long time to figure out that it's alright to be what you are, and not what they said about you. It shouldn't take half of your life to figure that out. You should know who you are when you first begin and then deal with the rest of the world ...

Sometimes I feel like a bridge. It's good that I have the responsibility of being a producer and director with the National Film Board of Canada. It's good to be in a position of power. It's important. The decisions of what goes into the films comes from us. It doesn't come from the outside. It comes from the people who are in the films and from myself. I can consult with the people who are involved and we can decide together. I'm really a bridge between two worlds. It comes through in my songs, my stories and my film work. I'm a fighter, a free spirit, but to be a free spirit at this time is very painful. You're choked by everything around you. You go outside and you're choked by the pollution. You're choked by the cars. You're choked by the traffic lights. You're choked by the law that tells you what you should be, what you have to be. How can you be free if you have to think of all those things they tell you to be. It puts to sleep what you are.

So to become free you have to fight. You have to fight and there is no war. Your soul, your spirit is wanting to breathe, wanting to express itself but you walk outside and you can forget it. So you have to be damn strong to be able to allow your spirit to live the way it should. You cry all the time. It's like dying and nobody buries you. Your real feelings are constantly being suppressed. You're not even allowed to be a child. Just like when the different tribes signed the treaties and they were told, 'As long as the grass will grow, as long as the water will flow.' The people never knew that the newcomers would be able to turn rivers the other way and pretty soon there would be no grass. No one thought that would happen. So who knows what they will do. All I know is that the power of soul, the spirit and the brain is extraordinary.

I'm sure that long ago all beings were able to communicate without traveling. Communicate through their brains, through their souls, through their visions. People were able to do magic. They didn't have all this shit we have to put up with. That's why they had peace in themselves. They

could spend time and become very well educated with what they were –
through their brains, through their experiences. They could perform
operations. They could cure people. They could bring down good or bad
people. They had powers which today cost millions and millions of dollars
to have just a tiny bit. People have forgotten this. Thank god there's an
underground movement in terms of our religion, in terms of our medicine
men and in terms of how it is important to not listen to the threatening
force that tries to manipulate you. You have to look at what is, and work from
that. In other words, work from inside. Work from your heart, and then you
go out. Not out, and then tear up your heart – there's nothing left.

I think the damage done to human beings starts in school. It's the
teaching. To be stamped by the title teacher is not a compliment. Some
people who have that title take it for granted that they're smarter than
other people. They begin to oppress those they feel are inferior, which is a
word that came with the newcomers. In our language there is no word to
say inferior or superiority or equality because we are equal, it's a known
fact. But life has become very complicated since the newcomers came
here. And how does your spirit react to it? It's like they're going to bury me
tomorrow at five o'clock when the door bell rings. It's painful. You have to be
strong to walk through the storm. I know I'm a bridge between two worlds.
All I ask is for people to wash their feet before they try to walk on me.

Free Spirits: Annals of the Insurgent Imagination (San Francisco: City Lights Books 1982) 49-52

▶ Lenore Keeshig-Tobias, born on the Cape Croker Reserve in Ontario, is a
founder of *Sweetgrass* magazine.

Running on the March Wind

I

i have talked
to you in twilight
before sleep
but never
for very long

i have wondered
about you despairingly
but never
for very long

knowing you
to be a trickster
i have
been cautious

and yet this morning
i dreamed of you
you were running
on the wind

going north
in disguise

ii

the others said
LOOK there
goes Santa Claus

that's not Santa Claus
i said
that's Nanabush

you wore a long serge
coat bound with a most
colourful sash, but i knew

it was you i saw
your glinting eyes brown
face and long black hair

but the others didn't
seem to care
the card game and table

talk were
too involving

iii

i hurried to the door
Nanabush i said calling
where are you going?

you stopped and
huddled in the snow
neath a prickly bush

Nanabush i said
why don't you visit
you looked back at me

were you goading me?

iv

then i held you
you cuddly old
teddy bear rabbit

i said things to you
and tried not to
frighten you

where are you going
Nanabush where are
you going why haven't

you come
this way before?

v

i held you you cuddly
old teddy bear rabbit
then let you go

north
somewhere

don't forget
to come back
i called

don't forget
to come back

we need you Nanabush

vi

i dreamed of you passing
through my dreams heading
north this morning

were you goading me?

II

so, Nanabush
where have you been
all these years

down south
somewhere

in some
Peruvian mountain
village maybe

i wondered about
where you had gone

thought maybe
you had died
rather than just
faded away like
some dusty old robe

but ah ha
i caught you trying
to slip through
my dream unnoticed

Nanabush
where have you been
all these years

Machu Picchu?

the women there,
i hear, weave such
colourful sashes

Ontario Indian, v, 4 (May 1982) 56

▶ Jim Morris is an Ojibwa from Big Trout Lake in northern Ontario. His
play, *Ayash*, a stage adaptation of an ancient Ojibwa legend, was performed
in its full version in Sioux Lookout on 18 February 1983 and went on to
tour northwestern Ontario. Several scenes of the play are reproduced here.

SCENE ONE

(THE NARRATOR WALKS ON STAGE)
NARRATOR: Pooshoo! This play is based on the legend of Ayash, one of the
most popular stories among the Cree and Ojibway. It concerns the plight
of the Son of Ayash who is punished for something he did not do.

The son did not know that he had been falsely accused by one of the
wives of Ayash.

As punishment, the son was left by his father on a small island far out
in the great waters.

The journey home was difficult. He had to overcome certain evil characters along the way who tried to kill him and stop him from going home.

The son was able to reach his home again and to confront his father Ayash, the one who had wrongly punished him.

Come! Come with me into the land of Ayash ... we will see why he was punished ...

(The scene will open inside a wigwam. The Son of Ayash and his mother are inside, the mother is sitting on the ground on the left and the son is still sleeping, covered with a blanket. The son gets up. He wears few garments.)

MOTHER: My son! Be careful today ...

SON: (LOOKS STARTLED) Why, Mother?

MOTHER: I had a dream last night about your father and ... Kitōosis ... your father's young wife. (SHE ALMOST JUMPS UP AND BLURTS OUT) I dreamt that she was chasing you ... running after you ...

SON: (STANDS UP) She would not do that.

MOTHER: You do not know Kitoosis ... (GOES BACK TO HER SEAT ON THE GROUND) ... and you do not know your father Ayash ... if he is unable to keep her satisfied, she might look for someone else more her age ... someone like you ...

(AYASH ENTERS THE WIGWAM)

AYASH: Koosis! We are going hunting today.

SON: It is early to go out now.

AYASH: No, it is not. I say we go now. (MOVES BETWEEN THE MOTHER AND SON) Have you eaten your morning meal yet, my son?

SON: No, father.

AYASH: What ...! (TURNS TO THE MOTHER) You haven't fed my son yet? (RUNS OVER AND KICKS THE MOTHER; KNOCKS HER DOWN) Feed my son! We are going hunting today ... for moose ... for beaver, and partridges ... (MOVES TOWARDS THE DOORWAY) We will leave as soon as you are ready, my son! (HE LEAVES)

SON: (RUSHES TO THE MOTHER) Mother ... are you hurt?

MOTHER: (SLOWLY RISES) No ... I am not hurt. I must go out now and do my chores ... I must get more wood. (SHE STANDS UP AND WALKS TO THE DOORWAY; THEN SHE STOPS AND SPEAKS ONCE MORE TO THE SON) Eat your food, my son. Take your time. There is no need to rush.

SON: Yes, mother.

(THE MOTHER LEAVES AND THE SON SITS DOWN AND BEGINS TO EAT FROM A BOWL. THE YOUNG WIFE COMES INSIDE.)

YOUNG WIFE: Have you seen your Father this morning?

SON: He came to tell me that we are going hunting today ... and that we would be leaving as soon as I was ready.

YOUNG WIFE: That's what he told me! ... and then, he just disappeared!

SON: If he told you that already, why didn't you wait for him inside your wigwam?

YOUNG WIFE: Oh! I ... wanted him to help me untie this belt ... so that ... I can take my dress off. I cannot wear this dress to the hunt. Your father ties it around my waist so hard. It's hard for me to untie behind my back. Will you untie it for me? (SHE TURNS HER BACK. THE SON STANDS UP AND BEGINS TO UNTIE THE BELT. SHE REACHES BACK AND FEELS HIS HAND.) You have such warm hands. They are smooth and yet so strong ... Not like your father's. His are so old and wrinkled, and cold ... (SHE TURNS TO FACE HIM) And ... your arms are so strong. Hold me ...

SON: (SOFTLY) No ... (THE YOUNG WIFE TRIES AGAIN)

YOUNG WIFE: Come ... it will do no harm ... you and I are friends.

SON: (AFTER A WHILE) No! (TURNS TO THE AUDIENCE) You are my father's wife.

YOUNG WIFE: (ANGRILY) Your father is an old man. He makes me feel old. (STOPS; BECOMES SEDUCTIVE AGAIN) Look at me ... am I not young? I want to feel your strong arms around me. It will give me a feeling of being young again ... if only for just a little while. Hold me ...

SON: No!!! (OUT TO THE AUDIENCE) My mother had a dream ... She warned me of you.

YOUNG WIFE: Your mother!!! ... your mother is a decrepit, old woman! She is sterile and sexless ... What does she know about loving a young man?

SON: I will have nothing to do with you! I want you to leave this wigwam ... Now!

YOUNG WIFE: AKAIEE! I'll get even with you for this! I'll make sure that you get into real trouble with your stupid father! You're going to be sorry for this! Just wait! (SHE RUSHES OUT)

THE VOICE OF AYASH: My son! It is time to go!

SON: I am coming, father. (EXIT)

NARRATOR: They went out hunting that day, the three of them ... Ayash the father, his son and Ayash's young wife. The young woman checked her snares. They were set up to catch just about anything: rabbits, squirrels, weasels ...

On this day, she caught a partridge. It was still alive.

She bared her thighs and held the kicking bird close, and through her anger felt no pain. At day's end, they returned home. The son of Ayash, to his mother's wigwam. Ayash and his young wife, to their own.

Now, let's see what happens.

(NARRATOR MOVES OFF STAGE)

SCENE TWO

(The scene takes place inside the wigwam of Ayash the father. It is evening. Ayash and his young wife are inside the wigwam and they are getting ready to retire for the night.)

AYASH: (LYING DOWN IN HIS SLEEPING PLACE) That was a very good hunt we had today. Ten partridges, four rabbits, and one young beaver. Now, we will have enough to eat for a few days.

YOUNG WIFE: (SHE IS SITTING DEMURELY, UNTYING HER BRAIDS) Yes, we will.

AYASH: There. Now, I am ready for the night. (HE HAS FINISHED LYING DOWN. HE LIES THERE WITH HIS HANDS BEHIND HIS HEAD FOR A FEW MOMENTS, LOOKING UP INTO THE DARK SKY, PAST THE POLES OF THE WIGWAM. THEN HE TURNS HIS GAZE AT HIS YOUNG WIFE AND HE GETS UP ON ONE ELBOW) Come, lie down with me.

YOUNG WIFE: Wait! I will be ready in a while. I must go outside first before I lay down. (SHE LEAVES)

AYASH: (HE IS STILL UP ON ONE ELBOW, LOOKING WHERE SHE JUST WENT OUT) Hurry up! I can't wait all night. (SHE COMES BACK INSIDE AND KNEELS DOWN BESIDE THE OLD MAN WHO IS UP ON ONE ELBOW. SHE TAKES THE BLANKET OFF HER SHOULDERS. THEN HE CARESSES HER ARM WITH HIS RIGHT HAND. THEN SHE TAKES OFF ANOTHER GARMENT.) Ahh ... that's better. (HE LIES DOWN) Now, come! Sleep with me.

YOUNG WIFE: (SHE STRETCHES) I am so tired tonight ... (SHE YAWNS) I must be all tired out from that hunt today ... Are we going to sleep right away?

AYASH: Maybe. Maybe not. (SHE TAKES A BLANKET AND COVERS AYASH WITH IT. THEN, SHE CRAWLS UNDERNEATH THE BLANKET, TOO, BESIDE HIM. SHE MOVES AROUND UNDER THE BLANKET AS SHE TURNS TO PLACE HER BACK TO HIM. MORE MOVEMENT CAN BE SEEN UNDER THE BLANKET NOW AS AYASH MOVES UP CLOSER TO HIS WIFE. THERE IS MORE MOVEMENT UNDER THE BLANKET AND SOME MUFFLED MURMURING. SUDDENLY, AYASH SITS ABRUPTLY.) You have scratch marks on your legs! (LOUDLY) What happened to you?

YOUNG WIFE: It was nothing. I accidentally scratched myself.

AYASH: (HE STARTS TO GET UP) You couldn't have scratched yourself that much. Someone must have done that to you ...

YOUNG WIFE: (STARTS TO SIT UP) It was no one. It was an accident.

AYASH: You're lying! (HE GRABS ONE OF HER WRISTS AND PULLS HER UP INTO A SITTING POSITION. HE GRABS HER FACE IN HIS RIGHT HAND.) Look at me ... tell me the truth ... Did somebody do that to you?

YOUNG WIFE: No.

AYASH: (SLAPS HER) You're lying ...

YOUNG WIFE: Don't ... (SHE HOLDS HER HEAD AWAY FROM HIM)

AYASH: Tell me the truth! Did someone do this?

YOUNG WIFE: Yes ...

AYASH: (HE STANDS UP AND FACES HER. SHE HAS HER HANDS OVER HER FACE. HE HAS BOTH FISTS CLUTCHED TIGHTLY.) Who was it?

YOUNG WIFE: It was nothing. Let us forget it.

AYASH: (TURNS TO THE AUDIENCE WITH ANGER, FISTS CLENCHED) No! I'll find the man who did this to you. I'll kill him! Nobody can do this to my wife and get away with it.

YOUNG WIFE: (SHE SAYS THIS IN A PLEADING VOICE) There was no harm done ... I was able to get away from him ... without him doing anything to me ... (SHE REACHES UP AND GENTLY TAKES ONE OF HIS HANDS IN HERS. HE STANDS THERE IN ANGER, TAKING DEEP LABOURED BREATHS.) Let us forget it. There was no harm done. Come on, let us lie down ...

AYASH: No! Whoever did this to you must be punished ... (HE GRABS HER BY THE HAIR AND TURNS HER HEAD TO FACE HIM) Who was it?

YOUNG WIFE: Owww! ... You're hurting me ...

AYASH: I said, who was it?

YOUNG WIFE: It was your own son! He did this to me! (SHE SAYS THIS PRE-TENDING THAT SHE IS SOBBING AND CRYING)

AYASH: (HE LOOKS SHOCKED. HE RELEASES HIS GRIP ON THE YOUNG WIFE'S HAIR. HE LOOKS BEWILDERED.) My son? (HE LOOKS AT HIS HANDS) How can this be? (HE LOOKS AT HIS WIFE) Did you do something to attract him?

YOUNG WIFE: No, I didn't. (SHE IS WHIMPERING) I didn't want to tell you ... but you forced me ...

AYASH: It is a good thing I noticed. Otherwise, my son might have gone unpunished for this crime against me. But, he will pay. (HE SHAKES HIS FIST AT THE SKY AND SAYS OUT LOUD) He will pay for what he did to me! I'll make sure of that.

(HE MOVES TO HIS SLEEPING PLACE AND SLUMPS DOWN)

YOUNG WIFE: (SHE MOVES TO AYASH) Will you turn around and hold me for a while?

AYASH: (BRUSQUELY) No! Go to sleep! Tomorrow ... I will deal with that no good son of mine. I'll show him that he can not make a fool of me. (HE PULLS HIS COVERS OVER HIMSELF. THE YOUNG WIFE LIES DOWN BESIDE HIM)

SCENE THREE

(THE NARRATOR WALKS ON STAGE)

NARRATOR: The next day, Ayash told his son that they were going out to look for seagull eggs. This time, there were only two of them; this time, with no weapons. Ayash told his son that he was looking for a certain island. They paddled and paddled, passing many islands along the way with many seagulls, far away in the great waters, until they came to a rocky, little island.

(THE NARRATOR MOVES OFF STAGE)

(AYASH AND HIS SON WALK ON STAGE)

AYASH: Well, this is it. (SPREADS HIS ARMS) This is the island ...

SON: (HE IS LOOKING AROUND AND UP IN THE SKY) But ... there are no seagulls around.

AYASH: (LOOKS UP AT THE SKY, STARTLED)

Huh! I wonder where they are? (SCRATCHING HIS HEAD) There used to be a lot of them around here. They must be out somewhere ... probably hunting for their own food. Why don't you go up and look around?

THE SON: Okay. I'll go up and take a look. (THE SON MOVES OFF, LOOKING HERE AND THERE ON THE GROUND. AS SOON AS THE SON IS OUT OF SIGHT, AYASH TURNS AROUND AND HEADS BACK. HE IS ALMOST OFF STAGE WHEN HE HEARS THE VOICE OF THE SON.)

THE VOICE OF THE SON: Father! There are no eggs around here!

AYASH: (STOPS, TURNS AROUND AND YELLS BACK) Keep looking, my son! There must be some eggs around somewhere. You'll find them. (HE TURNS AROUND AND LEAVES)

(AFTER A WHILE, THE SON WANDERS BACK ON STAGE, LOOKING THIS WAY AND THAT WAY. WHEN HE ARRIVES AT THE SPOT WHERE HE HAD LEFT HIS FATHER, HE LOOKS AROUND, PUZZLED.)

THE SON: Father, where are you? (HE STARTS TO LOOK AROUND. HE RUNS TO WHERE AYASH WENT OFF STAGE.) Father! (HE LOOKS BEWILDERED) Father! Where are you going? Are you leaving me? (THERE IS NO RESPONSE) Father! Are you leaving me behind?

(NOW WE HEAR THE VOICE OF AYASH)

THE VOICE OF AYASH: Father? Who is your father? Didn't you scratch the thighs of Kitoosis?

THE SON: Father! I didn't do anything! (NO RESPONSE) Father ... come back. (HE FALLS TO HIS KNEES) Don't leave me here. (HE SUDDENLY REALIZES THAT HIS FATHER IS NOT COMING BACK, AND HE BECOMES FILLED WITH GRIEF. HE BEGINS TO CRY. HE LOOKS OUT ONCE MORE OVER THE WATER BUT HIS FATHER IS ALREADY OUT OF SIGHT. HE FALLS ON HIS HANDS, HANGS HIS HEAD AND WEEPS.) Father ... (HE SLUMPS DOWN ON STAGE AND REMAINS STILL)

[The Son of Ayash, marooned by his father on the barren island, is fed by the birds and animals, but they cannot get him to shore. He is rescued by a Giant Snake, his grandfather, who is struck down by the Thunderbirds. His grandmother gives him food, clothing, and weapons to defend himself on his difficult journey home against the likes of Old Man Legs and two blind old women with long, sharp elbows; through her guidance he sees through their trickery and removes the threat of their evil ways from his people. He arrives home to avenge his father's unjust action.]

SCENE SEVEN

(THE LIGHTS BECOME VERY BRIGHT. THERE ARE BIRDS SINGING; BRIGHT AND CLEAR IS THE SONG OF THE ROBIN, AND CHICKADEES. THE MOTHER WALKS ON STAGE FROM UPSTAGE LEFT. SHE WEARS A SHAWL. SHE WALKS TO CENTER STAGE AND SITS DOWN, DIAGONALLY FACING RIGHT. SHE IS CRYING. THE SON WALKS ONSTAGE FROM UPSTAGE RIGHT. HIS HAIR IS BRAIDED. HE STOPS TO THE LEFT OF THE MOTHER.)

THE SON: Why are you crying?

THE MOTHER: I have lost my son.

THE SON: Don't cry. Your son is home.

THE MOTHER: Do not make fun of me ... I am already very sad as it is ... I do not need you to make fun of me.

THE SON: Mother! I have arrived home! (THE MOTHER LOOKS UP STARTLED. THE SON WALKS A LITTLE TO STAGE RIGHT TO FACE HER)

THE MOTHER: My son! Is it really you? But you are a MAN ...

THE SON: Mother, stand up. (THE MOTHER STANDS AND WALKS TO THE SON. SHE TOUCHES HIS FACE.)

THE MOTHER: My son. It is you. (THEY HUG EACH OTHER) You have really arrived.

THE SON: Why do you have these burn marks all over your face and hands?

THE MOTHER: (SHE TURNS TOWARDS THE AUDIENCE) It is your father. Whenever I want to hold his new son, he tells Kitoosis not to let me hold it.

209

He says I will dirty the baby. He scoops up hot coals and cinders from the fire and throws them at me ... this is why I am burned up like this.
THE SON: Go back to the camp and put wood on the fire. Make an opening in the fire and ask to hold the baby.
THE MOTHER: He will say, 'No. She will dirty it.'
THE SON: This time, he will allow you to hold the baby. I want you to cast the baby into the fire and run back here to me.
THE MOTHER: But why ... why must this be done? Is it not enough that you were lost and now you are home again? Why should there be more trouble now?
THE SON: My father and his foolish young wife must be punished for what they did to me. My father must not be allowed to think that he can do this and get away with it. He must be punished. (HE LOOKS AT HER) Go! We must hurry.
(THE MOTHER RUSHES OFF STAGE LEFT. THE SON EXISTS UPSTAGE RIGHT.)

SCENE EIGHT

(THERE ARE VOICES BACKSTAGE)
THE VOICE OF AYASH: Run. Run. That's the way. That's where you'll find your son. (THE MOTHER COMES RUNNING FROM UPSTAGE LEFT, ACROSS CENTRE STAGE AND FALLS STAGE RIGHT. THE SON WALKS ON FROM UPSTAGE RIGHT. AYASH RUNS ON STAGE, HOLDING A BIG AXE, STILL SHOUTING, 'RUN, RUN.' HE RUNS INTO THE SON STANDING CENTRE STAGE)
THE SON: Let's see someone harm my mother. He will die.
AYASH: Ehhhh! My son is home. (HE TURNS AND YELLS BEHIND HIM) Koosis TA-GO-SHIN! Bring my furs here! (HE TURNS TO FACE THE SON) Ah, my son, it is good to see you. Where have you been?
THE SON: You know where I was. But now, I am home. (THE YOUNG WIFE WALKS ONSTAGE WITH BEAVER PELTS)
YOUNG WIFE: Here are your footpads.
AYASH: Put them where he is going to walk. (THE YOUNG WIFE BACKS OFF STAGE, THROWING DOWN THE BEAVER PELTS AS SHE GOES. AYASH WALKS TO STAGE LEFT. THE SON WALKS TO THE FIRST TWO BEAVER PELTS AND KICKS THEM OUT OF THE WAY)
THE SON: I have walked a long way on this earth without footpads. Why should I walk on them now when I am home.
AYASH: Ehhh! Ki-shoo-sheh Koosis! (THE SON AND MOTHER EXIT UPSTAGE LEFT. AYASH FOLLOWS THEM REPEATING THE LAST PHRASE: 'MY SON IS ANGRY.')

SCENE NINE

(THE NARRATOR WALKS ON STAGE)

NARRATOR: The son of Ayash made his journey in an evil world. He found that he had powers of his own as he went from one challenge to the next. He had become a man in his own right. He discovered that he could change the world as it was so long ago to a new world of hope and promise.

(WHILE THE NARRATOR SPEAKS, AYASH AND THE YOUNG WIFE WALK ON STAGE, WITH BOWLS OF FOOD AND SIT UPSTAGE CENTRE. THE NARRATOR EXITS. THE SON ENTERS. AYASH AND THE YOUNG WIFE ARE EATING.)

AYASH: Ehhh, Koosis. Sit down. Eat.

THE SON: Father. Once while I was sleeping along the way, I had a dream. I dreamt that the water was on fire and the land was burning. (THE YOUNG WIFE LAUGHS)

AYASH: Ehhh, Koosis ... I had those dreams all the time ... that is what I used to see in visions, too ... but it never came true.

THE SON: You have that huge cauldron of bearfat. If you have a feast with your bear's fat, this will not happen.

AYASH: Koosis. I have seen it before. It will pass. (AYASH AND THE YOUNG WIFE CONTINUE EATING)

THE SON: You have put my mind at ease. I will go now and leave you to your eating. (THE SON EXITS)

YOUNG WIFE: Who would want to set the whole world on fire?

AYASH: No one. Come. Let us go hunting for more food. (THEY STAND UP AND EXIT)

SCENE TEN

(THE SON AND THE MOTHER WALK ON STAGE FROM LEFT. THE SON IS HOLDING A BOW WITH TWO BRIGHT RED ARROWS.)

THE SON: Today, I shall destroy the world.

THE MOTHER: Koosis. What will happen?

THE SON: I will shoot one arrow far out into the great waters ... and one arrow deep into the forest ... and the earth will catch on fire.

THE MOTHER: What will happen to us?

THE SON: Nothing will happen to you or me. I have drawn a big circle all around this wigwam. The fire will not come inside that circle.

(THE SON FACES LEFT STAGE AND SHOOTS ONE ARROW UP IN AN ARC. HE TURNS AND SHOOTS THE OTHER ONE RIGHT STAGE UP IN AN ARC. HE STOPS AND LISTENS.

(THERE IS A ROARING SOUND – LIKE FIRE. THE SON AND MOTHER SIT DOWN CENTRE STAGE FACING AUDIENCE. AYASH AND THE YOUNG WIFE ARE SHOUTING BACK-STAGE. AYASH RUNS ON STAGE.)

AYASH: Koosis ... The earth is on fire ... and the water, too. Let us throw a feast with my bear's fat.

THE SON: It is too late. I told you to do it before.

AYASH: But what will happen to your brothers and sisters?

THE SON: Put them in your bear fat – let their heads stick out of it.

AYASH: ... and what will happen to myself and ... Kitoosis?

THE SON: You can be in the bear fat too ... you will fit.

(THE ROAR OF THE FIRE GROWS LOUDER. SHADOWS OF FLAMES FLICKER IN THE BACKGROUND.)

AYASH: What will happen to you and your mother?

THE SON: We will stay here in the wigwam. We might as well burn. My mother has burn marks all over her face and hands, anyway.

(AYASH RUNS OFF STAGE. THE ROAR OF THE FIRE BECOMES LOUDER. IT GETS VERY BRIGHT. THERE ARE SCREAMS FROM THE VOICES OF AYASH AND THE YOUNG WIFE. THE ROAR SUBSIDES UNTIL THERE IS SILENCE.)

THE SON: Ehh! I am being too cruel to my father to kill him off completely. (THE SON STANDS UP.) Come ... let us go find his bones. We will make him a new person in the new world! (THEY EXIT)

(THE NARRATOR WALKS ON STAGE)

NARRATOR: The son of Ayash destroyed the world as it was before. When they saw the new world, they saw a pile of bones, bleached white from the intense heat of the fire. That was Ayash and his family. The son gathered up the bones and he flung them into the water. Soon, they saw a white duck and his family. That is Ayash.

(THE SON AND MOTHER ENTER)

THE SON: Mother, in the new world, you will be the beaver. You will help our people. If one dreams about a female animal, that is the beaver. I will be the moose. I too will help all people. The moose will always know when he is being hunted. I will know when someone is approaching me. One should always think of the moose as human when one dreams of him and when one dreams of any animal, one should think of it as human, because the animal will know that he is hunted. That is the new world.

Listen to the song of Ayash (LISTEN) × 3
Listen to an unknown world (LISTEN)
Listen to the ancient voices (LISTEN)
Listen to the flood and the fire (LISTEN)
Listen to the people and things (LISTEN)

Listen to the Old Man's thoughts (KILL)
Listen to the Son and the Fox (KILL)
Listen to the Red Fox kill (KILL)
Listen to the Old Man die (KILL)
Listen to the Son change man (LISTEN)

Listen to the Mother cry (LISTEN) × 3
Listen to the Son come home (LISTEN)
Listen to the world on fire (LISTEN)
Listen to the raging fire (LISTEN)
Listen to the dying voices (LISTEN)

Listen to the fire die (LISTEN) × 3
Listen to a new world come (LISTEN)
Listen to the white ducks fly (LISTEN)
Listen to the beaver swim (LISTEN) – stop
Listen to the blackbird sing.

Acknowledgments

Grateful acknowledgment is extended to the following for permission to use material quoted. Every reasonable precaution has been taken to trace the owners of copyright material and to make due acknowledgment; any error or omission will be gladly rectified in future editions. Sources and full bibliographical information are given in the text; the text pages on which quoted material appears are given here within parentheses.

The Champlain Society, Toronto: permission to reprint from Gabriel Sagard, *Long Journey* (4); Chrestien Le Clercq, *New Relation of Gaspesia* (18-21); La Vérendrye, *Journals and Letters* (24); James Isham, *Observations on Hudson's Bay* (25); John McLean, *Notes* (32)

Coles Canadiana Series, published by Coles Publishing Co. Ltd., Toronto, Canada: permission to reprint from Anna Jameson, *Winter Studies and Summer Rambles* (2, 51, 59); J. Long, *Voyages and Travels* (14); Alexander Morris, *Treaties of Canada* (62-3, 64); George Copway, *Traditional History* (107-10); John MacLean, *Canadian Savage Folk* (130)

Alexander Mackenzie (27): Reprinted with the permission of R.R. Donnelley & Sons Company from the Lakeside Classic, *Alexander Mackenzie's Voyage to the Pacific in 1793*

William L. Stone, *Life of Joseph Brant* (36-7): Reprinted with the permission of Kraus Reprint, a division of Kraus-Thomson Organization Limited

A. Grove Day, *The Sky Clears* (50): Reprinted by permission of the University of Nebraska Press

L.F.S. Upton, *Micmacs and Colonists* (53-4): Reprinted by permission of the University of British Columbia Press

J.W. Grant MacEwan, *Portraits from the Plains* (64, 65): Reprinted by permission of McGraw-Hill Ryerson Limited

Daniel David Moses, *Delicate Bodies* (194-6): Reprinted by permission of the author

Verna Kirkness (196-8): By permission of the author

Alanis Obomsawin, *A Bridge between Two Worlds* (198-201): Reprinted by permission of the author

Lenore Keeshig-Tobias, *Running on the March Wind* (201-3): Reprinted by permission of the author

Jim Morris, *Ayash* (203-13): By permission of the author

Picture credits

The Public Archives of Canada: **Poundmaker** C13001, **Four Kings** C92416, **Joseph Brant** C10350, **Piapot** C3864, **Peter Jones** C4840

Glenbow Alberta Institute, Calgary: **Crowfoot** NA29-1, **Big Bear** NA1270-1, **Henry Bird Steinhauer** NA352-4, **James Gladstone** NA1524-1

Metropolitan Toronto Library Board: **Tecumseh**, Benson J. Lossing, Pictorial field-book of the War of 1812, BR971-034 L59; **John Sunday** JRR2450

Vancouver Public Library: **Maquinna's ancestor** From a drawing by Tomas Suria, circa 1788; **Dan George** Province Newspaper Collection, 44681A

Peter Jacobs: from *Journal of the Reverend Peter Jacobs* (New York 1858)

Parry Sound Public Library: **Allan Salt**

County of Grey Owen Sound Museum: **Catherine Sutton**

Manitoba Archives: **James Settee** N80, Cowley, F.P.V. 2

George Copway (pictorial drawings, p 109): from George Copway, *The Traditional History and Characteristic Sketches of the Ojibway Nation* (London 1850) 135

Francis Assikinack: from James Cleland Hamilton, 'Famous Algonquins: Algic Legends,' *Transactions of the Canadian Institute*, VI (1898-9)

Louis Jackson: from Louis Jackson, *Our Caughnawagas in Egypt* (Montreal 1885)

Ontario Archives: **John Brant-Sero** William Kirby Papers MV1638

Brant County Museum, Brantford: **Pauline Johnson** (both photographs)

Saskatchewan Archives Board: **Dan Kennedy** R-B4598; **Edward Ahenakew** R-A8788(1) part

Alanis Obomsawin: from Alanis Obomsawin

Jim Morris: *Wa-Wa-Tay News*, Sioux Lookout

Lenore Keeshig-Tobias: Sue Young

Walter Currie: from Dr Walter Currie

Index